Queer and Catholic

Queer and Catholic

Amie M. Evans
Trebor Healey
Editors

NEW YORK AND LONDON

First published 2008
by Routledge
270 Madison Ave, New York, NY 10016

Simultaneously published in the UK
by Routledge
2 Park Square, Milton Park, Abingdon, Oxon OX14 4RN

Routledge is an imprint of the Taylor & Francis Group, an informa business

Printed and bound in the United States of America on acid-free paper by Sheridan Books, Inc.

Library of Congress Cataloging in Publication Data
Queer and Catholic / Amie M. Evans, Trebor Healey, editors.
p. cm.
1. Homosexuality—Religious aspects—Catholic Church. I. Evans, Amie M. II. Healey, Trebor, 1962-
BX1795.H66Q44 2007
282.086'64—dc22

2007045471

ISBN10: 1-56023-712-0 (hbk)
ISBN10: 1-56023-713-9 (pbk)
ISBN10: 0-20388-948-7 (ebk)

ISBN13: 978-1-56023-712-9 (hbk)
ISBN13: 978-1-56023-713-6 (pbk)
ISBN13: 978-0-20388-948-0 (ebk)

For all of the kind Catholics who told us
to never be ashamed of ourselves.

CONTENTS

NUNS

SAINTS

Trebor's Preface

This book was born on Royal Street in the French Quarter of New Orleans, a fitting place for such an idea to have its genesis, what with the city's myriad esoteric and exoteric varieties of Catholic expression—from Afro-Caribbean and Voodoo to Irish, French, Spanish, and more recently Vietnamese, and even Central American—making it one of the major American crossroads of the various morphologies of the Church of Rome.

Amie and I were chatting outside the opening party of the third annual Saints & Sinners LGBTIQ Queer Literary Festival, when one or the other of us had mentioned something Catholic in such a way that we immediately recognized each other as coreligionists, or ex-coreligionists anyway. From there, we were on a roll, reminiscing and laughing, sharing a common outlook regarding issues of eroticism and ritual, guilt and redemption, spontaneous altar-building and superstitions, humor and absurdity—all courtesy of Roman Catholicism.

I'd been wanting to put together such a book for years. Though I'd turned my back on Catholicism as a militant homo in1980s San Francisco, the Church's imagery and presence continually reasserted itself. For not only was I crucifying and beatifying crushes and exes in my own spoken word poetry—when I wasn't reimagining them as Our Lady of their various qualities and habits—I was witnessing nuns in full drag traipsing down Castro Street almost daily. These were the Sisters of Perpetual Indulgence who showed up at ACT UP demonstrations, fundraisers, and all number of street protests; who published some of the first safe sex pamphlets; and who, in an admirably real way, put into practice the very teachings of Christ that the Church supposedly espoused, but didn't always practice. The Sisters were saving the lives of those rejected by society while the Pope in Rome stood firm against condoms, helping fuel a worldwide pandemic that is now far larger than it would have ever grown if it weren't for the strictures and insensitivity of the Holy Roman Catholic Church, among other negligent forces. And yes, Pope John Paul II himself did show up in San Francisco during those years. But he would only visit hemophiliac children, and passed on invitations to visit AIDS hospices, one of which—Coming Home—I volunteered at, and which it turned out was rented by Most Holy Redeemer Catholic Church across the street to Visiting Nurses for just $1 a year.

No one ever claimed Catholicism wasn't a mixed bag, and my experience with it as such didn't end there. When I took part in an AIDS Buddy program, it was the Catholic Hospital, St. Mary's that took in my schizophrenic client when all the public health facilities would only treat him as either an AIDS case or a mental health case, but never as both. This same client bounced all over the city, and in the end, no one would give him a place to die, except Gift of Love, Mother Theresa's Hospice on Oak Street. The little nun there told me, "We take anybody." Having been blocked by one social service agency after another, and betrayed personally and socially by the Church in countless ways myself, I burst into tears I'd been holding back for eight months, and ran out the door, unable to square my feelings of disdain for the church with this little nun's Christ-like act of simple and essential compassion. Emotions aside, and my tears dried, I had to face the hard truth that the Church seemed more than willing—and even good at—embracing death, but not in any way prolife; not in our community.

So it was with that openness to the contradictions inherent in religion that we embarked upon this project. We knew we would get pro- and antichurch essays, as well as numerous examples of the conflicted and unresolved experiences of the vast majority of us. It seemed a wonderful and fruitful opportunity for discussion and exploration at a time when religion is literally threatening to tear our nation and the larger world apart. We wanted to explore what was good about our religious upbringing, what was bad, what was insane, what was salvageable, and what of it we could use to build a better, more just world of compassion for those many of us who had outgrown religious institutions as well as for those few who had resolved to stay and reform those institutions from within.

The submissions we received were legion, and wide-ranging. We got dozens of memoirs of Catholic grammar school bizarreness of course, and just as many tales of tortured seminarians and nuns, struggling with adolescent and adult vocations. So many stories of spiritual alienation and betrayal, from the shocking to the comedic. And right alongside them were essays from those who have healed the rift and found peace between their queerness and Catholicism as they continue to practice to this day. Numerous entries arrived expressing their Catholic upbringing in highly poetic terms, sometimes beautifully rendering the ephemeral and mystical aspects of the Catholic mythology in a way that a logical argument never could. And since Catholicism, though a mega-culture on one level, is also defined and influenced by the ethnic and national cultures it inhabits, we received fascinating and enlightening derivations of the Roman model from Polish, Irish, French, Cuban, Mexican, Filipino, English, German, Italian, and Spanish perspectives, among others. There were lots of stories of sexual exploration, not surprisingly, as Catholicism seems to be one of the most erotic religious traditions the world has ever known. We received countless recountings of first sexual encounters between boys in the rectory, tales of nun crushes and lesbian dalliances, and lamentations on the denial of the sacrament of marriage to gay couples, as well as a disturbingly high number of pieces dealing with priest abuse of minors. To say we weren't surprised by the latter is perhaps the greatest indictment of the church's negligence in this area.

But, we resolved early on not to let such issues as priest abuse and gay marriage dominate this collection, and so, though we have included stories that address these extremely important and difficult—even criminal—issues, they are but part of a larger effort to assess the full experience, range, catastrophe, blessing or pathology of a Catholic upbringing vis-à-vis our queer selves. We wanted to hear from—and about—the frustrated altar girls and nuns in full drag; the enlightened feminists and angry intellectuals; the horny bondage aficionados and lyrical poets; those earnest gay and lesbian parents and self-discovering students; the young heretics and often hilarious apostates; those creepy as well as likeable priests, and those kindly as well as strict, ruler-wielding nuns; those few and rare ingenuous angels and the sweetly pure of heart; the practicing as well as the nonpracticing—and we organized the collection accordingly.

We even received work from non-Catholics, who at times reminded us that Catholicism is sometimes best understood (as is the case with so many things) objectively by those who were never trapped within its confines.

And so, this collection includes what we hope is the widest variety of expressions of Catholicism by queer writers. While many of us consider ourselves ex-Catholics, most of us are aware that we are part of a culture of origin that can never be wholly eradicated from our psyches. Some of us have moved on to pagan practices, Buddhism, Hinduism, Sufism, and Wicca, among other traditions. Some of us are atheist or agnostic, and some of the work in this book is by those who have remained members of the church, sometimes peripherally, and sometimes in a fairly orthodox way though none in an unconscious manner as coming out queer has challenged each one of us to fully examine our social and spiritual relationships in a way few heterosexuals ever do.

I understand my own relationship to Catholicism so much better after reading all these submissions and having some incredible dialogues with Amie along the way. I was rather shocked to wake up the morning after completing my own essay dealing with Marian heresy to discover I'd actually never even been a Christian. Yet I was Catholic to the marrow!

It is our hope that this book will provide those kinds of revelations and myriad opportunities for discussion and self-exploration. It's a rich vein we've mined here and we humbly offer it up to you and hope it is worthy (insert altar boy bell-ringing here).

In nomine Patris, et Filii, et Spiritus Sancti, Amen.

Amie's Preface

Growing up Catholic has been both a blessing and a curse for me. Editing this anthology with Trebor has made me realize that this is true in differing degrees for most of the queer authors included in this text.

Catholic traditions filled my childhood with joyful memories that none of my non-Catholic friends or colleagues share, and these traditions have had a profound impact not only on the adult I have become, but also on how I continue to interpret and interact with the world at large. Catholic ideology was the first moral grid I learned to use to navigate life. All other moral systems that I have encountered—and there have been many—have been compared and contrasted against it. Some came up short, others illustrated the deficiencies of Catholicism, but ultimately, none were perfect or infallible. And so, while I no longer am one of the faithful, I find those elements of Catholicism that originally charmed me—the ritual of the mass, the repetition of the rosary, the grandiosity of the sacraments, the passion of the Stations of the Cross, and even the excesses of the ornate gold altar instruments and elaborate vestments—echo throughout my adult life.

I find I miss the rhythm of the cycle of the year that was dotted with holy days and punctuated by Lent and Advent. I yearn not only for the ritual of the events—receiving ashes on Ash Wednesday and palm fronds on Palm Sunday, keeping vigil on Holy Saturday, attending Midnight mass at Christmastime—but for the deeper human symbolism that they represent: sacrifice, celebration, renewal, communion. And while I can locate the origins of all of this in non-Christian traditions, I am drawn back to the place where I first discovered them in the folds of the Catholic Church.

And, on a more cultural level, I admit, I miss bingo. I also miss bake sales, church bazaars—complete with raffles, potato pancakes and beer—and all those feelings of community they provided during my childhood. I still decorate my house with plastered statues of the saints I once envied and now purchase at religious stores and yard sales. I still think of Saint Anthony when I lose something, and I am hard pressed not to make the sign of the cross when I hear an ambulance's siren. Plaid, Catholic-schoolgirl uniforms with knee socks, scapulars, and mass cards call me back to a time when things seemed ordered, simple, and easily navigated—when the entire universe seemed to be clearly laid out with divine purpose. I miss the poetry of it all!

But, even before I realized I was a lesbian or embraced my queerness, I was aware of the ideological problems in Catholic doctrine that would eventually lead me away from the church of my childhood. My faith—because I truly did want to believe—led me down a path of unanswerable questions. I had no problem accepting the mystical elements of the Church's doctrine—miracles, including the Immaculate Conception, weren't an issue for me. Nor were tenets such as three persons in one God that required what seemed to many to be a giant leap of faith. Instead, contradictions between the teachings of Christ as I interpreted them in the New Testament and the Church's doctrine (ostensibly based on the same text) were what ultimately prevented me from fully embracing Catholicism as I grew into adulthood. The Church's position on so many issues seemed then, and still remains, at odds with the ideals Christ offered up his life for in the New Testament.

Limbo for unbaptized babies and heathens who didn't have an opportunity to hear the word of God was especially problematic for me. Likewise, the inequality inherent in the priest/nun dichotomy was troublesome to me long before I knew the word feminism or had a working understanding of misogyny. The guilt and self-loathing fostered by the Church's attitudes toward masturbation, sex, birth control, abortion, homosexuality, divorce, and a host of other issues were all at odds with my personal belief system and didn't seem to have much to do with what Christ taught either.

The reactions to the AIDS crisis in the 1980s, the recently revealed cover-up of the priest sexual abuse scandal—and the ill-informed and homophobic response the Church fathers issued in reaction to it—as well as the relentless pronouncements from the Vatican regarding the inherent evil of homosexuality and the so-called threat to the family that gay marriage poses have all contributed to my further alienation from the church of my childhood.

Honestly, I think I have more fond memories of my Catholic upbringing than I do scars, but unfortunately, the scars are the result of deeper wounds, and so they are more profound than the often superficial joys I recall.

Catholicism—whether we embrace, modify or reject our faith—colors who we are as queer authors and as citizens of the world. For if we had not been raised Catholic, if we had not been blessed with queerness, we would likely not be the authors we are today; not written the insightful, humorous, emotional, tragic stories that make up this anthology. And so, I am truly thankful to the Catholic Church. And Trebor and I are pleased to offer up this collection of stories that run the gamut from integration and epiphany to betrayal and madness, but have in common one vital spiritual truth: they are queer.

APOSTATES

The Fifteenth Station

Austin J. Austin

I. JESUS IS CONDEMNED TO DEATH

I never understood how Jesus could be born, age thirty-some-odd years in three to five months, and then die in time to shrink and climb up into Mary's womb for a little nap until the following Christmas. I was unclear on the concept of commemoration versus occurrence for at least a decade, encouraged in my fallacy by a family that spoke of religious events as current ones: *tonight, Mary is looking for a place to have her baby. Today, Jesus is standing before Pontius Pilate*. The time-lapse nature of the devotional year gave me vertigo. I really grossed out my father when I relayed to him my interpretation of Jesus' great zygotic trek, as if up Mount Kilimanjaro, to the unsuspecting womb of Our Lady. *That's not how it happens,* my father intoned, looking stricken. But how else could a two-thousand-year-old dead guy end up germinating in the same uterus, over and over again—and more importantly, how could Mary ever endure two millennia of this? I was unaware of kegels at the age of eight.

II. JESUS RECEIVES THE CROSS

Because of state laws prohibiting underage gambling, my grandparents would have to cross over into Connecticut to take me with them to play bingo. In the Quebecois church cellar, smoke rose from the mouths of weathered, blue-haired angels. God didn't care if you gambled or smoked or swore or showed children how to polka or set up a bingo card, as long as you paid your admission fee to the church. I always spent at least half an hour setting up my shrine until it was perfect: lucky horseshoe, lucky penny, lucky dauber, orange-haired troll, pink plastic elephant with trunk upturned. I learned to talk to God in those bingo basements, starting and ending our conversations politely as I waited for O-69. I had no words yet for what I did not even know I wanted—which was the undying love of the human embodiment of Pebbles Flintstone—but I was utterly at peace near the whirr of gently tumbling numbered balls.

III. THE FIRST FALL

In the basement of Saint Hedwig's, I scowled into the crossed eyes of the praying plaster Madonna, Our Lady of Medjugorje. Quality control wasn't a big priority at whatever convent or convenience store she was purchased from, nor at my church itself. The basement stank of mold and stale bake-sale *chrust,* and every Monday it got harder and harder to go to CCD where Father Barnyard visited the faith sweatshop only to offer his snide condemnations. After taking turns reading aloud from a cartoon where Billy was a Catholic and Jimmy was a Jew, and not only was Jimmy going to go to Hell for being a Jew, but Billy was going to end up in Hell, too, for failing to convince Jimmy to come away from the Dark Side, Father Barnyard gave our class a lecture about the holiness and sanctity of the body. He lifted up his middle fingers and pointed them straight to Heaven. *You see? When I do this, it isn't a sin, because of my love for God.* I let my forehead touch the cool Formica desktop and I prayed. Out of the corner of my eye, I watched Leah scratch the back of one bare leg with her shoe. The afternoon before, in my backyard, I had bound her hands with my lavender Get In Shape, Girl! gym ribbon, placed a pink weighted ring atop both of our heads to give us halos, and beat her with a pastel juggling pin as Madonna sang "Like A Prayer" on my boom box. We were choreographing a dance that ended in the two angels dying, being freed from their bonds, and rising up to Heaven. Leah's mother Eve was cheating on Leah's father. The man Eve left town with died of cancer. Around that time, in Leah's father's basement, I found a keychain with a rainbow on it and a condom inside it. Leah made me promise not to tell; I was moved to comply, not by her tears, but by the knowledge that Leah had the dirt on me, too. She'd accidentally seen my mother's wig hanging on the back of the bedroom door, a synthetic, curly sheep, waiting to be shorn of its hair shirt.

IV. JESUS MEETS HIS MOTHER

It's a conundrum: what if the abortion you didn't have because it was against your religion could have kept one more queer from blazing across the sky like a rhinestone comet? For years, my parents hammered in the importance of their decision to remain virgins until marriage, going as far as to recite a litany of banal sex acts they'd never perform, despite thirty years of wedded bliss. Premarital or antimarital sex was out, and virginity was the new pink. My queerness laid waste God's divine plan for my intact hymen, which, incidentally, disappeared after an unfortunate string of preteen incidents involving a tampon and a bicycle seat. My mother did not want a queer, trans child; based on her contraceptive use, I am fairly certain that my mother did not actively want *any* child at the time she conceived, an Easter miracle. Despite my mother's religious, virginal, vaginal purity, she was using the sponge when she became pregnant with me, and my father had a vasectomy when I was still a babe in arms. *He did it for me, because the doctor said I would die if I ever got pregnant again,* my mother told me. I've always been curious as to why married heterosexuality absolves devout Catholics from having to defer to God's law when it's inconvenient. It must be that offering of a holy flapping hymen, vibrating in the breeze like the throats of a thousand angels.

V. SIMON OF CYRENE CARRIES THE CROSS

For almost the first decade of my life, I lived in a little, grey house at the edge of a used car lot. When we moved, my father became a Eucharistic minister. Whenever I was angry with him I would refuse to take the Host from him. Our new priest, Father Barnyard, wouldn't let my mother be anything but a lector, despite my father being my mom's employee when they were in civilian clothes. I lived in that town and attended that church for six years. Square and white, with iron railings up the many, many steps and realistic stained glass depictions of the stations of the cross, Saint Hedwig's was a Polish church, and the overtones were numerous, ranging from special feast days and early morning masses held in Polish to holiday services being conducted in both languages. In front of our usual pew, the flaming heart of the Lord blazed out of his chest from a large, demure painting that decreed *Jezu, pan z wami.* Next to him, the fierce, scarred face of the Black Madonna of Czêstochowa looked down at the priest, clutching her infant savior son protectively. When I moved out at fourteen, a sequence of events inspiring more *rashomon* than the holiest of Mysteries, I thought I was free from the dead weight of the Church, but my father was adamant that I continue to attend. The closest church to the school where I lived was four miles away, so I had to get up early and walk to church as the sun rose. With every step closer to Mass, I walked further away from the Church.

VI. VERONICA WIPES JESUS' FACE WITH HER VEIL

Every afternoon, I'd brush the leaves off my knees where they'd gotten stuck to my tights, and straightening my skirt, rush off to the library in the chapel. Right after I'd signed in on the library monitor roster, I would excuse myself and lock myself in the bathroom off of the periodical stacks. I'd run the tap in the sink and gently touch my wet hands to my face, wiping off the hardening, sticky cum. In the woods, I'd been pushed to my knees and had my boyfriend's hard cock thrust into my mouth until the moment when he'd pull my hair, pull out of my mouth, and come on my face. Sometimes I liked it, usually I didn't, but I never, ever knew it was sex. Sex was a penis ransacking a vagina, period. This rustling along the wooded trail was something else, like Limbo, or Purgatory. The last time I was on my knees was in a Confessional. Separated from him by a screen, a peepshow window that slid over so he could peer at my most private parts, the act was supposed to be anonymous. But he would sometimes say my name, or say other things that would make it clear he knew which child I was. He was always breathy—oh, he was so passionate about God—and in the dark I would make up sins rather than confess to the things I'd really done.

VII. THE SECOND FALL

Our little pink weekly kiddy offertory envelopes were stamped with "Stewardship is Time, Talent, and Treasure." Each capital "T" was a cross. I'm nailed right in. A little embossed number—corresponding to a different member of the church's flock—blazed red nearby so the priest could tell who had and hadn't given every week. His moral accounting system was better than Santa's had ever been. When I was younger, I would do anything to keep from being pulled aside by the arm during CCD, hearing the *whoosh* of his cassock as he yanked and admonished, *God only loves a cheerful giver.* I would save chunks of my allowance, using it to pay for being left alone. Eventually, just as I learned to dine and dash at Friendly's on my way to CCD, I learned to swipe from the change jar at home. With all the tiring fighting and conniving, how was I ever going to have time to converse with God? For instance, it was much more important to keep Vivian, the CCD friend I never slept with, from crying when I told her that her boyfriend asked me out (his hair, dark and introspective as lamb's wool, gleamed under the streetlight, lustrous as her wet eyes). As we scoured the streets in the car, looking for her after she ran away, my mother clenched the steering wheel and declared that I was going to get Confirmed, come Hell or high water. Lacking the power to summon either, I was forced to make a list of Confirmation names. The priest sneered at Lucifer and Jezebel, but allowed me to take Scholastica, sister of Benedict—who wrote all her brother's important works while *he* took all the credit—and Magdalene, my favorite foot fetishist of all. Scholastica flew to Heaven in the form of a flaming flock of doves, and Jesus flew into Magdalene's holy-holy in the form of a flamer. What good company. When the bishop laid his hands on me, it was Father Barnyard's eyes that burned my skin. Shortly thereafter, any time I touched myself, my tender skin would burn. Poorly diagnosed, it was a reverse miracle: vestibulitis, an inflammation of my vestibule. I cut up all my sex toys with scissors.

VIII. JESUS MEETS THE WOMEN OF JERUSALEM

I had to close my eyes and breathe deeply to keep from seeing the Pope sitting at the end of the bed as she fucked me. My heart was pounding so hard it felt like a length of thorns was wound around it. But how could anything that tasted, smelled, and felt this good be wrong? I had worked so hard to vilify myself, as per the usual ancient Catholic recipe. Ingredients: four cubits anguish, two fingers of guilt, and seven strides of shame, blended furiously until a crust of sin forms. In my blood family, there were no attempts to understand, to make holy this part of me. In a family like mine, family and faith were so inextricably intertwined that falling in love meant falling from grace the first time I said, "girlfriend." The crowbar of queerness pried me away from that faith, where once I'd found solace, before I'd ever had my face covered with chrism or jism.

IX. THE THIRD FALL

It was not from the mouth of the Holy Trinity—my mother, father, or grandmother—that I heard about it. Six months later, I read about it on one of the internet's watchdog sites. The original suit, filed on behalf of two anonymous brothers, cited abuse that happened when they were altar boys in the late 1980s. During those years, I would take part in the St. Hedwig Festival every year, parading through the church with thirty other little girls dressed up like the saint who gave up her fortune for God after she was widowed, hoping to win the look-alike contest. I never won because my mother made me dress up like St. Hedwig as a widow, in dowdy, black attire, but this outfit likely saved me. Leah dressed up to look just like the statue in the rectory, and though she won, I wonder what she lost at his hands. Father Barnyard's civil suits are still ongoing clichés, of course: in Massachusetts, a diddler priest is not just evil, but embarrassing. In the papers, it said that Father Barnyard threatened one of my peers that if he ever told, Father would make it so the boy would never, ever make his Confirmation. Unwilling to miss out on a Sacrament because of a pedophile, the kid replied that if he didn't get to make his Confirmation, he'd make sure the bishop and the entire parish found out, during Mass. This boy was ultimately Confirmed, perhaps even on the same day that I took Magdalene's name as my own. It's ironic, of course, that for years I was so worried about going to hell because I had hot and happy sex, while through my entire youth, my priest was raping young boys.

X. JESUS IS STRIPPED OF HIS GARMENTS

The choir loft was small. I preferred to sit there because the ancient, lathed oak bars of the safety rail protected me from what was going on below as I grabbed on tight and peered through with one eye like a strange, caged bird. Besides for safety, I was up there to sing hymns in Polish. Mind you, though Polish is certainly in my cellular structure, it's not on my list of languages spoken, read, or understood. I figured, hey, it got me away from my parents and my grandparents, so it's gotta be worth a good fake job. I wasn't too well-versed on the tune of most of these songs, either, so while the accompanist was blowing dust puffs out the organ pipes with every keystroke, I was the one standing straight and tall, holding my hymnal like the proudest castrato, words tumbling and splatting from my mush-mouth, at least one beat too late. Next to me, Emily Zakrzewski: platinum-haired, blue-eyed, angular, and expressionless—God's gift to annoying the shit out of me. God and I had been having some trouble since my pépère's death. Our conversations, once as prolific as the Holy Prepuce, had dwindled with my lack of faith, morale, or attention span. Most of my time was now spent thinking curious thoughts of pushing pious Emily up against the stained glass pane of the tenth station, her hymnal falling over the balcony rail as I kissed her on the mouth, hard. Sometimes, when she looked down her nose at me with a little too much enjoyment, I thought about how much it would humiliate her if, somehow, the buttons on her cardigan came undone—and in this part of my vengeful reverie, only Emily and God and I were upstairs in that balcony, my anger turning to tears as I bathed in her hot shame.

XI. CRUCIFIXION: JESUS IS NAILED TO THE CROSS

Made in San Francisco, I was born in a blizzard on the other coast. I was baptized on my thirty-first day, wearing my father's baptismal gown, white as a bride. I made my First Communion in a white dress speckled with tiny purple flowers. I was the tallest child. The priest did not have to lean over to offer my mouth the Host. We had rehearsals for the ceremony, during which time we took wafers and drank wine. *Why don't those wafers count?* I wanted to know. *They haven't been blessed, so they haven't turned into Jesus' body and blood.* Right now, they were just crackers and liquor, of questionable value to the juvenile digestive system, but on the day of my First Communion, they would be transformed. Every year, without fail, my grandmother sends me a packet of Polish *wigilia* wafers through the mail for Advent. One for each week, they are rectangular host crackers embossed with various scenes from the yuletide season. The eldest in attendance cracks off a piece and gives it to another loved one around the table, saying something nice about them, and expressing love and good wishes. I marvel that they never arrive crushed into pieces, and every year, no matter where I am, the last thing to be eaten is always the regal white eagle crowned in glutinous bas-relief. Everyone knows that Poland is in Jerusalem.

XII. JESUS DIES ON THE CROSS

For two years, I was an HIV counselor at a needle exchange. Every day, I stocked bleach kits and measured vitamin C into little plastic zipper bags. I had to be careful to label each bag because anthrax was arriving at clinics just like mine, in powdery baggies just like those. In half-hour blocks, I asked about her unprotected partners, his unprotected partners, hir unprotected partners, for shooting and sniffing and fucking. I filled in little bubbles with a number two pencil, driving home the pedagogical aspects of the test. Tedious as the Via Crucis in a language I couldn't understand, the long litany of bar codes written out number by number in my anonymous book, and a return date—two weeks—issued on the back of my business card. Gabriel came to Mary one day, announcing the news of what was growing inside her, and this role model of nonconsent prepared me for my inevitable role. One Christmas Eve, a woman came in for some 27-gauge needles. She refused anything thinner because she said they broke off in her skin, for twenty years she'd had needles disappearing in her skin and resurfacing again in little chunks. *Here,* she said, and peeled off a long scab on her arm. Pushing it hard into my hand, she said, *there's one, right there, do you see it?* Neither virus nor her co-infection—or any related condition, symptom, or illness—ultimately caused her passing, nor did the mysterious breaking needles; I cannot say whether overdose is really a fancy word for ascension.

XIII. JESUS' BODY IS REMOVED FROM THE CROSS

Being marked as queer is a complicated issue of, among other things, passing, kinship, survival. The same thing that saves you in one context can easily betray you in another. On Ash Wednesday morning, my parents, grandparents, and I would go to church together. Lining up in two straight rows, the parishioners took off their hats and accepted a thumbprint of palm soot on their foreheads. Inevitably, the ash would fall into my eyes, making my eyes red and watery, and would dirty my clothes. When I would show up at school, it looked like I had gotten into a fight with a vacuum cleaner bag and lost. As Jesus must have said, *What a pity.* What didn't Jesus say? Certainly, nothing about how to feel proud of being fat and girl-crazy and Catholic, with big puffy eyes and dirt all over. I didn't want to be marked. Marking made me dirty. Marking made me the same as the heavy-breathing priest who stood between me and God. One Ash Wednesday, as I fasted, I decided what I was giving up for Lent. Not chocolate, not television. Catholicism. I liked it so much after the requisite forty days that I decided to make it a habit. Much like a nun's, this habit has stayed around, at least in spirit.

XIV. JESUS IS LAID IN THE TOMB

One of the best times I ever had as a pro-Domme was with a client who had a fetish for chloroform. I wrote him elaborate stories with him as the main character, I mailed him carefully researched and mixed bottles of chloro-faux, and we would meet with a very particular agenda. He would come into the dark hotel room, turn on the light, put down his briefcase and jacket, and begin to remove his tie. As the tie hit the bed, I would silently step out from the corner of the room, clamping a cloth over his mouth, heavy with camphor and brandy. A brief, passionate struggle would ensue, with labored, heavy breathing, and I would hold the wet cloth fast to his nose and lips. Ultimately, he would fall onto the mattress, still struggling weakly. I would climb up onto him, straddling his chest, and with one hand on the rag, begin to undress him. As I tormented him with various implements, I would often think about my ancestor who had come to what is now Quebec from France, preaching hard to the locals. His tongue was cut out when they got sick of his prattle, and I can't help but think: *it served you right*. My client would pretend to rouse slightly, and I would make a big deal out of rewetting the cloth and covering his face again. I never took off my clothes. Only occasionally would I touch his penis myself. I was quite surprised to learn that he was not trans. One time, he paid for the whole nine yards, and I covered it up and saddled up while the cloth still hung from his gaping mouth, a fish without water, a cave with no door. It was a short session, which he rounded out with tales of his impending divorce, the scandal at his company. Shortly thereafter, a terrible, stinging plague descended upon the land—and by land, I mean my pants—perhaps God's wrathful punishment for playing Him for the afternoon.

XV.

Usually, the Mysteries conclude on such a wretched note, and any happy ending is the Resurrection. Spending the majority of my life scrubbing Catholicism from my skin like any unwelcome contact, I've discovered that there is no way to separate myself completely from all it culturally and mythologically altered. And really, when life hands you lemons, make a rosary out of anal beads and pull them out of someone's ass one at a time while you make them recite each decade. I like iconography. I like making martyrs in my bedroom. I liked going to a play party wearing a black shirt with a white stripe on the collar, and spanking my lovely slut with a hefty King James until the cover flew off; and I liked that someone pulled me aside later, and in hushed tones, asked, *did you see that priest with the butt-beads who was beating that schoolgirl with a Bible?* Now I know what it is to be legendary during your own life. It's not blasphemy; it's how I worship and navigate this long and challenging territory. I enjoy turning over my Magic 8-Ball in the shape of a pink rubber Jesus, and asking if everything's going to be alright: YES MY CHILD. My ideal scene involves a large, welded cage, the size of half a room, or a sheet of Plexiglas bisected by a countertop, with a phone receiver on each side. Two prison guards would escort him in, with his orange jumpsuit. Father Barnyard would be seated, and look through the bars or the glass. His eyes would widen and then narrow again as he recognized me. I would be the one to speak: "Bless me, Father, for I have sinned."

Objective Disorder

Gregory Woods

Propriety once segregated us from girls,
and passion followed suit. No laws or papal bulls
applied to adolescent guile within these walls.
For all that we were rendered regular by bells,
each body's pulse subordinated to the school's,
mortality's unsentimental chisel gnarls
a boy's credulity, and scepticism kills
his faith. The gods he worships then are human pals,
imperfect but more beautiful than bloodless souls.
Beneath a plaster Virgin's blindness, like a doll's,
a pair of us replace cold prayer with spattered vowels
of inarticulate delight. Each of us feels
himself, unlike the sheets our ecstasy defiles,
unspoilt by the division of our bodies' spoils.

Excerpts from *The End of the World Book*

Alistair McCartney

INTRODUCTION

I think the best way to explain the effect growing up in a strict Roman Catholic family had on my psyche is to tell you about Catholic boys, the boys I went to school with for twelve years at Christian Brothers College, Fremantle, Australia. Italian boys mainly, sons of immigrants, with fathers who were fishermen and builders. Dark-haired, olive-skinned boys, compact and muscled, with deep brown eyes and pencil mustaches. At night I still dream of them, find myself entangled with them, in their father's fishing nets, in the bathroom of the house I grew up in, or find myself muttering their names David Pensabene, Angel Bario, Paolo Schiliro, Karl Cicanese, Marco Vitali like the beads on a rosary. Whether I like it or not, in the realm of my sexuality, and in the realm of my imagination, Catholicism's influence has been indelible. It's left me with a very Catholic desire, not to observe doctrines, but to pervert them. Here are some of my perversions.

CHRISTIAN BROTHERS COLLEGE

One day when I was in fifth grade during recess at Christian Brothers College, the Catholic Boys School I attended, I was playing handball with my friends, when all of a sudden, a boy in twelfth grade—

"Excerpts from *The End of the World Book*" were first published in their original format in *The End of the World Book* by Alistair McCartney (University of Wisconsin Press), 2008.

who, with his raggedy, dirty blonde brown hair bore a passing resemblance to the pop singer Leif Garrett—came up behind me, grabbed me by the neck and proceeded to stuff a half-eaten apple core down my throat. I felt like one of those geese French peasant women wearing polka-dot head kerchiefs force-feed, so the geese can get all nice and fat and their enlarged livers can be used for pate, which is a delicacy.

The boy continued shoving the apple into my mouth, until one of the priests came down and put a stop to things. By this time, the Leif Garrett look-alike or impostor had pushed me down onto the concrete. I remember that as the priest hovered over me, I got a look up his black gown. I saw that he was wearing long, black socks that went up to just below his knees, and that his legs were very white, but covered in thick, black hairs. His shoes smelled of the pink cakes of disinfectant that lay at the bottom of the bathroom urinals. I was seized by a desire to suck on the heavy, black hem of the priest's robe, but held myself back.

Up on my feet, I remember that the skin of the half-eaten apple looked very red against the sky, which was gray and pigeony. The priest held the apple between us as evidence, and the older boy claimed that I had thrown the apple at him. I denied having done this, but I can no longer recall whether or not I was being truthful. Either way, I was left with a lifelong erotic though ambivalent attachment to red apples.

Just the other day, I was at our local Venice Farmers market, surrounded by the usual hordes of white mothers with their gaggles of white babies. Stopping at a stall selling only red apples, I picked one of them up, and was taken back, transported on a rickety horse-drawn cart of red apples, to that incident. I felt an intense longing to once again be held in that boy's grip. The apple in my hand seemed to almost glow, and somehow it felt terribly heavy. As the stall owner asked me if I was interested in purchasing some apples, his comment dragged me out of my reverie, and I was transported back on a cart—this time the cart was wholly devoid of red apples—to the present.

FLOOD, THE GREAT

I think my favorite story in the Bible is the one about the Flood. It happens early on in the Bible if I remember correctly, very early, in the first few pages, and to be honest I've always thought it a bit funny that God decides to destroy all flesh (even the creeping things!) so early on, but still, I suppose he had his reasons.

There are so many good parts in this story it's hard to pinpoint why it's so good. I like everything about it—the whole business with constructing the Ark—out of Gopher wood no less—and how specific God is in his instructions to Noah re: the dimensions. God's very specific. And I like how everyone thinks Noah's a crazy, old fool, a very old fool—when the Flood finally comes he's six hundred years old—but then when the waters finally come, of course everyone wants to get in. But they obviously can't, because of the business with the pairs, only one pair of everything.

And then when the waters rise and don't stop rising it's of course very exciting. I think that's what I like most about the story. It's very visual. You can really see everyone getting blotted out. Ever since I was a kid I've had a very clear picture of this.

I remember in first grade, when it rained heavily, the courtyard of my school—Our Lady Queen of Peace—would often flood. And on those days, when morning recess or afternoon recess or lunchtime came, we would leave our desks in an orderly fashion and file into the hallway, where our raincoats and rain hats and galoshes were hanging on hooks spaced at regular intervals. We would put on our bright yellow rain gear as quickly as we could and run outside to play and splash in the rain, which filled me with a deep delight.

As we played, I liked to imagine that the Ark was passing by, bobbing on the water, and that I could see the animals in the Ark, their faces pressed up against the windows. Our parish priest, Father Lions had made it perfectly clear that when, once again, the rains refused to stop and the waters steadily rose until they covered the earth, our rain gear would be no use to us. I could picture exactly the big buttons on my raincoat coming undone from the force of the rushing water, and my galoshes slipping off my feet. And long after I and everyone else had drowned, I liked to imagine all our bright yellow rain hats, bobbing brightly on the water's flat, gray surface.

And then in the actual story it's nice when the waters gradually recede. Even today when it stops raining, I can almost imagine how Noah must have felt, filled with unimaginable hope and unimaginable dread, and how orderly everything must have seemed, the world so quiet and empty, and everything in it divided into pairs.

GOSSIP

I thought I had stopped believing in God, probably when I was around fourteen. How strange then, yet how sweetly predictable, twenty years later, to find myself having discussions with him, usually at night, when my boyfriend's away, and I'm in bed by myself, just after turning off the bedside lamp.

The voice I speak to God in is quite particular, hushed yet deep, like I'm having phone-sex, and trying to sound sexier than I actually am. It's my God-sex voice, a voice I use for no one else.

I realize that one never really stops believing in God: it is not a question of belief; one simply stops talking to him, gives him the cold shoulder.

This is very interesting then to pick up the thread of the conversation so many years later. And despite the time that has passed, it feels surprisingly natural, quite convivial. I gossip and chat away with him, just like my mother did when chatting with her sister Helen on our olive green telephone.

HEAVEN, RESTROOMS IN

Recent findings have revealed that there are public restrooms in Heaven that have those warm hand-blowers (not paper towels), and urinals that are silver, just like the urinals here on earth. In Heaven's urinals, attendants also place those little pink cakes of disinfectant soap. And just as men frequent certain restrooms down here, for anonymous and passionate and fleeting encounters, in Heaven there are also restrooms where it is known that you can get a bit of quick action. Apparently there is one restroom in particular, that, whatever time of day—or should I say eternity—you visit, there you will encounter a young man kneeling at the base of the urinal, waiting for you, in a little patch of light.

Though it remains to be seen if the concept of fleeting even exists within the confines of eternity. Perhaps, in Heaven, all passion is enduring.

INDEX LIBRORUM PROHIBITORUM

Begun in 1559, the Index Librorum Prohibitorum is an official list of books the Roman Catholic Church strictly forbids its members to read, considering these books to be antithetical to the Church's teachings. In the Vatican there is a library housing every one of these books, staffed by young priests. More than anything, I want my book to find its way onto the shelf of this library. I keep sending a copy to the Vatican. I even had my mother write a letter, the gist of which was "My son's book is evil," signed not only by my mother, but also by our parish priest and the parish's choirboys, and enclosed the letter inside the book. But the Index keeps on sending my book back, with a letter of their own saying that they don't think my book is sinful enough. They aren't fully convinced that my book poses a real threat to the faithful.

LIPSTICK

Our parish priest would refuse women Communion if they were wearing too much lipstick. He'd give homilies, referring to the passage in Revelations that talks about the time when there will be only one stick of lipstick left in the world.

Sometimes, after mass, he'd confiscate the lipstick. He kept the offending items in a metal box above the stove in his house behind the Church. There were rumors that he'd redistribute the lipstick to the choirboys who came over on Tuesdays and Thursdays, put aprons on over their robes, and cleaned and cooked him kippers, and did the dishes. There was talk of choirboys kissing, coloring in the Holy wafers, but these are just rumors.

PEWS

At our Church the pews were smooth as skinheads. As the priest gave his homily, I would sit there, trying to induce the pew to give me splinters. Trying to seduce the pew.

RESURRECTION, THE

In Rubens' miraculous tapestry from the 17th century, depicting Christ emerging from his tomb three days after being crucified, the fact of the Resurrection pales before the fact of the legs of the Roman guards, who are all wearing these short tunics, which reveal their strapping calf muscles and powerful thighs. One forgets all about the Resurrection. One has to be reminded to pay attention to the Resurrection. The guards are cowering before the unbelievable terror and beauty of what is happening—just like me, they are frightened by beauty. Our eyes linger on one soldier in particular, the hem of whose tunic is flying up, ever so intriguingly, and who is attempting to flee, just as I find myself doing when confronted with unbearable beauty.

SAINTS

There are currently more than 10,000 saints in the Roman Catholic Church. In the chapel at my school there was a wooden statue of a Saint, I forget which one in particular, but somehow over the years a hole had formed right where the asshole should be, and, over the years, boys stuck their fingers in the Saint's asshole, finger-fucking the saint as it were, making the hole smoother and smoother, so you didn't have to worry about splinters.

SALOME

They say that when Salome kissed the decapitated head of John the Baptist, she could still taste honey and locusts on the prophet's breath. However, in requesting the head of the prophet on a platter, she didn't go far enough. In my opinion, her request was far too modest. She didn't ask for enough. She should have taken her desires one step further, and asked her stepfather Herod to bring her, not only the head, but the unconscious of John the Baptist, on a silver engraved platter.

That said, ever since the giving of this gift, in AD 28, no gift has quite matched up. All gifts are not quite what we wished for. The exchange of gifts takes place in the shadow of Herod's gift, and, in this shadow, we all smile and say thank you, but the look on our faces gives away that fact that we are all severely disappointed.

SODOM AND GOMORRAH

After the Flood, my favorite bit in the Bible is Sodom and Gomorrah. I think I like it because I can relate to it. I particularly like the part when the angels come to Sodom, and all the men hear about this, and go to Lot's house, where the angels are staying, and they all want to know the angels, and they're at Lot's door, and they're just about to open the door, when the angels blind them, so they're left, blindly groping around the door. I know just how they feel. Though I also like to think about Sodom and Gomorrah prior to all the destruction. More often than not I feel like those men must have felt just a little bit earlier, when they were still very excited, about the possibility of knowing the angels.

THE WORLD, THE END OF

When the world ends, and it is time for God to announce who the winners are, and who the losers are, I just know that I will be so nervous, that I will not listen very carefully, like when I am meeting people for the first time and their name goes in one ear and out the other.

I better be listening, because imagine how embarrassing it will be if, when God reads my name off the list, I am so distracted that I don't hear it. Or, even more embarrassing, imagine if I hear my name, but I can't be 100 percent certain if he told me to go on the right side with all the people going to Heaven, who are condemned to eternal bliss, or to go stand on the left side, with all the dogs and sorcerers and fornicators condemned to eternal damnation.

If my eternal fate goes in one ear and out the other, this will make for a very awkward situation. I will have to put up my hand, like in primary school, and ask God if he could please repeat where it is he wants me to go. Most likely, he will get so annoyed with me, he will tell me that although he initially wanted me to go with him and the angels, just to teach me a lesson, a very harsh lesson, now I need to go stand on the left side with the dogs and the sorcerers.

But more realistically, I will be too shy to even raise my hand, and I will just sort of loiter around the middle, in between the wet snouts of the dogs and the quivering wings of the angels, trying to make myself appear inconspicuous.

Two Poems: "Noose" and "Tattoo"

Susan McDonough-Hintz

NOOSE

The light turns green
I close the door and kneel.
The mahogany box stands like an upturned coffin
It's pitch black inside and
Smells of worn velvet and hearts.

Say three Hail Marys
Two Our Fathers
Genuflect on your way out
Return next week
Perfect mortal sinner.

In the pit of my stomach
Words unleashed are bubbling up
Like lava, brimstone
Hellfire wanting to spit.
Outrage about to erupt.

Memorized words, meanings instilled
Syllable by syllable, from the Latin root
Shrouded in mystery
Clouded in frankincense
Embellished with gold leaf, sterling, and amber.

Infallible. Virgin. Unworthy. Submit. Be silent.
Words that strangle me

Like a crucifix on a chain
A noose around my neck.
I choke on their intentions.

Almighty Hangman
Give me a ladder.
Heaven is just out of reach.
And when I climb to the
Top rung
And stretch my fingertips
Toward salvation,
Kick the ladder out from
Under me, and
Watch my wings unfurl.

TATTOO

The indelible mark
Bears witness to the offertory.
My outstretched arm humbly, gratefully
Braces for the wound.
A healing infliction.

Your gift, the needle's dart.
Stab, release.
Again.
Again.
Steel pricking, injecting
Ink. Pain. Pleasure.
Like thorn through brow
Spike through palm
Relentless loving pierce.

Your black blood pumps into me
Like sacramental semen
Mixing with my crimson flush
Stinging the very core.
Sweet agony.

My body quakes in desperate resistance
As ancient rusted hinges are torn
Off the soul's heavy door
Thrust open
Like a sinner's lips
Awaiting communion.

Needle ceased.
Pain absorbed.
Gift accepted.
Saved again.

The Erotic Education of Elmer Rosewater

Ernest Posey

It is 1948, and nine-year-old Elmer Rosewater has been enrolled at a strict Roman Catholic boarding school, St. Stamen's School for Boys, on the Gulf Coast about an hour's drive east of New Orleans. In this excerpt, Elmer vividly remembers two lectures by Brother Severance, the religion teacher, who expounds on the Roman Catholic views on atheism and masturbation.

BROTHER SEVERANCE ON ATHEISM

"Good morning, class."

"Good morning, Brother Severance!"

"Today we're going to learn about God's plan for humanity and why God made us. Can anybody tell me why God made us?" I raised my hand. "Yes, Elmer."

"It's in the Little Catechism. 'God made us to know Him, to love Him, and to serve Him in this life, and to be happy with Him forever in the next.'"

"Very good, Elmer. That's correct. But what happens when we refuse to know God? What happens when men refuse to acknowledge God? What are such men called? Anybody? Such deluded men are called atheists. These men are so lost in the snares of Satan's web that they even deny the very existence of God."

"The Lord particularly hates the sin of atheism, and punishes it with a terrible vengeance."

"How many of you have heard of the ocean liner called the Titanic?" A few hands went up.

"Well, the Titanic was the largest passenger ship ever built. But the bankers who put up the money to build her were all atheists. So were the shipyard owners and the engineers. They claimed that the Titanic was unsinkable. They said that even *God* couldn't sink her. So just before the Titanic was launched, they ordered the painters in the shipyard to paint these words in big, black letters on the underside of the hull: NO GOD—NO HELL. After the ship was in the water, nobody could see those words, but the Lord could read them, and He decided to take vengeance."

"One night, on the ship's maiden voyage, the atheist bankers and their hired crew were having a party. The orchestra was playing and they were dancing around and drinking champagne. Then God sent a huge iceberg floating into the path of the Titanic. The two collided. The iceberg tore a long gash into the side of the ship. The hull filled with water within minutes. People were jumping into the ocean in panic, but they froze to death immediately. In the last moments, the atheist captain ordered the orchestra to play "Nearer My God To Thee" but it was too late. The Titanic sank like a brick to the bottom of the North Atlantic. Thousands of people died and all because of the pride and folly of a few atheists."

Bradley's hand went up. "Yes, Bradley."

"But Brother Severance, all of the people on the Titanic weren't atheists, were they? Maybe there were some Catholics on board."

"Sometimes the innocent must suffer with the guilty, such as when the Lord rained down fire and brimstone on the wicked cities of Sodom and Gomorrah. But I believe that the Lord arranged for the Catholics on board the Titanic to get places on the lifeboats, so they didn't drown with the rest. Any more questions?"

The classroom was silent while the students digested this terrifying story. Then a hand went up.

"Yes, Phillip, you have a question?"

"How does a person get to be an atheist? Didn't their mother and father tell them about God when they were little?"

"Good question, Phillip. It's the Devil who tempts men with the sin of pride. They begin to think that they can do things without God's help. The Devil leads them to finally deny the existence of God altogether. Sometimes very intelligent people become atheists, because the Devil blinds them with pride."

"There was a man named Robert Innersole who became an atheist and started to preach atheism. He became famous, and he wrote articles for newspapers and magazines. He even started to travel all over the country, giving lectures to spread his devilish ideas. He would tell his listeners that disbelief in God was a good thing, and that human beings did not really need God because science would take care of everything. Well, when Innersole was on his deathbed, he realized that he had made a terrible mistake. He realized that his soul was going to burn in hell for all eternity. He started screaming for a priest to hear his confession, but no priest came. He died screaming over and over, "Dear, God, forgive me!"

Once again, not a sound was heard in the classroom as the frightening tale sunk in.

"Any questions?" I put up my hand. "Yes, Elmer."

"Brother Severance, how long is eternity?"

"Eternity is always and forever. It's hard to understand, but think of it like this. Imagine that there is a little bird. Every year he picks up one grain of sand from the beach in his beak and flies to the moon and drops it. The bird does this every year for millions and billions and trillions of years, until he has emptied all the sand on all the beaches in the world. When the beaches are all empty, then the first second of eternity is just starting."

"Does that mean that the atheist has to burn in hell for all that long? He never gets out?"

"No. Never. God's justice is very stern, and He hates atheism most of all." I put up my hand again.

"You have another question, Elmer?"

"Yes, Brother. Suppose that there was a little baby boy who got shipwrecked and grew up all by himself on a desert island and didn't have anybody to tell him about God. So since he didn't believe in God because nobody was around to tell him, when he died, would his soul have to burn in hell for all eternity?"

Brother Severance's lips cracked into a rare thin smile. "Don't worry, Elmer. You have been fortunate enough to have received the word of God, so it would be impossible for you to succumb to the sin of atheism. Besides, such little boys on desert islands don't exist, and if they did, God would find a way to instruct them, like a catechism book rolled up inside a bottle would wash up on the beach."

I raised my hand again, because I wanted to know who would teach the little castaway to read?

Brother Severance ignored my hand and said, "Class dismissed."

ANGEL'S ROOST

At the beginning of the fall semester, I was transferred to an unfamiliar dormitory, nicknamed "Angel's Roost." Located in the attic of one of the older buildings, it was a low-ceilinged room with three large dormers, each big enough to hold two single beds. One of the dormers had been fitted with a door to make a private room for the dorm prefect, Brother Damon.

I much preferred this cozy room with only ten beds to the larger dorm I had known with those penitential rows upon rows of beds. The low ceiling of Angel's Roost made it easy to heat in winter, and, in warm weather, the window above my bed could be opened to catch the night breezes from the Gulf. Certain nights, the moonlight would pour in this east-facing window, bringing a celestial magic to the Roost.

Last and best, the layout made it very easy to jerk off. Since my bed was against the wall of one of the dormers, I would simply lie on my side facing the wall and masturbate with impunity. Besides, I could hear Brother Damon's door when it opened or closed, because one of the hinges made a distinctive grating sound. My ears became attuned to this sound, so I could always tell if he was patrolling the dorm.

My sleep was deeper and more refreshing in Angel's Roost than it had been before at St. Stamens. But one Thursday night, about a month after the beginning of the semester, I was awakened by a hand gently rubbing my shoulder. It was Brother Damon.

"Wake up, Elmer," he whispered. "Come to my bedroom. Don't knock."

As soon as my mind cleared, I tiptoed over to Brother Damon's door. It was slightly ajar so I pushed it open and went in. The prefect's room contained a single bed, no different from mine, a small desk, a chair, and a desk lamp. A tiny bookcase held a few books. A dim amber-colored nightlight was plugged into the wall behind the bed. A window like mine looked out over the waters of the Gulf.

Brother Damon was sitting on the edge of his bed, wearing a dark-colored dressing robe. "Close the door, Elmer." I closed the door as quietly as I could. He motioned to the empty chair. "Sit down, Elmer. I want to talk to you." I sat down and waited. My heart was pounding, and my mouth was dry as cotton wool. The alarm on the desk ticked softly and its hands stood at 12:10 a.m.

"You have seemed sad since you came back from summer vacation. I remember seeing you very happy last spring. Is something bothering you, Elmer?"

It seemed as if he had seen through me, all the way into my soul. I was indeed sad and lonely. I missed Boudreaux something awful, and whenever I thought about him, I wanted to cry. How could I explain these sinful feelings to a Brother who had taken the vow of chastity? I was too ashamed.

All these thoughts and feelings came up in an overwhelming rush. Brother Damon must have seen the expression on my face. "You can confide in me, Elmer. I'm here to help. Tell me what's wrong."

It was all too much for me. I started to sob, deep gasping sobs from the bottom of my lungs. Brother Damon grasped my shoulders gently and pulled me to his chest. He encircled me with his arms and held me until my blubbering stopped. Then he sat me on his knee and dried my cheeks with his handkerchief. He stroked my hair and rubbed the back of my neck.

"There, it feels better to let it all out, doesn't it? I've seen boys cry before, and it's always better after a good cry." He smiled and stroked my chin gently. "You miss Boudreaux very much, don't you?" He brushed my forehead lightly with his lips.

I was thunderstruck. How did he know about Boudreaux? All the effort we spent keeping our meetings secret had been useless? My astonishment was evident. I'm sure that I turned red as a strawberry.

"I've known about you and Boudreaux for a long time, Elmer. I could see what you were doing at the end of the pier by looking out my window."

I realized that Brother Damon's view included the benches at the far end of the pier. I looked over at the window and noticed a set of binoculars on the windowsill. How many times had he spied on us? Why had he not reported our sins to the principal? Why had he waited until now to say anything to me?

"Don't worry, Elmer, I'm not going to punish you. I want to help you. Now tell me, did Boudreaux ever touch your private parts?"

"No, Brother, never even once."

"But he let you touch his private parts, did he not?"

"Yes, Brother."

"Did you touch his penis or his testicles, or both?"

"Both, Brother."

"Now think carefully, Elmer. Did Boudreaux coerce you—force you—to touch his privates?"

I thought for a moment before I answered. "No, Brother. He didn't force me."

The prefect let out a little puff of breath. "In other words, Elmer, without being forced, you wanted, you desired of your own free will, to play with Boudreaux's sexual organs?"

"Yes, Brother Damon, I wanted to do it!"

I was starting to cry again. My eyelids burned and the tears started to wash down my cheeks. My body started to shake. Brother Damon put his arms around my waist and pulled me close to him. I sensed a wetness on the back of my neck and realized that the prefect was crying too. He hugged me closer. Then I felt a hard lump against my thigh through his dressing gown. Brother Damon's prick was erect and throbbing. I reached down and pressed it gently.

It calmed me down to feel a man's hard prick in my hand, the thing I had been missing since Boudreaux graduated. I reached under the dressing gown and fondled Brother Damon's erection. He started to shake and sob, the way I had done a few moments before. His sobbing turned to low moans as I started to stroke up and down in a regular rhythm.

I knew what I needed to do. I knelt on the floor between his legs and pulled open his robe. His prick was engorged with blood, red and throbbing in dim light. I spat on my palm and started to jerk his dick in earnest. He fell back across the bedspread with a grunt. His whole body was trembling, and a moment later a torrent of sticky cream jetted across his belly, his chest and even landed on his nose. And it kept coming and coming and coming. So I kept stroking and pulling and milking, until he grabbed my hand and whispered hoarsely, "Enough, Elmer, enough."

Time seemed to freeze for a few minutes. We both remained still, and then Brother Damon took a small hand towel from under his pillow and wiped up the spunk from his face, his chest and belly. He seemed deflated, like a balloon emptied of its air. He handed me the towel to wipe my hand.

He smiled weakly. "You're a good lad, Elmer. A good lad. Now go back to bed. Be very quiet. And don't mention this to a soul."

As I was opening the door, he whispered, "Come back here at midnight on Sunday."

BROTHER SEVERANCE ON MASTURBATION

"Good morning class."

"Good morning, Brother Severance!"

"Today we're going to learn about a very important topic, so I want everyone to listen very carefully."

"Can anybody tell me what the word "virgin" means?"

Brother Severance paused gravely. Everyone looked around uneasily. Finally, Bradley raised his hand.

"Yes, Bradley."

"I think I read somewhere that it means pure and white, like new-fallen snow. But I never saw snow, so I don't know for sure."

A few boys giggled, but Brother Severance silenced them with a scowl.

"That's right, Bradley. It means untouched, unstained, unpolluted, unspoiled. The pure sinless soul is like a beautiful white garment like the one our Lord wore when He ascended to heaven. When a person commits a mortal sin, it's like taking handfuls of slimy, dirty mud and dung from the bottom of a pigsty and throwing it all over until the pure white garment of the soul is black and polluted."

Brother Severance looked around the classroom as if he were examining our dirty little souls. The boys shifted uncomfortably in their seats.

"Right now, some of you may be in the state of mortal sin. And how do you clean the white garment of your soul?"

Bradley raised his hand. "Yes, Bradley, you seem to know all the answers this morning."

Bradley blushed and stammered, "By the Sacrament of Penance?"

"Correct. Our Savior gave us the Sacrament of Penance, so that by confessing our sins, we can wash away the black stain of sin and return our souls to their virginal condition. If you die while your soul is in the filthy state of mortal sin, you will go directly to hell for all eternity. So you must be vigilant and confess your sins regularly and receive absolution.

"Now, one of the sins which boys are likely to commit is the sin of self-abuse. Describing this filthy sin is not necessary at this time, because you know what I'm talking about." He looked sternly around the room. The entire class was on the edge of their seats waiting for what was to come.

"The body is the temple of the soul. The Lord intended that our bodies should be kept pure and virginal as suitable vessels to contain our immortal soul. Abusing your God-given body is one of the things that the Lord hates most.

"Here's an example. There was a boy I taught a few years ago. On the outside he seemed very innocent and pure. He went to Mass and took Holy Communion practically every day. He went to Confession twice a week. He got straight As on his report card. Nobody suspected that he practiced self-abuse on a regular basis. When he confessed his sins, he lied to the priest, and never mentioned his secret vice. Then, one night he died in his sleep. They took his body to the funeral parlor and put it in a coffin. But when they tried to close the coffin lid, the Lord caused his right arm to stick straight up, stiff as a board. The morticians tried to push the arm down so they could close the coffin, but they couldn't budge it. It was that very arm that he used in his self-abuse. Finally, the morticians had to use a hacksaw and cut the arm off at the shoulder. They buried him with his severed arm."

The classroom was as still as a tomb. Brother Severance paused for dramatic effect and then continued.

"Self-abuse affects every part of the body as well as the soul. Every act of self-abuse is like a series of electric shocks which travel up the spinal cord to the brain. Eventually, the whole system degenerates and collapses. The senses are afflicted. Sometimes the unfortunate sinner will start to go deaf in one ear, then in both ears. The taste buds degenerate so that chocolate will start to taste like feces. A root beer will smell like urine. Often, the self-abuser's body will begin to tremble violently, or it will collapse in a faint. Finally, the eyes will start to shrivel like prunes and the sinner will go blind.

"Self-abuse is like an addiction and the self-abuser is like a dope fiend. The more he gets, the more he wants. He begins to crave these electric shocks to the brain, and finds it impossible to stop. Every time he commits this abominable sin, he simply digs his grave deeper.

"I am reminded of a case which I heard about that happened in New Orleans. There was a boy who practiced self-abuse every day, sometimes several times a day. He started to show symptoms of illness and depression. His parents took him to many different medical clinics, but nobody could diagnose his disease. One night, his parents were startled to hear loud screams. They rushed to his bedroom. The boy was stark raving mad, and a gray slime was oozing out of his ears and his nose. When the ambulance arrived, he was already dead. The autopsy revealed that his brains had turned to jelly, and simply drained out of any available orifice in his skull. His parents were so ashamed that they had his corpse cremated and then they flushed the ashes down the toilet."

Brother Severance paused. Every boy in the classroom was frozen, barely daring to breathe.

"If you should find yourself afflicted by this horrible vice, pray to Our Lady for help. She should be our model of purity and chastity. Ask her to relieve you of your addiction to self-abuse. Confess your sins and resolve to make a new start. Return the white garment of your soul to its virginal condition."

Brother Severance looked at his watch.

"Class dismissed," he said.

This lecture gave me a lot to think about, because I was abusing myself at least once, sometimes several times a day. I knew that my soul was doomed to burn in hell for all eternity. I also knew that there was no way that I was going to be able to give up jerking off. My little child's soul became a battleground, and I seemed helpless to change the outcome of the struggle.

HERETICS

Jesus Is My Father

A. Lizbeth Babcock

I first learned the word "illegitimate" when I was seven years old. It was perfect timing since my first confession was just around the corner. I always knew that there was something "wrong" with my father's absence. I knew because of the barrage of questions from classmates and teachers and other people's parents about where and who he was. With that first confession fast approaching, and me—the ripe old age of seven—not feeling like I had a whole heck of a lot of sins to choose from, I thought being illegitimate sounded like a good one to lay before Father Walter, my parish priest. Turns out it was, because I had to say four Hail Marys and an Our Father as penance. I imagined each act of contrition washing over me like a storm-tossed wave from the nearby lake, washing over the dirt of me and making me clean.

The kids who couldn't think of anything to admit at their big confessional debut resorted to making things up about stealing cookies and other such frivolities. I didn't have the wit back then to suggest that they just confess to being liars. Nor did I have the insight to scrutinize the irony of the whole preposterous liturgy. I was just glad I didn't have to fib about *my* sin. Glad I had one of those good sins that I could keep using over time, because it would always be there, like dirt beneath my feet.

The nuclear family reined supreme in 1970s small-town Ontario, and it was even more pronounced in the little Catholic community that surrounded my school. I not only stood out because of my paternal deficiency, but also because I wasn't taxied around town in a family station wagon chock-full of siblings. I lived in the low-rental apartment units—not in one of the nice houses by the school, and I was the only child of a single parent. My mom got pregnant with me in high school, the same one I would eventually attend, and she went to college when I started kindergarten.

So, of course the other children asked questions about the ways in which I was different from them. They asked *lots* of questions. And there was no escape and there were no answers. I felt a bit like a piñata strung up in the air, getting bashed again and again for colorful details that might fall out of me if only someone could hit the right spot with enough force. I hated all of the space between myself and others. I decided I should consult my mother for advice.

"Just tell them you don't have a father," were her words of wisdom. "It's none of their business." It seemed reasonable. But then there was the whole problem with the scientific validity of the explanation. And those kids from big families know all about the nitty gritty details of conception. Basically, the problem was that no one believed me. And they didn't believe me because it wasn't true.

The truth was, I had a secret dad that no one could know about. I called him by his first name, John, because that's what he wanted. He visited sometimes on Sunday evenings, and brought ice cream—the main ingredient of *our* root beer floats—and I got to stay up late and watch "All in the Family" with him on those nights. It's a memory that has stayed with me all of these years, because it's a good memory. Sometimes I catch the reruns. I think about the animated expression on his face, the big mug of frothy drink in his hand, how he laughed. But I know that for the most part I felt terribly awkward around my father, and terribly unloved. I could feel the distance he constructed between us. That distance was like thick layers of stone that I couldn't climb over, couldn't bust through.

John was married and had one of those big families of his own. It appeared that he had a lot to lose should the knowledge of my paternity become public. I heard him talking one time about taking his kids on a trip to Florida. He could have knocked the wind out of me just as easily by kicking me in the stomach. I wondered what it would be like to go somewhere like that with him, to be with him like that. I wondered what I'd have to do to be one of the kids who got to go. But that trip to the sunshine state came and went, and I wasn't a part of it. He brought me back a key chain.

I felt pretty awkward and uncomfortable around dads in general. I had no idea how to interact with them, and I worried that they could see that thing inside of me that made me bad; that thing you had to look a little closer to find, like dirt at the bottom of a glass. Even if they didn't see it at first glance, it was just a matter of time until they looked a little deeper, their expressions giving them away. Being alone with one of them was like being held under water.

Still, I hoped that things would change. Someday, he would be proud to be my dad and would want everyone to know that I was his. And if he could see the good inside of me, everyone else would see it too. There would be no need for questions. The strings that held me up would sever, and my bright colors would fade to gray. Finally, I would be one of them.

I went to school with a girl named Holly McKenna, who could run faster than anyone else. And another girl named Tara Sullivan wore the most beautiful dresses and competed in national beauty pageants. If only I could show my dad that I was especially good at something, things might be different. We could be a real family, like the McKennas and the Sullivans. Or maybe my dad could just be "out" about having two families. Maybe it didn't all need to be so secret. But I watched Archie Bunker carefully, and I learned that the status quo was hard to change.

The problem was that I wasn't the fastest runner in school, and my mom couldn't afford beautiful dresses or beauty pageant entry fees. I tried really hard to be good at things, but I was never the best. I got a lot of second and third place ribbons at track and field, but I never got first place. I was a finalist in a county-wide art contest—I painted a picture of a dead girl in the grass that they called "sleeping girl"–but I didn't win. I prayed that God would make me more like someone else.

One day when I was struggling to answer some particularly direct and contentious questions, a boy named Sean Kirkpatrick said:

"Jesus is her father."

Everyone went silent, including me. For some reason, this seemed to make some kind of sense in our little distorted world. And for some reason, this felt better to me than having a secret dad who wanted me to call him John. "Jesus is my father" became my only defense.

That week at Church, I looked at the big mural of Jesus above the altar with a longing I had never known. I imagined floating up to him, like an angel, and stretching myself across his image. I could almost feel the ridges of his slender frame against me, his skin spread tight across his bones, little muscles underneath. I could almost see his arms drop down from the holy cross, fall forward, wrap around me; his bloody hands pressing hard against my back, like he had been hanging there waiting to hold my little body for a long time. I started to resent the space between Jesus and my church pew. And I started to pray a lot:

Dear God,

If Jesus is my father, which I believe he is, I'm wondering if you can send him down for dinner sometime this week? I could invite my friends over and we could eat around the kitchen table like a real family. I'll make sure that he's back in heaven early because I know you keep him busy up there. Could you think about it? And if it's not too much to ask, could you make sure that all little creatures are safe tonight and always?

Thank you Lord,

Amen.

I always felt a special kind of affinity with animals and other little beings. Maybe I identified with their vulnerability, and to some extent, their helplessness when it came to humans. I went to school with a girl named Joss Robinson. She was a bully through and through, but she liked me in particular because I cried at the drop of a dime back then. To make matters worse, her mother was my after school babysitter. So, I spent countless hours being terrorized by her. We would walk back to her house at the end of the day, following a narrow dirt path through the grassy field behind the local college where my mom went to school. The thick grass stood tall and stiff above my head—tickling, poking—unwanted up my skirt; the air breathed through the dark blades in a slow, deliberate pant. I would say it was beautiful, but for all the murders.

It was in that field that Joss would always manage to find a baby frog or a bird or rabbit; she could spot a rabbit like a lynx in the Rocky Mountains. She'd get me to name the little creatures, and then she'd stomp the living shit out of them while I screamed and cried—the desired response. She was the kind of girl who liked to burn ants with a magnifying glass, and pull the wings off flies. She was the kind of girl I wanted to put my foot on and squish into the ground.

I felt that in some warped way I was responsible for the suffering of all of those tiny beings, since they died for the entertainment value of my reaction. I wished that I could carry the little carcasses to a special place where, if I prayed really hard, God would breathe life back into their bodies, because he can do things like that. But finding all of the remains after the fact proved to be an impossible task. So instead, I prayed for their protection. And I spent my lunch hours carrying grasshoppers to the other side of the school yard fence so they wouldn't get trampled upon, singing songs along the way, like "We Shall Overcome."

But Jesus never stopped the killing, nor did he ever come for dinner. I'm not too certain what we would have served him anyway. Dinner was always a quick fix at my place because my mom had to study hard in the evenings so she could get a good job. She wasn't much of a cook either, and most meals started off frozen. We didn't even say grace or thank God for the perfect little compartments of frozen peas, mashed potato, apple crumble, and (what I think was) meat.

When I was told of my father's death, I secretly grieved; I grieved mostly for the loss of my hope for our relationship and all of the things that would never be, all of the things *I* would never be. The grief grew and grew like thick, dark grass that held the blood and guts of animals and the breath of little girls. And even all of the secret tears I cried couldn't wash away the dirt. I became more invested in the idea that Jesus might come to earth in flesh and blood, and legitimate me. That he might come to fill a void that hurt as much as being stomped to death:

God Almighty,

You know you have my dad with you now. And I know you bring people to you for good reasons. But I was wondering if, now that he is there, you could tell him a few good things about me. Because I didn't get a chance to show him anything good. If I had, he would have been proud for me to be his girl. And I thought maybe you could make him proud of me from heaven. You could whisper the good things in his ear.

I know that I should not ask for too many things, Lord. But my dad won't be coming to visit anymore since he is busy with you. And I was wondering if you could send Jesus down in his place one Sunday night, in flesh and blood. If you send him with ice cream, I'll make him something that I know he'll enjoy. And he can leave right after.

I hope you have time to hear this prayer.
Amen.

I sent that wish to God every night, until eventually the nights turned into weeks and the weeks turned into months, and soon a whole new school year smacked me in the face. But Jesus never came with ice cream, and there were no root beer floats after that.

By the time confirmation rolled around, I made friends with a man named Cedric. I never did catch his last name, but he was an older man who drove for the local taxi company, and he was pretty well-known in the community. He drove me everywhere and gave me money to shop with. He did some of those things that dads do, like taking me and my friends from point A to point B. And my friends thought it was neat to ride in a taxi and not have to pay for it. I thought so too. My new Sunday ritual was driving around with Ced while he picked up his fares, and chatting and noticing things around town. He had his flaws, but he filled some of that void that hurt so much. He made me feel like there was less distance between myself and others. And he occupied some of that space that sat between:

"Dad" and "John"
Ontario and Florida
Jesus and my church pew

And for a while, all I thought about was Ced. I thought about how fast his car could go and how far away we could drive. It didn't even occur to me that there would be a price to pay for his attention. But nothing in life is free. He wanted me to pay in ways I didn't even know existed. And I held my breath every time it happened. There wasn't much to notice anymore, except for the dark, velvety roof of his car, and the blue and white of heaven behind the bodies of insects on his windshield. But by then, I questioned the existence of heaven. And I had given up on prayer. "Do you like this?" he would ask. But I wasn't even there to answer.

I entered grade nine with dirt all over me, like sand from the beach that you just keep finding, ground into every crevice of your body. It fell from my hair when I brushed it; it oozed from my pores when I sweat. There were smears on my face that not even a body of lake water could wash off. I started making myself throw up that year because I didn't know what else to do. I spent a lot of time in the girls' bathroom. And I noticed that there was always a pale gray cloud of smoke hovering above the last stall. It didn't bother me though—if anything it helped me feel nauseous. Then one day a voice emanated from the haze. "Are you okay?" it asked.

"I'm fine. Leave me alone," I grumbled. Annoyed.

"Why are you doing that?" the voice persisted. It was above me now, and when I looked up I saw a girl I had never seen before. She was standing on the toilet, leaning over the wall, a cigarette pinched between her thumb and index finger.

"Why are *you* doing *that*?" I charged back, swiftly gathering my things and departing for Sister Marnie's math class. "I'm late," I offered apologetically as the bathroom door caught and closed gradually.

It became a bit of a ritual. Her and I in the bathroom between classes: her smoking, me barfing. "You could get in trouble, you know," I teased one day.

"You *are* in trouble," she said with the most serious of tones. And we had . . . the greatest discussions of all time. Her name was Sunny Campenelli. Soon, we were skipping class to be there among the flushing tanks and running faucets, skipping class to plant our asses on the cool, tile floor, and talk. She was different from any girl I had ever known. She was tougher. More like a boy than a girl, with long sandy bangs that guarded her eyes. Most of our questions to each other started off with, "Do you . . . ?"

"Do you like guys?" she asked one day, her body tipped forward for my response. I hesitated for a moment.

"Yes!" I said emphatically, wrapping my arms around my knees. I was trying to give all the right answers.

"Do you do it with guys?" she pursued. I knew what she was driving at. Did I go out on dates with guys my own age, and did I have sex with them, etc . . .

"No." And I hadn't done *that,* so it felt like the truth.

"Do you want to know *how* to do it with a guy?" she probed with one eyebrow raised behind her shield of hair.

"You've done it with a guy?" I squealed, my jaw on the ground.

"I'll teach you how. You won't be nervous if you've practiced."

I actually didn't feel like I *would* know how to "do it" with a guy in a normal everyday circumstance. So I agreed to love lessons. The next day Sunny and I met in our regular spot, the handicapped booth at the back of the "spa," or so we now called it. I wasn't quite sure what to expect, or even what I had agreed to exactly. She had her school bag with her, which I had never seen before, and she directed me to stand up. I looked at her, perplexed, because I was already standing. "No, here," she instructed, and she gave the pearly white toilet a tap with her hand. I climbed up and placed one palm on the wall, and each foot on an opposite side of the plastic seat. I watched curiously as she shuffled through her bag for God knows what, then watched her pull out the biggest fucking carrot I had ever seen.

"What's *that* for?" I said to no response. "What's it for?" I whined insistently.

"Just relax, it's for when you're ready." *It* stood ominously beside me on the big toilet paper container. Erect.

"I'm not sure I'll ever be ready for *that,*" I said.

"Shhhh," she urged, busily pulling saran wrap from the bottom of her tote and placing it beside the bright orange spectacle.

"Um—" I began again.

"Just relax. Holy Moses!" she groaned. Exasperated.

"How can I relax with—"

And then she touched me. Slipped her hand up under my kilt and ran her firm fingers across the silky material of my underwear. It was . . . divine. My nipples went hard beneath my cardigan, my blouse, my white cotton bra. And I breathed heavy breaths that made me feel full and present. When she felt my moisture against her hand she said, "We're going to have to take these off." And I helped her. My underwear clung pointlessly around my knees, just above my tall, woolen socks. And Sunny's head disappeared under the rough pleats of my navy blue uniform. I pulled her face in even closer, harder, from the other side of the coarse fabric.

"Do you like this?" she asked, sounding smothered.

"Yes!" I confessed as the bell sounded and girls raided the bathroom to fix their hair and makeup. "Oh my, God, yes!" I cried out like I had seen the light.

"Quiet!" she scolded, her lips tense with controlled giggle. I hunched down to avoid detection. And eventually, after the girls left our sacred hideaway, Sunny fucked me with the colossal vegetable. Oh, I mean, she *prepared* me for sex with guys, see. And two years later when I actually "lost my virginity" to some random doofus from fourth period, I couldn't help but think of Sunny, and the second floor spa. I couldn't help but wonder if she saved me that day.

I came out as queer years later when I moved to Toronto to study social work. I still don't know what happened to Sunny. One day, she just wasn't there anymore. I used to lock myself in that bathroom stall and remember her, between classes. I think of her sometimes. She had talked about running away to Toronto, the closest urban center, and she had wanted me to come with her. But I could always think of reasons not to go. I like to imagine her here in the big city, maybe not so far away from me, out and proud, and fucking women without the unnecessary guise of training them. But sometimes I wonder if she was one of the casualties, one of the kids who wound up on the streets and got swallowed, like so many small-town escapees.

For the most part now, I live in the present. And my present doesn't include much thought of church or God or religion. But I still dream about my little hometown, dream that I'm flying, just like an angel, in the little stone church where I confessed my first sin.

I'm floating in the air, and I do not need strings to hold me high. I soar up to that mural of Jesus, stretching my full-grown body across his image, my breasts pressed hard against his chest. I touch his cheek, slowly, carefully, trace the lines of his features; run my fingers along the thorns of his crown. I am so gentle. There is no space between us; our bodies meld together, soft breaths bouncing back against the flatness of his face. This is the moment I have dreamed of for a lifetime. The details are overwhelming: his flesh, his blood, his bones, all perfectly etched. Even his expression seems different: more peace, less suffering. These are the things you can't see from the pew. Everything is dark and close and blended. In the backdrop of caliginous sky I see the souls of little beings who once walked the earth, but who now fly with God.

I press my lips hard against the mouth of Christ, staining his perfect skin with the red of my lipstick. My hand evanesces beneath my clothes, and my underwear descend willingly, effortlessly to my knees, and stay taut there. My legs are spread; my thighs wet with the warm overflow of my desire. My body is mine to touch, and it is cleansed and purged and beaming—my fingers twitching, rubbing beneath my layers of beautiful gown. I moan in exaltation. I am ready to receive him, if *only* he would say the word. My eyes, my mouth, my heart, my cunt—everything open.

"Jesus?"
I am breathless and not worthy.
"Am I still your child?"

I Was Always a Marian Heretic

Trebor Healey

It wasn't something I decided upon or thought out. It was just that, on some level, church was a big, BIG room you walked into, and you looked around for a nice or safe person to talk to. It was crowded and you were supposed to "behave" as there was something vaguely threatening in the air.

Its name was God.

You crossed yourself to appease him when you entered, and genuflected at the pew to humble yourself again just for good measure.

And then there was this quiet lady with a kindly face over in the corner, a big bank of candles in front of her.

Mary.

It wasn't something I ever had to think about or decide upon. Infantile, I toddled toward my mother. With a smile. The church was always that kind of refuge to me: a lap; a pretty place to be quiet and alone with one's thoughts; a place where no one was allowed to beat you or berate you and humiliate you; a place where you could actually reach out and shake someone's hand and offer them peace; you could smile and they'd smile back with nothing to sell.

The Eucharist was like a cookie. Hospitality.

I knew it was God's house, but what was best in it didn't seem to have much to do with him. People talked about God as mighty and good and loving. But if he was, why did they have to keep reiterating it? Besides, from what I read in the Bible he seemed to be somebody prone to violence, punishment, and tests. I didn't like violence, punishment or tests. I liked hugs and smiles, candlelight and quiet.

Mary.

It was God's house, but it was her home.

Perhaps then, it was all because of my mother who was kind and a closeted Marian heretic herself. In fact, I come from a long line of

Irish women, all Marian heretics. They saw Christ as having set the example, done us all a big favor. *Don't bother him, he's done enough.* God was beyond reach, probably the ever-unfolding rose of Dante's *Paradiso* to them, if not the Godfather whom you simply did not piss off or annoy under any circumstances. They always claimed how loving he was, but when things got desperate they always turned to *her,* not him.

During Mass, with its Old Testament first reading, we weekly received the message that God was an ornery, old grandpa, dyspeptic and cranky. This was supposedly fatherly, but I never saw him as a father, and would have run away if he was mine. My Dad was nice, a sort of comic jokester kind of guy who never hit us.

In the second reading we were subjected to one of the letters of Paul, God's attorney general, who droned on and on, scolding us in bad epistolary prose. I thought him a piss-ant.

Jesus, being the star and hero, or prince (God, the sequel), got the good parts—the Gospel—but he was unimpressive to me, his stories kind of obvious, and he wasn't very warm. Besides, he was doomed, a tragic figure, and a willing one at that. God living out his dreams through his son, like half the Dads with kids in Little League. I even felt a little sorry for Jesus. He was like one of those brilliant-colored Swallowtail butterflies, pinned (literally) on velvet: pretty, but dead and from some past inaccessible world of drama long gone. He never stood a chance. And I never really believed he was around; never prayed to him. I mean, they'd go on and on: *Christ has died, Christ is risen, Christ will come again.* When? He's 2000 years late. I wasn't holding my breath. He was a no-show is what he was.

Mary, she was accessible, and well, a mother—I knew what that was as I had one. I didn't have a Jesus, a God, or a Holy Spirit. They were like superheroes, something for the imagination. Mary, being a mom, was real. She had to deal with you, and would. An intercessor, she would deliver your prayers. All the saints could do this of course, but only for specific things: St. Anthony for lost objects, for instance; St. Francis for wounded squirrels and birds; St Jude, when you felt especially desperate. Mary, she was like the queen of the chess board, and those saints were just pawns, or rooks or bishops at best, restricted by their various specialties. No such limitations were set on Mary. It was as if she had that doomsday phone they say Nixon had where he could call straight through to Brezhnev in case of nuclear war. Mary could barge right into a private meeting God was having with the devil or whomever. *She* was the connection to have. And what was God? The boss, the principal, the chief of police. The bumbler. The threat. Faceless authority. God really was the King of the chessboard, silently waiting for Checkmate, while Mary rushed about winning the game. I wouldn't have known what to say to him if I ever did meet him. I'd likely just duck or run. So Mary handled it for me. I knew I could tell her I was queer when it dawned on me as a boy. She might even help me get rid of it. I wouldn't dare speak of it to God or Jesus. I wasn't stupid. Men didn't like fags.

So I addressed my prayers in her direction. And Mary developed quite a track record between my own requests and those of my mother, who petitioned her often in my presence. I watched Mary find my mother parking spaces; watched her help my mother negotiate black ice, and save a soufflé from falling. She was always on call and amazingly attentive. She continually came through for me in myriad ways: saving me from German Shepherds; helping me understand my algebra; fixing it so I'd win at Monopoly; or, that I didn't catch my brother's cold or chicken pox; delivered on aisle five when I'd say a *Hail Mary* and ask that she please make Mom buy the Oreos. Bingo. I prayed that I would not be insulted, bullied, beaten—at least not too much. I sealed it with the sign of the cross, and kept a rosary under my pillow, along with the occasional lost tooth, my scapular, and my shiniest, JFK fifty-cent piece. And I felt invincible. *"You've got a friend . . ."* James Taylor sang melodiously.

Maybe it worked because I asked for small things. Later my demands would get bigger—and poor Mary, she didn't do big. Which made her all the more special on some level. A true Mom.

Like my own dear Catholic mom, who after her fourth child was told in no uncertain terms, she'd likely die if she carried another. What was a Catholic girl to do? She went looking for a priest who'd okay birth control. Priests were intercessors as well. And she found one. Later she'd find one who would okay homosexuality when I confessed that unpleasant truth. Because it was never about moralizing, or any kind of 'now you've done it'. If I'd killed someone, my mom would have simply found a priest who could secure my forgiveness, and she'd be back in the kitchen making up care packages to take to San Quentin. So I knew priests weren't really holy men. They were more like agents, lawyers, advocates—*homies*? None of us were good enough for God apparently—his standard was an ideal after all, like the Constitution or the Bill of Rights—so we had to hire attorneys to plead our case. Intercessors. I knew early on I was never going to pass muster with God the father, so I needed Mary's advocacy. She petitioned. She would go to God for you. She was a lawyer, like all the priests and saints were lawyers. They couldn't change the laws, they couldn't mete out sentences, but they could argue your case. A good lawyer is always better than a good judge, and Mary knew the laws of the human heart, better even than God himself did. She was an expert witness.

When my mother had finally admitted her use of birth control to me years later, I'd wondered how exactly she'd found a priest who would allow it. Without missing a beat, she answered: "I prayed to the Blessed Virgin Mother, of course." An intercessor for an intercessor.

My mother was a devotee of the rosary, and along with the Blessed Mother, she was into the Holy Spirit more than she was ever into Jesus or God. I never got the Holy Spirit myself. He sounded sneaky and hard to pin down, being invisible and all. My mother was sort of psychic, seeing lights and having strange supernormal encounters. She was always getting messages: nudges from sick relatives, flashes of light when old aunts died, pats on the back from the dead. She'd bug out her eyes and tell us it was the Holy Spirit. Okay then. But he never talked to me.

Be that as it may, there's something for everyone in Catholicism. It was a spiritual candy store in many ways. I had my book of saints with my favorites—the cute ones: St. Martin de Porres, St. Sebastian, the several young, Italian boys with stigmata. But I never really prayed to them for whatever reason. Probably because Mary trumped them, and she worked—and, of course, she was a mom. Cute boys were narcissists, even if they were saints. Mary was sweet and seemed to take an interest in my welfare (I had hard evidence: dogs who abruptly stopped chasing me, miraculous cures of stomachaches), so I stuck with her. She was my true and erstwhile friend, just like my real-life Mom.

When I explicitly realized I was queer at eleven (a combination of the locker room at The Washington Athletic Club and that nearly nude poster of Burt Reynolds that was circulating in 1974), I asked Mary to please put a stop to it. I checked up on her progress too—or rather, was alerted to her negligence—as I found myself still gazing longingly at boys and their various parts: hands, elbows, chins, knees, and those shocking unmentionables that required the sign of the cross. Down at the lake—oh my god, how their nipples indicted me and sent me spiraling into gut-sinking, tragic hopelessness.

I figured I needed to say more rosaries (that was always my Mom's last resort). I'd pace around the house, my brothers looking at me with concern. They never teased me. Everyone respected the rosary and Mary, and both my parents were a bit obsessive-compulsive—switching off lights, checking the stove, locks, the mailbox—so what's another kid circumambulating the rec. room saying *Hail Marys*? Just don't step on the Lincoln Logs. Maybe it was because our mother was a saint, I don't know. We kids endlessly joked about everything else Catholic—using Cheerios and Ruffles as hosts, anointing each other's foreheads with Mazzola, or parading around with a tennis racket in place of a monstrance—until we were slapped for our blasphemous behavior. But Mary got a pass. We were all Marian heretics I think. Like I say, a long line of them. It's a hallowed, Irish tradition.

I took a rosary to school. Kids would ask me what it was, or tell me they knew. Some would defensively throw out: "Well, I'm a Christian too!" But I was quick to retort: "I'm not a Christian, I'm a Catholic!" Which was like saying, *I'm not a boy, I'm a man!* I was the real deal, and they were cheap knockoffs. Imagine my surprise when I began to meet readers of Chick publications, which claimed that Catholics were worshippers of Baal, and that the Holy Father, Pope Paul, was the devil incarnate. I didn't care about the pope really, but what about Mary? *Don't cast aspersions on my mother—she doesn't wear army boots*. But they never actually had a bad word for her in all their Catholic bashing. The only pamphlet she starred in was titled "Why Is Mary Crying?" and it said that it was because priests and popes had corrupted the faith. Well, I couldn't argue with that.

But the rosaries didn't work. After that, it was St. Jude, or find another means. I learned the Memorary: *"Remember O Most Gracious Virgin Mary that NEVER was it known that ANYONE who ever FLED to thy PROTECTION, IMPLORED thy HELP or SOUGHT thy INTERCESSION, was left UNAIDED."* A guarantee.

But I still found myself staring at boys—at their arms and legs, their chins, their brows; imagining them naked. Even as I droned along in the pew," . . . . *we believe in one God, the Father, the Al-*

mighty, maker of heaven and earth, of all that is, seen and unseen. . . ." Indeed.

I became sad more than angry or freaked out, because I knew boys' beauty spoke to my heart, and I trusted my heart even as I was told not to. A conundrum. The dread was never hell in the afterlife, but some version of it in the here and now. The dread was loneliness and the shame of social failure. But I knew Mary didn't judge me. God and Dr. David Rubin did however. Dr. Rubin, who wrote that book my father had on his shelf that I'd referred to in my confusion, as it was the only thing at hand: *Everything You Ever Wanted to Know About Sex But Were Afraid to Ask.* Dr. Rubin pretty much relegated me to "sicko," informing me that I'd spend my entire adult life in subway toilets seeking out "meat." I was shocked. *Say it ain't so, Mary!*

I prayed to be straight, looking into the naves where she played second fiddle to the men.

Because it was all about men, wasn't it? My attraction and the proscription regarding it—though I'd heard even my mother quip that homosexuals were selfish, because they didn't have children. But that was something I could rectify as I figured I could always adopt. Selfish was something I could handle, but what came out of the mouths of my father and brothers I could not, as they laughed, mocked, and carried on, all agreeing that faggots were sick, disgusting and should be killed.

At Mass, Paul railed about abominations (I hated him); the Old Testament God ranted about impurities and disobedience (blah, blah, blah); Jesus ignored me and droned on with his parables about mustard seeds and thieves in the night. It all seemed more and more irrelevant. I mean, I was a good kid; I *got* the gospels; I was good with the golden rule. In the end, the only words of *His* that ever really struck me were about leaving one's family to follow him. Was he gay? Follow him where—to the subway? I didn't know—he was an enigma. He'd never tell. *Men.*

So I prayed to Mary, my heart a mess, weeping its way toward my divine mother, longing toward my classmates—and during Mass at our parish, Sacred Heart, toward the altar boys. They looked SO CUTE in those dresses.

Since my father had been beaten as a youth in parochial school by Jesuits, he gave us a pass on both Catholic school and being altar boys. We were public school crossing guards instead. But I admired altar boys from afar. I loved them as I loved all Catholic boys. I thought Catholic boys were special like I thought the Catholic Church was special. After all, I and my Catholic crush boys were ancient. We were Romans. Part of history. To be part of an ancient tradition was a kind of succor. It gave me an odd kind of hope, like maybe I could make it through somehow. The balm of longevity. I suppose I began to hide in it, like people have always hidden away in the folds of tradition–in the mantle of Our Lady even, I cowered.

So, while other boys grew proud of their looks, athletic abilities, or maybe the sudden girth and length of their dicks, I reached for whatever I could to bolster my flagging little ego. I was on no team; I chased no girls; I had no posse; according to Dr. Rubin, my dick was some sort of rotten meat. But I had a glorious Roman history. I was of the One True Faith. My mother told me so. It was self-evident, besides, as the Catholic Churches were always the oldest and prettiest in town. They had more stained glass, special holy waters and oils, and cool gothic wood-carved confessionals. Even in history class at the public schools, we learned that most of the important buildings of the past were Catholic cathedrals—Chartres, St. Peter's, the Duomo, Notre Dame, etc . . . Leonardo da Vinci, Michelangelo, Raphael—the Renaissance was a Catholic affair, right? Go team. I was an elitist, a nationalist, a tribalist. I found I had a pedigree to console me for all the things I didn't have or *wasn't.* I fetishized the glory I was heir to, reveled in it. I let my hands linger when I dipped them in the holy water font; blessed myself slowly and with gravity like a bishop; genuflected like a knight in full armor before his lord; my tongue was offered as a grandiose gesture, like a lady's velvet glove, when I kneeled to receive Holy Communion.

I was royalty. And to think, my poor Protestant friends had to drink grape juice and eat Wonder bread, while I sipped wine and worked the Holy Eucharist off the roof of my mouth. I worshipped in big cathedrals with an organ soundtrack by Bach, surrounded by stained glass, statues, and incense, while they sang lame hymns in whitewashed rec. rooms. Our priests wore robes while their ministers wore suits and looked like car salesmen. They didn't even have monks or nuns—and they didn't have Mary! They'd put Mary out to pasture. Which was like leaving your mom on the porch. How could the Protestants expel her? Imagine a religion with no mom. That would be like a house with no mom. I knew without my mom, I'd probably die. How could a church not have a mom?

The One True Faith. I became ever more devoted, following my mother's lead, hoping that through devotion, one day I'd turn miraculously straight. And though I may have been off about the results, I was on the right page with my focus on sexuality. *This is my body,* the wafting incense, the tortured expiring young male in a loin cloth upfront on the cross, forever playing out the divine orgasm of death. We kept our eyes upturned to the ceiling, shivering penitents on our knees—we kissed Jesus' wooden feet on the feast of Mary Magdalene; we kneeled and bowed our heads for a smudge of charcoal on Ash Wednesday—and then we wore it out on the streets proudly like a scarlet letter. He wasn't God's son; he was my sexuality.

But I never went so far as to consider the priesthood. They weren't mystics like me and the rest of the pagan Marian heretics. On top of that, I thought their sermons embarrassingly apologist and contemporary, cheesy—or like bad, English essays. I didn't like polyester and I didn't want to stand out in front of the church and be fawned over by all the kiss-asses. It made me sick. Priests weren't real holy people to me; their Catholicism seemed a Lite version. But I did consider becoming a monk. They were cool: silent, reclusive, mysterious, sexy, eighty-proof, old-style Medieval Catholicism.

Our parish, Sacred Heart, looked like the Ritz-Carlton compared to the humble manger Jesus was born in. But that was for the glory of God. Protestants just had no sense of glory or grandeur. They weren't Romans. And besides, we Catholics were allowed grand churches because we were often poorer than our Protestant neighbors—which just proved how good we must be. Our reward was in Heaven, while Protestants took their reward here in this world. Well, good luck at the Pearly Gates! My mother told me all hardship and suffering was a gift that brought us closer to God. Worked for me, I felt chock full of such gifts. My hero was Eduardo, a sweet Mexican kid who lived with a local family, ostensibly because his own in Mexico was so poor they couldn't afford to raise him. We used to give him rides to C.C.D. class. Mexico must be especially holy with all that poverty I thought in my youthful, suburban naiveté. Thus Eduardo had the mystique of a near saint. He also had a divine face and angelic smile, divine arms, a divine little waist, and the sexiest brilliant white, bleached, oxford shirts to match his shimmering white teeth and the whites of his eyes—all of it complementing his dark, Indian complexion. I wanted to see him naked as the host. Oh, the Glory.

That's how sex enters a Catholic boy's mind. Like a thief in the night.

And oh, how Eduardo filled my dreams. Perhaps he was a saint, and I was just overwhelmed by God's love. But the things me and Eduardo did in my dreams were clearly not going to lead to beatification (I was yet to learn of the ecstasy of St. Theresa), even if they meted out enough suffering for my waking hours to guarantee me a pass right through Purgatory and on into Heaven on the fast track.

I lost hope.

It wasn't going away, and Mary clearly wasn't getting anywhere upstairs in the boardroom. And if Eduardo was a saint, then it couldn't be a sin. Or maybe that made it more of one?

I shunned him. I gave Mary the cold shoulder too, withdrawing at full speed, hoping it might inspire her to feel bad and DO SOMETHING! Of course, I still asked her for good grades, and to cover my tracks when I broke one of Mom's favorite dishes, or to make sure no one began to suspect what a hopeless fag I in fact was.

I was mad at her, but I guess I was growing up. I mean, poor Mary, she lost her son. She must have pleaded, but to no avail. In the end, God was mean and stubborn. She lost her son; I was a fag. It wasn't her fault. She'd tried, I was sure of it, sure as that A- I didn't deserve on an English essay I'd begged her to assist me on. She'd given it her best shot. She'd look at me from those candles and prayer cards, bearing her heart with never a moment's rest, and I had to say: *Mary, it's not your fault.*

So I embraced tragedy. I took an interest in martyrs. The Kennedys specifically. Because they were handsome and Catholic and Irish. And tragic. "That's what happens to Catholic presidents," my mother shook her head and crossed herself.

Well then, I wanted to be president. To hell with the priesthood or monkdom. I wanted to be loved and missed and mythified—and assassinated! That would make up for my shameful, sexual failure. JFK was a saint, and maybe I could be too. I mean, really, what was the difference between "do unto others as you would have done unto you;" and "ask not what your country can do for you, but what you can do for your country"? Not a lot. Along with a plate bearing his likeness hanging on my wall, I had stacks of half-dollars and a record album of his speeches which I'd listen to and mimic. "Ich bin ein Berliner," and "I look forward to a nation, honored not for its victories or defeats on the battlefield or in politics, but rather, for its contribution to the human spirit." Yeah, me too, John. He was a man, not a wandering boy hippy who knocked on doors and bothered people with lectures. He got elected. I wanted to be him, and I felt blest to have been born under his reign, in 1962. Another pedigree. A prince and heir. He was the first; I'd be the second.

But who would be the first lady? Mary? Eduardo?

Things imploded. I sank like a stone. I knew I'd never be straight; I'd never be married; I'd never be president; I'd likely never be martyred. I hung up my cleats, or my scapular as the case may be.

We moved. I entered high school, I read Jack Kerouac (yes, because he was Catholic and ruined just like me), and I drank. Catholic to the bitter end. I only attended Mass when my mother made me.

I turned to art, the last stand of religious thought in the modern mind. Drawn toward the abstract to relieve me of the pain of the heterosexual paradigm that infused figure-drawing, I sought out mostly color and composition, and the inarticulate emotional states that let me *be* in my heart even though I didn't know what to do with what was there. I wrote my first poem—about Mary actually—and sent it to the *New Yorker,* and got my first rejection slip. God.

I spent a lot of time backpacking in the High Sierra, and I got into yoga and Zen. Once, while hiking, I noticed that Half Dome in Yosemite looked like Mary in her mantle. I imagined she was speaking to me. I thought it kind of sweet. I really missed her.

She became Gaia I suppose. Again, it wasn't conscious. Of course the earth is my mother. The universe was a big, BIG room and the earth seemed sweet, a refuge.

Nowadays, when I go home for the holidays, I never go to Mass. Sunday mornings, my mom and I hop in the car together, and on the way, she drops me off at a trail where I hike for an hour while she's at church; then she picks me up, both of us having partaken of sacrament. Two Marian heretics. And it suits her fine.

She tells me, "When I went into labor with you, I had this flash from the Holy Spirit: *This one is your priest.*"

Perhaps, in my own way. For I look about my room and see the church I've built around myself. There are many altars, from my desk to each bookshelf, to the windowsill, and atop the computer. The whole room is piled with books like offerings: each a Eucharist of wisdom and knowledge. They lean against one another and shine, swell and put forth color and imagery, like a great, ramshackle pantheon of saints. There are photos of clowns and rock stars, divas and Teletubbies—all of them holy to me; there are tankas of Buddhas, pictures of landscapes and towering peaks, and images of Our Lady, including a large poster of her (Guadalupe is always my preferred image—Mother of the Americas, don't you know), a glue-on dashboard Mary (also a Guadalupe, from the Zocalo in Mexico City, hometown of a boy I once knew named Eduardo); there are several candles of her various incarnations: black madonnas such as *Our Lady of Czestochowa* and *Our Lady of Einsiedeln; Our Lady of the Angels,* patron saint of Costa Rica; another still of *Our Lady of the Sacred Heart,* with her open, pierced heart; the iconic rendering of *Our Lady of Perpetual Help* (perpetual—I always liked that). There is, as well, a candle of the *Miraculous Virgin,* rays of light blasting from her palms, and Guadalupes galore. I light these candles whenever I feel powerless or want to make a good wish for something: my health; the health of a friend; the health of the world; the loss of a friend or relative, or another soldier in Iraq, his picture propped up in front of this cheap, dimestore Mary surrounded in stained glass, holding a glowing flame, the jar like two hands protecting it.

Even the Buddha on my meditation altar is her. Mary's a Buddha now, a quality, and a relationship, a refuge and a teacher. In other words, she hasn't changed a bit.

And I was right about Eduardo. All the men I've made love to have been as angels, sacred visitors, soon to become saints in my pantheon, their bodies holy as altars where I make my offerings; where the Buddha nature in my heart honors the Buddha nature in theirs. Every relationship is a rosary, with joyful mysteries, sorrowful mysteries, luminous mysteries, glorious mysteries. Anoint your lover's forehead with oil. Is there anything sweeter than washing his feet?

Love is a continual flow of sacraments. Communion.

Coming out is a sacrament. Confirmation indeed.

My spiritual matriculation has been queer from the start and remains so. A blessed heretic am I, and I sing my heretical songs when I kneel in her grotto, grateful she was there for me, and thanking her from my little boy's heart for being that one flickering flame, that Virgil who carried me through the dark, confused place the church is for those like me, and I whisper that old prayer . . .

Hail Mary, Full of Grace, Blessed art thou . . . and blessed has your grace made me.

Thanks, Mom.

Binding the God

Jeff Mann

I

The fascination goes far back. Probing memory, what I first find is an illustrated book of Bible stories for children in the optometrist's office in Lewisburg, West Virginia. My parents, both liberals, free-thinkers, and agnostics, bless them, kept me fairly insulated from orthodox religion and the narrow-minded Baptists that surrounded us in Southern Appalachia, but they didn't stop me from picking up that colorful book in the waiting room. God, how old was I? Ten? Leafing through that book, was I even then admiring the bearded men in robes, the savior with long hippie-hair? The savior in a loincloth, stretched out and nailed down, the muscles of his chest and arms swelling, his hair falling down around his bare shoulders. Did the illustrator bother to give him chest hair, belly hair, nipples? I can't remember, but I hope so. Did the child I was think about how the savior tasted and smelled? Did I want both to wield the nails and also kiss his bleeding feet and comfort him? I hope so. If not, it wasn't to be many years before all those desires would well up in me like a mountain spring.

My sadomasochism might not have consciously kicked in by that age, but I know I was an occult enthusiast by then. I reveled over vampire protagonist Barnabas Collins' exploits on the ABC-TV gothic soap opera *Dark Shadows*. I spent my pubescence and adolescence reading huge tomes about pre-Christian religion, books like the abridged edition of Sir James George Frazer's *The Golden Bough* and Robert Graves' *The White Goddess,* along with classics like Margaret Murray's *The God of the Witches* and Gerald Gardner's *The Meaning of Witchcraft.* These interests, needless to say, made me a complete freak in Hinton, West Virginia, my hometown of 3,500. Everyone who knew of my occult proclivities (and everybody knows everything about everybody in a town that size) assumed I was a Satanist. The Baptists were especially nasty and judgmental, and I responded to them with unconcealed hatred (still do).

The Catholics, well, there weren't many of them around, and the few that were—mainly folks of Irish descent—impressed me with how private and dignified their approach to faith was. Unlike the Baptists, with their pompous, sanctimonious high-school Bible Club and their revivals, their pamphlets, and their church camps, the Catholics I knew never pushed or proselytized. I appreciated that. I also appreciated their sense of ritual, for I'd been to a couple of Christmas Eve Midnight Masses with friends. Catholic observances reminded me of the incense, robes, altars, and chalices of witchcraft and ceremonial magic. The drinking of transubstantiated blood reminded me of how much I relished *Dark Shadows* and *Dracula* movies. My readings in Wicca had pointed out the ways in which the Virgin Mary was the sanitized Catholic version of the pre-Christian Mother Goddess (the Egyptian Isis, after all, being the first bearer of the honorific "Queen of Heaven"). Jesus, on the other hand, was the latest in a long line of sacrificed gods, in the tradition of Tammuz and other Green Man vegetation deities who spring to life with forest greenery and garden grains in the spring, reach maturity and fullness in the summer, and are sacrificed beneath scythe and frost in the fall. The nearness of Christ's supposed birthday and the birthday of the sun god on the Winter Solstice was just too much of a coincidence. I felt somewhat at home in Catholic churches when I translated their icons into pagan equivalents, glimpsing the old Gods beneath the Christian facade.

As if being a Wiccan in the Bible Belt weren't enough of a predicament, when I read Patricia Nell Warren's novel *The Front Runner* during my sophomore year and realized I was gay, that uncomfortable epiphany made things even more difficult. Another secret to try to hide, though, with the recognizably lesbian friends I had, that secret didn't stay concealed much longer than my paganism. Now the Baptists despised me even more. Other than spending time with my lesbian buddies, I kept to myself, escaped into ancient Greece through the queer-friendly historical novels of Mary Renault, and dreamed of the day I would graduate from high school and get the hell out of Hinton.

But the most inconvenient facet of my identity had yet to surface—or, rather, I had yet to acknowledge it. By the seventh grade, I was jacking off, and the images that aroused me the most involved beautiful men struggling in restraint, strong men forced to submit and to suffer. There were the comic-book images of my favorite heroes—Batman, Tarzan, the Flash—tied up by villains. There were the stubble-rough cowboys on TV always getting overpowered or outnumbered or knocked out, only to end up bound and gagged, doing a lot of sweating and struggling in their bonds and making a lot of muffled noise. There were, ubiquitous in southern West Virginia, those Christian images of the crucifixion and the events leading up to it: the muscled, half-naked man bound, tortured, beaten, suffering on the cross.

Why did these perverse images carry so much erotic power? I didn't know (still don't). I only knew that this was another secret I'd damned well better keep to myself. Nevertheless, despite my confusion, by the time I was in high school, I was, in fantasy, vigorously wrestling down and tying up a few of the younger, handsomer substitute teachers. My bearded buddy Mike, only a year older than I but already possessing the muscles and body hair of a *man, inspired fantasies in which* I would strip him to the waist, chain him to the wall of a garage, and gag him with a dirty cloth. I would beat him till he bled, till his body was wracked with sobs. The blood tasted good licked from his broad back. (I was, after all, not only a Wiccan but a vampire aficionado). Other times—already a Voracious Versatile, as I jokingly call myself these days—I would take off my shirt, tie my feet together with laundry cord, wrap the cord around my chest, and imagine being the powerful, heroic prisoner of some dangerous Western robber.

Even as I filled Kleenex after Kleenex, I was convinced I was sick. Don't most leatherfolk for a while? Such desires had no context. They were shameful, twisted, not to be shared. Sometimes, seeing the way that bondage was portrayed in movies and television shows—always in scenes of nonconsensual violence—I feared that my aroused response to these scenes was proof that I was on my way to becoming a crazy kidnapper or a psycho killer.

Despite my guilty confusion, however, I sensed in these fantasies an almost spiritual power, a religious mystery. Seeing the relationship between BDSM (what we called S&M in those days) and Catholic imagery was a real help in solidifying this sense of the sacred and escaping my self-hatred and self-doubt. In this regard, Patricia Nell

Warren saved me again. I'd fled to college by then and started classes at West Virginia University in August 1977. My freshman year, inspired by Warren's gay biracial biker Vidal Stump in *The Fancy Dancer,* I started wearing a black leather jacket to the local gay bar but still had no real understanding of what my regularly savored fantasies about hot men bound and gagged could possibly mean. Then, in the autumn of 1978, I read Warren's *The Beauty Queen,* a novel based on Anita Bryant's campaign against gays and lesbians in Dade County, Florida. Two of the book's queer characters were leather-wearing cop Danny Blackburn and his lover Armando. Both were big, masculine guys, the kind I wanted to be, the kind I wanted to love. In Chapter 7, the lovers visit "the little St. Francis of Assisi Church on Wade Street" and pray together in the candlelight. Danny recalls "the guilty pleasure that he felt in parochial school. . .when he read in the prayer books about the torments of the martyrs" and was "enthralled by this fusion of pain with love." After they worship, they return to Armando's apartment, where Armando is stripped and chained down to the bed, and Danny pushes pins through his nipples. Armando suffers like a saint, like a savior, and Danny lies "beside him with the next pin, devastated at being both the instrument and the witness of this passion. There was no desire to hurt Armando, nor pleasure in it. He was the flaming angel. He was almost God, willing it to happen and knowing it so intimately" (Warren, 155-157).

Reading that book, relating to Danny and Armando, getting my first glimpse of the leather community—where bondage and suffering involved not madness and crime but mutuality, love, and passion—so many disparate pieces came together for me on a deep, unspoken level. My sadomasochistic fantasies. Christian images of restraint, torture, suffering, endurance, redemption. The relationship between the spiritual and the erotic, a connection most people I knew would find sacrilegious.

Given courage by these revelations, I began to identify as a leatherman (well, leatherboy at that point—I hadn't tied anybody up but myself) and sheepishly began to admit my bondage interests to queer friends. When the film *Cruising* came out in 1980, like many gay men I boycotted it for its negative depiction of S&M aficionados as dangerous killers, though newspaper articles describing the film gave me pause, making me wonder what kind of world I was getting myself into. (Years later, I would guiltily rent it and get hard seeing a young

Al Pacino, in a maddeningly brief scene, naked and hog-tied.) In my junior year, I ran across a guy who was very much into BDSM, but I wasn't really attracted to him, plus I really didn't know what I was doing, plus he was what I've since learned to call a pushy bottom, so our evening together was a major disappointment as first leather experiences go: silly, not sacred, and uninspiring enough to end up in my repertoire of cruelly satiric tales told for friends' amusement.

It was the summer of 1982, just before I started graduate school in English at WVU, that a handsome, flirtatious, red-moustached bartender named Steve finally gave me a chance to experience firsthand sex that felt sacred. I'd studied Steve for weeks, and the beauty of his face and body seemed as close to the presence of deity as I'd ever experienced, other than brief and solitary moments of transcendence I'd experienced in the natural world. Having read *The White Goddess* years before, I was heavily influenced by Robert Graves' belief that the poet's inspiration comes from a beautiful human muse who serves as the embodiment of the goddess. It was hardly a leap for me, then, to see beautiful men as embodiments of Wicca's Horned God, the deity of masculine energy, wilderness, and untrammeled sexuality, and of the Green Man, the god of vegetation who is sacrificed in the autumn, the muscular Savior—God immanent in bread or wine—whose body is devoured by his worshipers. Steve inspired in the lonely, horny, passionate boy I was a crazy, violent, devouring reverence. I wanted to bind him, gag him, suck him, fuck him. I wanted to eat him, drink him, incorporate him, make him a part of me. Like an Aztec priest, I wanted to hold his heart in my hands. That ache for fusion, for union, reminded me of Aristophanes' myth of love as recorded in Plato's *Symposium:* two halves of a previous whole yearn for completion, and sexual desire is a manifestation of that yearning.

I was lucky. For a few weeks, before he moved on to greener pastures, Steve wanted me too. One evening I rode home with him. He lit tiny votive candles around the room. He pulled off his clothes in that flickering shrine, that stuffy bedroom down West Virginia Avenue. Oh yes, he was my Christ in the Candlelight. I tied his hands behind his back with a belt and knotted a dark blue bandana between his teeth. I sucked his big cock, chewed his hard nipples, reddened his ass with my palm, ate his smooth, perfect butt—white as a communion wafer—and I fucked him for a long time. I had found my religion that night, I knew without question, lying beside him later, watching him sleep, wishing I could keep him prisoner forever. Here was the Muse, the God, the Savior, manifested in this beautiful nakedness snoring softly by my side. I was the priest, the Roman soldier wielding the whip, the nails and the spear, and the sinner redeemed by tasting the Sacrificed God's bound body, his moustache, his armpits, his nipples, cock, asshole, spit, and semen. Theophany had become not intellectual abstraction but physical and emotional experience. My heart swelled with gratitude as I rose to quietly snuff the candles out.

Robert Graves differentiates clearly between the human embodiment of the Muse—often fickle and inaccessible—and the spirit of the Muse herself. I was to learn that the hard way, as Steve moved on to other men and then out of town. I mourned as only a passionate, despairing young poet can, but I was to find that Muse manifested in another man soon enough. In graduate school, I fell in love with Paul, who slept with me once and led me on for years. In literature classes, I studied the tradition of courtly love, the troubadours, the passion of Dante for Beatrice, of Petrarch for Laura, of Keats for Fanny Brawne, of Yeats for Maude Gonne. I read metaphysical poetry that effortlessly mingled the sexual and the sacred and called on Christ as the Divine Lover. Aching for Steve and later for Paul, I sat in Catholic churches staring at the beautiful bearded man suffering on the cross. I lit candles and whispered prayers that the God might return again and offer himself to me as a willing sacrifice. Though Christian concepts of sin and salvation were not ones to which I subscribed, I could certainly grasp how suffering and endurance might serve as paths toward spiritual and emotional maturity, and I knew even then that, if I were in need of redemption, my devotion to beauty—human, natural, and artistic—would be what would save me.

Writing lovesick poems about Steve and Paul and browsing again through Robert Graves' description of the muse in *The White Goddess,* I finally, belatedly, began to see how not only Christian iconography but related elements of neo-pagan religion might provide a much-needed mythic framework for BDSM. Graves hypothesizes that two powers, the God of Light—the Oak King, ruler of the Waxing Year—and the God of Darkness—the Holly King, ruler of the Waning Year—fight for the favors of the Goddess, a poetic mythology that has been since adapted by many Wiccan groups to celebrate the changing of the seasons. Light falls to darkness on the Summer Solstice, dark falls to light on the Winter Solstice, much like the Zoroastrian battle between light and dark that influenced early Christianity. Rival males fighting for a female was all too heterosexual for me, of course, but seeing those opposing gods as locked in a brotherly, loving struggle, that was another matter. As if Jesus and Satan were each to strip to the waist and wrestle away, till one overcame the other, bound him, and took his sweaty pleasure on top.

Graves gave me, in addition to this seasonal dualism, a crucial paragraph that summarized all my perverse fascinations with bondage, devouring, vampirism, sacrifice, and crucifixion. (Surely, in my adolescent first experience of Graves, I read this paragraph. Who knows how it might have, on some unconscious level, prepared me for my obsessions to come?) In his chapter "Hercules on the Lotos," he describes how Hercules, the sacred king, the lord of light, is, at midsummer, "made drunk with mead," led into a sacred stone circle where an altar stands, and behind that, an oak fashioned to form a T, a makeshift cross. He is bound to the tree in a "five-fold knot which joins wrists, neck and ankles together"—which sounds like a rigorous hog-tie to me—and then sacrificed. His blood is caught in a basin, much like a primitive chalice, and "used for sprinkling the whole tribe to make them vigorous and fruitful" (Graves, 125). Here is the literal sacrifice that leathersex makes metaphoric, as Catholic communion makes metaphoric Christ's command to partake of his flesh and drink of his blood. Finally I had a spiritual framework—reconciling, in my mind at least, Christian and pagan imagery—in which to comprehend sadomasochism.

Lonely, for the most part celibate, I spent the rest of my grad-school days teaching freshman composition and studying for my master's comprehensive tests, in my sparse leisure time reading Larry Townsend's *The Leatherman's Handbook* and bondage stories in *Honcho.* When I graduated with an MA in English, my creative thesis was composed of love poems to Steve and to Paul, my erstwhile Muses. To this day, no Catholic but still a cherisher of relics, I have, hidden in a dusty box, the blue bandana, never washed, that, over twenty years ago, I knotted between Steve's teeth and which, in the course of his trussed-up, rapturous struggles, grew soaked with his saliva.

As a priest presiding over sacrifice, I had a true vocation. After graduate school, it was time for me to take my turn as the suffering god. Jim was not a lover, just a fuck-buddy in Beckley, a well-built, deeply closeted country boy with a thick accent and a closely cropped beard. It took only one play session for him to admit that he preferred the dominant role to the submissive. I'd been almost exclusively a Top for years, but, as a true hedonist always ready to test any path toward pleasure and into intensity, I consented to bottom. When next Jim and I met, I was the Christos, naked, anointed with my own sweat, hands bound behind me, bandana knotted between my teeth, grunting and helpless as Jim propped my calves on his shoulders, put clothespins on my nipples, and gently pushed his condomed cock up my ass. Now I was the holy one, I was the one beautiful and desired. Now I knew how they felt, the heroic, handsome ones, the demigods and warriors whose fates led them to helplessness, to suffering, to crucifixion and penetration. Wicca holds that God/dess is in each of us, and that night, being topped by Jim, I felt my divinity inside, rather than projected outwards and honored in another. My role was not that of active worshipper but passive sacrifice, the god of the fallen stag, the scythed wheat, the crushed grape, Christ nailed gasping to the cross, Odin hung moaning on the World Tree.

II

Now I know what I am about. I am a collector of holy images, a participant in rituals of submission and surrender. I will be ruthless priest and helpless god as often as I can, before age dries up my sap and heaps wet earth over what's left of my bone-fire.

He meets me here when his lover's at work. It begins as experimental Sex Magick, invoking gods to descend into flesh, to wrestle and love through us. We drink wine, light candles, strip in the midsummer heat, press our young, hairy torsos together. He is the most beautiful man I've ever touched, and, were I able to choose my own endless heaven, it would be making love to him forever. I tie him spread-eagle to the bed, blindfold him, and buckle a cock-gag in his mouth. Then I sit back, sip Rhine wine, and study his struggle. He groans, tugs at his ropes, then falls back into acquiescent silence. Slowly, his cock grows hard, aroused by his own helplessness. He looks like Christ stretched out and crucified. I run one reverent hand over his forehead, taste the

sweat on his temple and in the hairy cleft between his chest's hard curves. I feast on a joy greater than any I've ever known. This love is meant to be, I know. This love will save me. I do not know that, by the Autumn Equinox, he and his lover will leave town. I do not know what agony and loneliness, greater than any I've ever suffered, will seize me then. I do not know that, in statues and paintings—the Stations of the Cross, the captive Christ bound, whipped, or nailed to his agonizing death, St. Sebastian's body strapped to the tree and pierced with arrows—in the churches of Sligo and Salzburg, the chapels of Bruges and Brussels, for decades I will continue to see the lover I lost. All I know is that a love as deep and reckless as this is bound to wrap my heart in thorns.

Appalachian Summer Solstice, the basement of a mountain cabin, and Hercules is about to be bound. "Get naked," commands Everett, and I do, stripping down to salt-and-pepper body hair and a steel cockring. It's hot outside, but the dark air here beneath the house is damp and cool. He pushes a wooden stool against one of the posts supporting the ceiling. "Sit," commands Everett, and I do. Using yards and yards of Wal-Mart rope, he ties my wrists and elbows together behind the post, secures my chest and shoulders to the post, then my thighs and ankles to the legs of the stool. "Let's get you a little drunk," he says, grinning, and pours out a big glass of red wine from a bottle he's fetched for that purpose. He holds the glass to my lips and I drink, I gulp. Most of it I get down, some of it trickles out of the corners of my mouth and runs down my chest. This continues till the bottle's done and I'm light-headed.

"Time for your gag," says Everett. The head-harness is a complex collection of black leather straps and metal rings, with a fat, black rubber ball Everett pushes between my teeth and buckles in place. With a few more cords, he ties the head-harness to the post so now I can't even move my head more than a few inches in any direction. He's got clamps on my nipples and is merrily tugging them and tightening them and savoring my pained groans when his husband Glenn descends the basement stairs.

"He's tough. He won't talk no matter how bad you torture him," jokes Glenn.

"He does seem to be one happy pig," Everett says, adding some weights to the clamps. He pats my head, licks the ball in my mouth, and strokes my very hard cock. "Nice, nice . . ." he mutters. "Okay, we're gonna be outside working on that damn ornery electronic gate. If you get into trouble, shout. I'll leave the door open. We'll hear you. We'll be right outside." I nod, and they're gone. Behind me, beyond my line of vision, the door to the driveway creaks open. I can hear their voices fading into distance, then the sound of hammering as they start on their task.

It's dim and quiet in here. I can't turn my head, but light from the open door behind me falls across the boxes of wine bottles, the leather sling in the corner of the basement. The post is cool against my bare back. My nipples are moving from fiery pain to dull ache. I test the ropes around my wrists, then those around my elbows and my torso. As experienced as I am, I can work myself out of a lot of roped-up situations, but not this time. If I really were a kidnap victim, held captive in this isolated place, I'd be shit out of luck. As much as I curse and tug, the ropes don't give an inch. I'd forgotten how good Everett is at what he does. Giving up, I settle back, content at being totally helpless. I chew the ball in my mouth, and pretty soon spit wells up and drips over my goateed chin, drops in slow strings onto my chest and belly. Pretty soon my chest hair is soaked with my own saliva. I close my eyes, sink into my wine-buzz, and hear the small sounds of insects in the weeds beyond the door, the murmur of Glenn and Everett talking over their work. I have no choice but to sit here in the dark, in the humiliation and helplessness I've asked for, at the "still point of the turning world," as T.S. Eliot put it in *Four Quartets.* Later, in an hour or so, Everett will return. He'll make me hurt, with any luck. He'll jack me off, then count the feet that my congested lust arched. He'll let me loose, and by then I'll be sore and stiff and ready to be freed. But right now I'm alone, fully aware of my tightly trammeled muscles, my steady heartbeat, the drip of cool spit on my belly. It's midsummer, and I am bound down like Hercules, like Christ, here at the sun's height, my body a small banked fire, thrilled with its own brief, intense heat.

"There's a little Jesus for you," John jokes, nodding toward the stage. He knows what kind of man heats me up. We're in the Dutch town of Alkmaar this sunny August afternoon, and there's an outdoor festival going on near St. Lawrence Church. A band of young guys is making evocative, electronic music: one plays a hurdy-gurdy and one a bagpipe, but the musician that John points out is the accordion player. He looks to be in his midtwenties; he's lean, with a closely cropped black beard and long black hair falling past his shoulders. Even from here I can see chest hair curling over his T-shirt top. Guys like me—beefy, hairy—are bears, according to queer slang, while boys like him—lean and hairy—are otters. I have, in fact, been joking for years, "Jesus was an otter." Here's Christ again, bending over his instrument, swaying to the tune, and here I am, entirely fascinated, briefly unaware of all the world but this furry young man on the stage.

Christ look-alikes always bring out the Top in me, the ache to overpower and dominate, but I'm almost fifty, and, more and more frequently, the scruffy saviors who attract me are young enough to be my sons, as is today's object of futile longing. According to the damnable law of averages, my long-haired accordion player is most likely straight and certainly not interested in submitting to a man of my age and knotty inclinations. Thus, loving Christ's human manifestations in the rough and tender way I want is a passion that, to my regret, recedes year by year from possibility into fantasy.

I sigh and pull my eyes away. I have spent my life desiring with great intensity what I cannot have. John leads me to a café along the side of the church, where we sit in the sun sipping coffee and devouring Dutch apple cake. I can't see the stage from here, and that's a relief. I don't like to look long on beautiful men who are utterly inaccessible; it maddens and saddens me.

In one Alkmaar, I'm chatting with John and planning a trip to Haar Castle. Maybe we'll tour the Maurithaus in The Hague to see the Vermeers, or track down some *rijsttafel,* or buy cheese in Gouda or ceramics in Delft. John and I have been together almost ten years. I love our life, our shared passions, our home, our pets, our travels. Despite the lacunae inevitable in any marriage, I expect we'll spend the rest of our lives together.

In another, an Alkmaar less secular, less solid, in fact entirely unreal, Jesus stands before me in the sanctuary. The dim church smells of burning wax, lilies, incense. I take him into my arms and kiss him, I stroke his thick hair, fondle a nipple through his T-shirt till he's gasping with gratitude. He bows his head in surrender. I pull his sinewy arms behind his back, rope his wrists and elbows tight.

When I have him helpless, I unsheathe the dagger. Staring at the steel blade, he begins a soft whimper. I cut off his shirt; it rends like the temple's fabled veil. I pull off his jeans, then carefully slice off his briefs. Now he's naked, trembling in the chilly air of the sanctuary, his long, dark hair falling about his face. In the restlessness of votive candlelight, his chest and belly are black with fur, his beard-framed lips are full and red, his brow is smooth and white. I lift him into my arms, stretch him out on the altar like a feast, an offering, a sacrifice. He lies on his side, panting, while I bind his crossed ankles together.

"Please . . ." he whispers. I know what he wants, and I oblige, stuffing his mouth full with the fragrant cloth I've cut from his loins. Gently I roll him onto his back. I strip, climb upon the altar, and lower myself on top of him. His eyes are long-lashed, wet, and wild. I kiss his chin, his gag-taut lips, his eyelids, cheekbones, and forehead. His cock is hard against my belly, and he mumbles muffled prayers into his gag as I bend down to take that thick flesh on my tongue. The packed cloth will keep his sobs down as I chew his nipples till his body gives me blood, as I hoist his legs up onto my shoulders and push into him, take him hard till tears streak his face. Upon our conjoined nakedness, stained-glass light will spill, ruby light, then darkness, then light again, as clouds surge and flicker over the sun. Sighing, rocking, sweating, suffering: this is how we enter eternity.

Hail Mary

Mallory Hanora

She is stone and I love her. She is plastic made to look like wood and the circle of her halo is missing a piece from when she fell off a shelf too high and I couldn't catch her. She is a magnet found outside the deli where he works and she reminds him of me. She is a candle burning unattended. I sloshed her green wax on the edge of the sheets and down the box spring of the bed when I extinguished her. She is a sticker he paid three quarters for in September, and saved until Christmas to give to me. She is ceramic, fist sized, the color and texture of my grandmother's skin when I was seven years old who gave her to my mother when she died and so she is an ancestor. She is paper: cut out, pasted, acrylic painted, and decoupaged to a table. She is underneath glass. She is an accident streaked across the side of an office building on Del Mar Drive. She is graffiti: a miracle above the bodega. She is a prayer I have said more times than my own name, some parts impulse, some parts a memory that has no other words. She is raised metal praying under an arc of stars and I have pushed her against my palm so hard she has left a mark on my hand that's still there.

Full of Grace

Her hands are small like mine. Mostly, they are pressed together but come apart ever so slightly at the seam which stretches from her index fingers to the base of her thumbs. That's where she hides her grace.

I am not graceful. Grace is the ability to drown without thrashing. The lack of blood. I was raised Roman Catholic and taught to love Mary because of an immaculate conception, a painless delivery. A uterus, cervix, vaginal canal, labia, and legs that didn't exist like I existed. And ached. And sweat. And broke. The birth that bent her into an impossible mother, forced her spine to curve so that Mary always hung her head until all the miracle was stolen out of her. Until she was shaped more like a question mark than a sigh.

I wonder if her thighs rub together like mine when she walks and if her leg hair is wild? When I stopped believing in the red and gold silence that shrouded her, I started seeing her robes as the folds of a harbor. Filling in the fullness of her breasts, drawing in nipples tough from the mouths of many children and many lovers. Reimagining the passive and apologetic expression on her face as one of subversive pleasure. As if her real miracle was being able to breathe underwater. Then grace must be the ability to exist in two oceans at once: the virgin and the mother, the stone and the skin, the prayer and my name. I have blind faith Mary was bowlegged.

Blessed are You Among Women and Blessed is the Fruit of Thy Womb

In the glass basin, the evacuated placenta dances in water doing steps thousands of years old. The edges are ruffled and feminine and it looks satisfying. The drowning pregnancy is a kind of birth, too, another kind of breathing. Woman, your insides are vivid as fruit—as brilliantly colored as you hope to be before your lover, or after in memory. Dancing purple, panting magenta, wild, wild, wild red. I watch among women. Learning how to care for these tender parts, to let them go when it is time, to choose to believe they are both blessing and curse. The doctor repeats like a prayer, a Hail Mary, it is a smart muscle that knows when to change its shape. It is a smart muscle even though it sometimes betrays the bones and skin around it. It is a smart muscle and it is yours.

Holy Mary Mother of God

Jesus. Mary. Joseph. They are kitchen words in my adult mouth for broken dishes or spilled milk. I can hear my mother yell them against me more clearly than Christmas mass. This year I am as old as my mother was when she first became a mother. Her life before motherhood, and those first years with my older brother are as mysterious to me as those of the Mother of God. She is fifty, and I still catch glimpses of her girlhood when I hope she was less afraid. Ninety-five pounds through high school, her bone skinny body gathered the strength to shape-shift for a baby a few months after she graduated. She got married like good Catholic girls do. This happened to four out of five of my grandmother's daughters. My mother wanted to be a nurse. I think she might have been amazing. Sometimes the Holy

Mary only invokes the tendency among the mothers in my family to kneel.

We never talked openly about sex, but there were always undertones of regret and magic that hovered around the unsaid like the hum of so many birds' wings beating at once. My virginity wasn't careful. It was stubborn and burned in my pockets. I never told the person it was my first time maybe because it would have been kneeling. Maybe because I lacked the grace to do it. Maybe because words can sometimes steal the magic out of a thing.

Pray for Us Sinners Now and at the Hour of Our Death

I don't know the Bible stories well enough to have sexual fantasies about them. But Mary—the way the corners of her mouth bend upward ambiguously, even as her head hangs down, in all the complexity of the female orgasm. Her eroticism, everywhere and nowhere, lies in her multiplicity. My tongue sweats up the winding stairs of her prayer, flights and flights of invocations, until I can't climb anymore because my faith is a ripped open building missing stories. But from up here, amongst broken and graffitied bricks, dancing on the last sliver of stair, I can see the birds hovering over the ocean where she might be breathing underwater.

Two Poems: "Just Like Jesus" and "Bastard"

Emanuel Xavier

JUST LIKE JESUS

Just like Jesus, I want nativity and childhood to be simple introductions
Summarized to make way for the mythology of adulthood
Evading early suffering and teen angst to grant the world peace
Not only celebrated with mass spending during my supposed birth but always

I want to encourage and motivate just like Jesus-
An uneducated peasant with spoken word skills
few academic literates could ever conquer
Simply by having faith in what I say I want to arouse revolution

I want to comfort just like Jesus-
make you believe there is a God above watching over us
Without need for proof or scientific explanation

Just like Jesus, I want to cast out your demons and disease
Cleanse your feet with mother's tears; the scented hair of prostitutes
Liberate your oppressed soul from the possession of others
Bring back lost friends from their tombs

Just like Jesus, I want to create my own family and break with tradition
Host gatherings and feast with sinners and whores
Be a shameless pervert and deviant
while indulging in the subservient role of feeding the hungry

Instead of miracles, I want to document my own history
Derail power hungry men from the possibility of integrating
sexism and paternalism to burden society with guilt and sin

I want to build my own cross with carpenter hands
Carry it down the streets where I will be found bleeding
Pierced with wounds not self-inflicted

Just like Jesus, I want to hear the voice of my father
Sacrifice myself in his name- arms stretched out
Bask in the brightness of stars with lifeless eyes
Aware this preposterous death is not an end but a beginning
Offering this body to be devoured by scavenger dogs and birds of prey
a sepia toned symbol of martyrdom

I want my image captured to snatch the breath out of the oppressor's mouth
Leave them powerless to recreate my looks to frame the minds of ignorance
launch crusades, sponsor slave ships and stage brutal wars
while blindly following the utterance of selfish leaders

Just like Jesus, I want to be nestled half naked against your chest
Sanctified, even after my time spent with over a dozen lovers
Claiming your spirit when I come
Baptize you with the promise of salvation

Just like Jesus,
I simply want to live before I die

BASTARD

Heard you got knocked up and I know you don't love him
Please, don't get wed for appearances
This is why I get pissed gays can't marry

Don't listen to family bullshit
Especially my mom's religious hypocrisy
(She didn't even know my pop's last name)

Remember Mary was also an unwed mother
Joseph wasn't even the *baby daddy*
She only claimed to be a virgin not to be labeled the whore
she was

Shit, back then, if I were Jesus, I would've claimed God to
be my father too

“Fragments from a Catholic School Girl’s Memory”

Excerpt from a memoir in progress
Remembered Fragments of an Identity
Amie M. Evans

I went to a Catholic school my entire life—kindergarten through twelfth grade—and a few things have marked my memory and contributed to defining me as an adult. Things I cannot seem to shake or package and put away.

In second grade, Sister Margaret Frances made us memorize the Ten Commandments. Each morning, we copied one of the Ten Commandments from the board into our black and white covered, thread-bound notebooks of white lined paper. For each commandment, Sister would illustrate the moral point with a story about a child obeying the commandment and being rewarded by God.

For homework, we wrote that day’s Commandment ten times and turned them in the next day. Sister would collect the papers, and then with our desk tops empty, she would call on students at random. Any of the Ten Commandments that we had covered would be fair game.

“What is the Second Commandment?” She would ask.

If one student missed one commandment the class would have to write all of them ten times that night in addition to the new commandment. This was my first experience with peer pressure, for anyone who missed a commandment question would be ostracized for the entire day by the entire class. No one would talk with that student at lunch or allow that student to play kickball or jump rope at recess.

On Thursday morning after prayers and the pledge of allegiance to the flag, Sister Margaret Frances wrote on the board: The Fourth Commandment: Thou shall honor thy mother and father. We all copied it into our notebook under the Third Commandment, skipping exactly one line between each commandment and printing as neatly as possible. When everyone was done, Sister Margaret Frances stood at the front of the class to begin what I considered the best part of the day's lesson—the magical story of God's hand impacting in a physical way on the lives of the faithful.

"Once upon a time, a little boy was doing his homework. He was practicing his neat rows of A's, forming the "A" one stroke at a time—the left side, the right side, the center. Pressing hard for each stroke." To illustrate this, Sister Margaret Frances drew in white chalk the letter "A," then turned back to the class, her hands disappearing into the long sleeves of her habit as she continued the tale.

"He had formed only the left side," she explained, turning back to the board and in white chalk making just the first stroke of a printed capital "A." "When his mother called out to him: Johnny!" Sister called as convincingly as any mother yelling for her son, "Come here."

"What do you think the boy did?" Sister Margaret Frances asked as she underlined the Fourth Commandment with white chalk and hands shot up around the classroom. She nodded her head, acknowledging the hands and continued with her story. "The boy, remembering the Fourth Commandment, immediately stopped forming the "A" and went to his mother."

"What do you think happened?" Again hands shot up, but Sister didn't call on anyone. "When Johnny was done helping his mother and returned to his homework, what do you think he found? God had sent an angel to finish the "A" for the boy," she said, walking over to the board and picking up the special yellow chalk only the teachers were allowed to use, "with solid gold as his reward for obedience." She turned and in the yellow chalk she finished the letter "A" she had started on the board.

"God did this because Johnny's love for Him was so great that God felt the need to reward him." She nodded and twenty little heads nodded with her. "Remember this as you go about your day. Never let an opportunity to serve God's will pass by you. God is always watching." Sister left the yellow and white "A" on the board all day as a reminder to us to obey the Fourth Commandment.

I was a believer. I spent the next month abandoning tasks. I ran when called by my parents, leaving uncompleted chores, homework—even play—in the hope that God would recognize my love for Him and my obedience and finish the task I left in order to obey the Fourth Commandment. I was eager to serve God. I wanted to fill His every want, for my body to become an extension of His divine desires, for His whims to be my commands. To serve, not out of purity of spirit, but for self-fulfillment—to enact God's will through my body to have Him provide me with physical pleasure in the form of a miracle.

My efforts were to no avail. God never finished putting away my clothes, straightening my room, or dressing my doll. My homework was never completed in solid gold, or for that matter pencil. Never once was one abandoned task finished by an angel of God. God didn't acknowledge my obedience or devotion. As far as I could tell, based on Sister's story, God loved little boys, not little girls.

I didn't understand that the story was a lie—"Thou shall not lie" was one of the Ten Commandments—and God became an ideological problem for me. As I saw it, God broke every rule He made. The pictures painted in the church and the classroom by the priests and nuns conjured up images in my head that I couldn't blindly consume nor dismiss. I wanted to know concrete answers. I wanted to know whom Adam and Eve's children married, why God had a son and not a daughter, and why the Church Fathers killed so many people who later became saints. I wanted to know what motivated God to cause so much pain in his followers' lives. And what motivated his followers to endure all of the pain? I wanted to feel the divine grace they felt. I wanted to rise above the earthly and become divinely spiritual.

I told Sister all of this.

Sister Margaret Frances' face turned red and she stumbled over her words. The only sentence she could complete was "Stand in the corner with your back to the classroom."

After conferring with the principal, she sent a note home all but accusing my parents of heresy. I was grounded for a week and ordered to stop asking questions, any questions. I stopped asking the questions, but not thinking them or trying to unravel the mystery that allowed God and His followers to create purity of the spirit and divine pleasure from pain and blind obedience.

The first time I ever heard the words "you are too fat" was in second grade. I was seven. In a few days I would receive my First Holy Communion dressed like the virgin bride of Christ in a short, white, ruffled dress, veil, and crown. The words cut through me like razors. My mother announced I was too fat in front of my school friends in the car. I was trapped in the back of the blue, Ford station wagon with nowhere to run or hide and no way to remove the focus from myself. When I look at the pictures of myself at that time, I don't see the fat that she saw, but I feel it now on my adult body. Ghost fat that I can see is not there, but I feel, nonetheless, clinging to my hips, stomach, and thighs.

As a virgin bride of Christ, I was to eat his body. We were told by the nuns that the symbolic host actually becomes the flesh of Christ in the mystical ceremony of Communion. It is an act of faith that gives the believer grace. We were not allowed to eat one hour before mass; our souls and our bodies had to be pure. We were not allowed to touch the body of Christ with our hands or to chew it. Chewing Christ would be rude; consuming his body was acceptable. The host was placed on the tongue by the priest, the only human allowed to caress, touch, and feel Jesus Christ's divine body in the form of the host.

Body of Christ

Enter me Lord.

We were to return to our places in the pew, kneeling upright, backs straight, hands folded, eyes cast down but not closed, in silence, until the priest released us from this position by sitting in his chair on the altar. We were to hold the host on our tongues, mouths closed, until it dissolved. It dissolved easily, clinging to the tops of our mouths before turning into a mushy, paste.

For six months after the first time Christ's body entered mine, I tried to keep my mouth dry enough to prevent the consecrated host placed on my tongue from disintegrating. I was certain I could quickly get it onto the roof of my mouth and pull my tongue away before it started to dissolve. I wanted to save it whole and examine it later in private. I wanted to see what the flesh of Christ looked like—to poke at the meat, skin, and bones of the savior I was consuming.

At my party, I ate white iced petit fours with my mother. Each square of white cake had an icing flower centered perfectly in the middle with two leaves that trailed off the edges to the sides of the squares. There were five colors of flowers: Pink, blue, yellow, orange, and lavender. I ate two of each, carefully keeping track of the number and color I had eaten, stealing and consuming them while no one was watching. After dinner, we had white cake with my name on it, next to two pinkish hands in prayer. The hands were tall and firm, not wrapped around each other and they looked like adult's hands with long extended fingers, not a child's short, stubby fingers. Icing roses tinted pink cluster in the corners of the cake. Scoops of vanilla bean ice cream were nestled next to each slice. My mother whispered to me that the cake and ice cream were because I had succeeded in making her happy. They were my reward. I entertained my guests, none of whom were children, with singing and dancing. I had won awards for these songs and these dances, and the ribbons and trophies lined the white shelves in my room. I was a wind-up doll in big curls and a white dress. My body was a shrine Jesus had entered to deposit his seed of grace. Amen.

When I was in third grade, a short, thin nun in a black habit instructed my class about "calls" from God. Sister Mary Agnes said God with awe in her voice and with a capitol "G." In order to become a priest, nun, or monk in the Catholic Church, a person receives The Call from God. As Sister Mary Agnes explained it, The Call is in reality a feeling, a sensation that God with a capital "G" sends to an individual's soul. The soul is somewhere inside your body, but it can't be seen or felt. For a long time, I believed it was attached to my belly button. I thought my soul kept my belly button in and that people with belly buttons that popped out had no souls.

So, God placed marks on the soul for sacraments—a small mark for baptism, a medium mark for confirmation, a huge mark for The Call. These "good" marks were permanent. No matter what evil you did in your lifetime the good marks would always remain on your soul. This was God's way of knowing you had a good Catholic upbringing and that you should have known better than non-Catholics about committing sins. There were tiny marks for small sins—venial sins, like lying—and larger marks for bigger sins—mortal sins, like killing someone or enjoying sex. The marks for sins could only be removed through confession and penance. One had to be truly sorry and repent, promising honestly not to commit the sin again in order to have these marks removed from one's soul. The soul is like a spiritual score board. God places marks on the soul to keep track of the good and bad you have done in your life so that when you die He can judge you. If you aren't Catholic, God doesn't keep score on your soul in the same way. Because you didn't know the rules and never had the chance to be good, God judges you on your intentions instead of on your actions.

I was afraid that when I died I'd go to hell and the other damned souls would make fun of me because I had had the "advantage of a Catholic upbringing." My first grade nun, Sister Mary Marguerite, indoctrinated this fear in me by bending down behind me and whispering in a breathy, deep voice into my ear: "Your soul was permanently marked with baptism. Because of that mark, if you go to hell, which you are surely on the road to doing, the Devil and all his demons will be extra cruel to you, missy."

Unbaptized babies and heathens in the African jungle, for example, are exempt from the rules regarding the sacraments. If they have committed sins, they are given "get out of sin" free cards to allow them to not go to hell. It wouldn't be fair to hold them to the same standards as good Catholics since they don't know better. However, since they are not baptized, they can't go to heaven and instead are sent to Limbo.

I knew I would go to hell because of these "good" marks. If I didn't have these good marks, I'd stand a chance with the heathens and unbaptized babies. Surely I was better than them or at least as good as them.

Often, Sister Mary Agnes explained, The Call was not immediately understood and caused great torment and upheaval in the individual's life. Ah, but never fear, God, with a capital "G" worked in mysterious and wondrous ways. Luckily, while God's Call might cause individuals confusion as to the specific meaning of The Call, there was never any confusion over the *vocation* of individuals who were called. God never called women to be priests and lead the Lord's sheep for a nice monthly income, and no men were ever called to be Sisters of Christian Charity, to give up all worldly possessions and wear those unflattering, but sensible black habits. Select members of my third grade class immediately felt the sensation, The Call to religious service. I was among them.

A few of the boys were affected, mostly altar boys who had greater aspirations of climbing the spiritual hierarchy and becoming priests, bishops, and perhaps, dare they even think it, The Pope. This was the first year that they could become altar boys, and in addition to the glamour of serving at mass on the altar in front of the chosen, they got to miss classes for funeral masses and even got paid for weddings on Saturday afternoons. Thus, they were already aware of the advantages open to them in the folds of the church. The girls, however, were far more affected by The Call. Half of the two dozen nine-year-olds in my class were bound for religious lives as unpaid wives to Christ. They would live in a woman-only environment with the other wives of Christ, Jesus' harem, so they wouldn't be stuck at home alone. They would not only be encouraged to have careers, but it would be demanded of them. The job of savior doesn't pay what it once did. Because everyone had taken a vow of celibacy, there were no children to worry about. It was the 1970s and feminism was just dripping into my small town. So being a nun sounded a lot like feminism to me.

My aspirations, however, were bigger than being someone's wife, even if it was God's wife. I was called by God to the ultimate sacrifice, "The Greatest Call." I was to be a martyr for God, sacrificing my life for my faith and dying in a most dreadful and painful way after hours of torture at the hands of the Church Fathers. I finally understood why God had not come to me and finished my homework; He was saving me for big miracles, for saint-sized miracles. I regretted that I had forsaken Him, but considered it an additional sign that I was being called to sainthood. After all, many of the saints had forsaken God—as had Jesus—in their moments of weakness before they understood that they were chosen to be saints.

I poured over the *Book of Saints* in which my name and likeness would appear decades after I died when the Church Fathers realized the mistake of persecuting me as a heretic. I considered the ways that the other saints had died and contemplated new ways for the church to kill me. I would have my own holy day, statue, and list of duties and responsibilities that people would pray to me to take care of for them. Old women would come to church to pray to me and young girls would choose my name as their confirmation names hoping my hand would steer their lives. Miracles would occur on the site of my death and a glorious shrine would be built in my honor.

If I was lucky, a new order of nuns would be established in my honor: The Sisters of Saint Amie. I sketched out their habits which were simple straight dresses because I wasn't very good at art and could only draw straight lines and decided on pink as the best color for the habits. It was different from all the other nun's habits which were drab and plain in brown, black, navy and white. I wanted the clothing my nuns wore to be colorful and show how much fun they had.

Finally, the misunderstood, wise-before-her-time, third grade girl would be understood by the masses for who she really was—a saint: by definition, someone who was divinely inspired. I'd hang out with Joan of Arc in heaven (my idol whom I had a secret crush on—even then, I had a thing for butches). I'd ask Eve what Lilith was really like. St. Bernadette and St. Margaret Marie Alacoque would join us for a hand of Old Maid.

I started a notebook to keep track of my sacrifices and sufferings as well as all of the miracles that would happen. This way, whoever wrote my story would have all the facts firsthand and nothing would be missed or lost in the details of my story.

The first opportunity for me to make sacrifices in the name of God toward my eventual sainthood came at Lent. It was traditional for the grade school students to make a group donation at Lent. Normally, we were sent home with a small cardboard bank with religious images printed on it and a letter that instructed our parents that we were being asked to give up something such as candy or soda for Lent and put the money into the bank. Each class would donate the combined offering to the charity selected for that year. The offerings were collected in the morning on Good Friday and the class totals were announced when school resumed after Easter break. The class that donated the most got a reward in the form of candy.

Our parish did something similar during Lent, sending home cardboard rice bowls, the offerings from which were used to sponsor a Vietnamese Catholic family's relocation to the area to start a new life and be part of our parish. These families normally arrived in June and were paraded across the altar at mass. Their children would be in our classrooms the next fall and everyone would go out of their way to help them to settle into their new life.

That year our cardboard banks had pictures of children from Africa and Asia on them. Sister Mary Agnes explained, as she distributed the banks and letters, that the school would be using the money toward supporting babies in third world countries. Each baby would cost $10—about three weeks allowance for a third grader in the mid-

1970s. The class that got the most babies would be the winner for that year's Lent-a-thon.

I'm sure Sister Mary Agnes explained that we would be sponsoring the babies, but all I heard was that we would get to name them and choose either a boy or a girl. She stressed that we were sacrificing during Lent for God, as Christ had for us when he died on the cross, but all I heard was we were buying babies and I desperately wanted a little sister. I was sure this was God's first test of me as His martyr.

I sacrificed. I went without candy, soda, and chips from the corner store. I didn't buy hair ribbons, '45rpm records of my favorite songs, or new clothes for Barbie. All during the four weeks of Lent I socked away my allowance in the bank while images of the children from far away danced through my mind. I wanted a baby girl, that much I was sure of; a little sister. I wasn't sure if I wanted an African or an Asian sister and I had no idea what I would name her. I'd only named stuffed animals and cats and felt that naming a person was a big responsibility. I decided I'd let her have the extra bedroom I now used as a playroom and quickly recorded the sacrifices I was making into my book. Not only was I going without things I wanted so as to bring her here, I was also going to give her my playroom for her very own.

I saved $10, the price of one baby, and turned it in on Good Friday. I was very pleased with myself all through Easter break. I saved a piece of chocolate, a modeled rabbit, from my Easter basket to give to her when she arrived. I also started to put aside some of my toys for her. I wondered when she would arrive and made up fantasies about how close we would be and what we would do together.

When classes resumed, Sister Mary Agnes informed us that she was very proud that we had raised enough money for three babies and we would select and name them as a class. I immediately thought that was unfair as one of the babies was clearly mine. Sister Mary Agnes had the class write boy or girl on a slip of paper and collected it. She did this three times and the class chose two girls and a boy, which worked out just fine for me. As I saw it, one of the girls was mine and the other girl and the boy belonged to the class.

The naming process was very stressful for me. Sister Mary Agnes asked us to raise our hands and offer up names which she wrote on the board. The names had to be Catholic Saints' names. I offered up Joan for Joan of Arc and Elizabeth for Mary's mother (though secretly I was thinking of Beth from *Little Women*). I was relieved when Elizabeth was chosen by the class, and when Sister winked at me I assumed we had an unspoken understanding that this baby was mine.

Sister wrote the names of the babies on preprinted certificates and hung them on the bulletin board. She told the class the pictures would come in a few weeks and we would also receive monthly updates about our babies. On the way out of the classroom to lunch, I asked her when the babies would arrive.

"Arrive?" She said, taking my hand into hers.

"Yes, when will Elizabeth arrive? I want to make sure her room is ready," I said, smiling up at Sister Mary Agnes.

She smiled back, "Oh, dear, the babies won't arrive. We send the money to them in their countries." I looked back at her blankly as she added. "We *sponsor* them." And then she smiled as if that made it clear to me.

"No, you said each baby was $10, and I gave you that much for my baby, Elizabeth."

Sister Mary Agnes bent down so we were at eye level. "Oh, you misunderstood. The babies stay with their mothers in their home countries and we help them to live a better life there with our money."

I pulled away from her, "You lied. You said if I sacrificed I could have a baby sister for $10. I did and I want my sister now." I stamped my foot for added emphasis before bursting into tears.

"Oh, dear, that isn't how it works. Let's go into the office and talk about it." By now the class had filtered down the steps toward the lunch room and Sister Mary Agnes and I were at the top of the stairs near the back emergency door to the playground.

"You lied. God lied. Everyone here lies!" I said before pushing the door open and setting off the fire alarm. I was faster than she was and I ran across the playground and up the street toward home. She jogged behind me calling out for me to stop and come back, but I didn't. I cried and ran until I was a few blocks away from the school, then sat down on some steps and put my head in my hands and cried as hard as I could.

I felt completely betrayed and confused. I wasn't going to be a saint. I wasn't going to be one of God's chosen because He kept changing the rules, but more importantly I wasn't getting a sister and I was out $10.

By sixth grade I had given up, at least on the surface, the idea that I would become a martyr and eventually a saint, though I still loved the genre. Every Friday during Lent the entire grade school would line up in the hallways and march over to the church by grade for the Stations of the Cross. As the priest, assisted by three altar boys, walked around the church stopping at each Station, we would kneel, stand, kneel and repeat our refrain as he called out the name of the Station. I found comfort in the repetition of the movement and the refrain.

The story of the Passion of Christ was always one of my favorites. Perhaps because of my early desire to be a martyr, it was more appealing then the nativity story. Christ was the ultimate martyr, suffering terribly and giving his life to save us sinners. I couldn't really wrap my mind around how Christ, as the son of God, would be willing to go through all of that for folks he didn't even know, even if his Father said he should. In sixth grade I became obsessed with the story.

As I read and reread the story, I wanted to know more about Judas. So much so that I started to make up things, fill in the small details that were missing in the story. Judas, as an apostle, was clearly one of the chosen. Peter was said to be Jesus' favorite but I started to think that Judas was. After all, Peter's character was such that he wouldn't even admit to knowing Jesus after he was arrested. Surely, Christ would have picked someone with more backbone as a best friend. Judas, on the other hand, loved Jesus so much that he was willing to turn him in to the authorities and forever go down in history as a betrayer of Christ. It seemed to me that someone had to turn Jesus in or he couldn't be crucified for our sins. Who would be the best choice for such an important job? Your best friend; the person you trusted the most in the whole world. Judas had to be Jesus' best friend.

What was problematic for me in the story was that just like I couldn't understand how Jesus would be willing to make such a great sacrifice for us, I couldn't understand how Judas—even if Christ had asked and he was his best friend (which I believed)—would be willing to turn Jesus over. The more I thought about it, the clearer it became that free will didn't exist. No one would agree to these things—no one. That was my first introduction to fate. The Catholic version of fate allows God to strongly suggest who becomes or does what. Sure Abraham had free will to choose whether or not he sacrificed his son, Isaac, to God, but when you look at the specifics of the relationship

Abraham had with God it becomes clear that to say "no" would only bring the wrath of God down on him and his son would ultimately end up dead anyway. Better to do it himself and prevent the additional plagues and destruction angering God Almighty would have caused. So most people couldn't say no to God. Since most people cannot say no to God, this disguises the reality of the unavoidability of the events and the lack of control by the actor, allowing free will to seem to exist without contradiction.

The Greek version of fate that I would learn through *Oedipus* at the end of the year was less shrouded. You were born with a very specific destiny, a life-events checklist. You couldn't help it; you had to kill your father and sleep with your mother because you were fated to do so. No matter what anyone did, no matter how hard you worked against fate, there was no way to change the way your life would turn out. So, though I had, at least on the surface, given up my dreams of martyrdom, I still felt like I was somehow marked, different than the rest of my class—the rest of the world for that matter.

Oedipus was fated to kill his father and sleep with his mother, and I had kissed a girl with my tongue and she had kissed me back. Oedipus' tragedy had redirected my life. Whatever was to happen to me would be beyond my control. My life was predestined, predetermined before I was born, possibly before my mother was born. This relieved an incredible amount of stress, but not guilt, over my sexual desires in my life. *Whatever* I did was now the responsibility of The Fates. Any trouble I got into was predetermined and destined to happen and beyond my control. Being raised a good Catholic girl, however, I would feel guilt for every fucked-up thing anyone ever did to me; for my own sexual desire; for my lesbianism; and for my needs—Catholic guilt would consume a great portion of my life despite Oedipus.

By the time I reached high school, I was taking the five dollars my mother put into the church envelope for me to drop in the collection plate at Saturday night mass, grabbing a bulletin as proof that I'd been to church, and skipping mass to hang out by the train tracks with my friends and smoke cigarettes and flirt with boys. Despite the fact that I no longer believed in the God of my youth, I had been brought up a good Catholic girl, and everything that I'd been taught was part of me.

Even if I no longer believed in God, I had been fully indoctrinated with shame, guilt, and the principles of ritual. As only a Catholic masochist could, I constructed a cure for my queerness. In high school, to cure myself of being queer, I stopped eating and started fucking boys. Fucking boys was easy. I knew exactly what they wanted and exactly how to handle them. They liked low cut tops that revealed cleavage, short skirts that exposed thighs, and tight jeans that when worn without panties allowed the folds of the labia to be clearly seen. They liked to feel smarter, stronger, and funnier than they really were, and they liked to think they were a good fuck even though they usually didn't know where or what a clit was. Boys liked to think they were manipulating you even when you were the one pulling all the strings. I could fuck boys sure, but it was getting the women out of my head that I had a problem doing.

Catholics believe thinking about committing a sin is a sin in and of itself. Thinking about having sex with women is as much of a sin as actually having sex with women. Penance is required even if the actual sin is never committed. I fasted. I fasted for one day every time I had a lustful thought about another girl or woman. Looking lustfully at a half-dressed classmate in the locker room was worth a day of fasting; masturbating to the image of my best friend was good for three days; and thinking about sex with girls while I was fucking boys levied a penance of five days without food. I fasted myself into an emaciated form in an attempt to stop my lust for women, to control my carnal desires, and to change my internal self.

I developed rituals of purification to cleanse my body—and with it my soul—of the stain my physical desires for other women's bodies continued to inflict upon me. I sliced chocolate laxatives into equal sections and consumed them Eucharist-style by placing them on my tongue and sucking each section until it dissolved as I knelt in my bedroom. The laxatives flushed my empty intestinal track causing severe abdominal cramping and forcing stomach acids to be expelled from my body through my already raw anus.

Locked in my room, by candlelight, I would place my naked body in an awkward position, holding it without motion until first my muscles ached, tingled, then burned. Holding it until the pain transformed itself, and with it my mind and body, into a purer state. The burning in my legs, back, and arms conjured up images of the soul in purgatory's fire burning off sins in order to attain entrance into heaven. When I ate, I ate only foods with no sensual value—white rice; boiled, plain chicken; lettuce with carrots and no dressing; no sugar, salt, or condiments. Every morning I took vitamins washed down with a mixture of hot water and aloe vera sap—slimy and thick, its healing properties entering through my mouth and spreading into my soul like the flesh of our savior.

All of this failed to cure me.

And I thought of God's Commandments. How come none of them asked that we love ourselves? At least He'd asked that we love others as ourselves. Jesus didn't qualify who the others were. And so why should I?

I have loved women with all my heart ever since.

The Tree and the Cross

Louis Flint Ceci

It's not there anymore, the church of my boyhood. The building still stands, of course, since nothing could have moved or even warmed that solid, rectangular, two-story cinder block and concrete structure on Milwaukee's north side. The only relief from its ruler-straight edges was a facade of irregular limestone around the entrance on Thirty-Fifth Street, as if by this cosmetic it could lay claim to some heritage from the great stone cathedrals. It was otherwise a featureless shoebox into which you could put anything, demanding nothing of the passerby, not even notice let alone reverence. So when the Archdiocese of Milwaukee abandoned its half-hearted mission to the German Lutherans of North Teutonic and Silver Spring Road and retreated to its Polish heart further south in the city, they had little reason to preserve the building, but even less to demolish it. Instead they sold it and its half-acre of woods to the Milwaukee public schools. It was as easy as that to turn sacred space into real estate, and St. Albert's itself—the parish, the church, and the school where I learned the dark heart of my faith—was gone.

Attached to the parish had been a woods whose old oak trees had been spared by the farmer who cleared the land and later by developers who, during the building boom of the mid-1950s, turned every pasture and former cornfield into grids of single family homes or clusters of public housing. Clarke's Woods was the scene of many an important boyhood initiation, including the climbing of and falling from various trees, for the woods contained the tallest ones for miles around. There was one whose top had tempted me many times, but whose lower branches I could not reach until I was at least seven. Even then, its branches tricked me into thinking they were stable when they were treacherously slick and rubbery, and on one occasion a rotten bough snapped beneath me, sending me plummeting to the ground where my sister Remy thought I had surely been killed. I finally succeeded in topping it one muggy summer afternoon as a thunderstorm darkened the western sky. I was on my way down when the wind picked up. Feeling that mighty creature begin to stir beneath me, I straddled a limb and felt its power rise up through my spine. I had an erection immediately, though I was scarcely aware of it. Instead, I was full of a wild freedom. I stood up on the branch and, grabbing two higher limbs like the reins of a horse, rode out that storm like a buckaroo, wild-eyed and howling. If God had wanted to strike me dead, that would have been his best shot.

The woods were also where the parish held its various annual fund-raising festivals, the most elaborate of which was the West-O-Rama, with its wagon wheels and bales of hay. What I remember most about these affairs were the German folk dances and the enthusiastic polkas danced on a temporary, raised stage. In my favorite dance, men in Lederhosen would take turns ritually slapping each other in the face while women in long dresses would turn in circles around them, their aprons to their eyes. These festivals were also where I could observe the adult males of my parish getting publicly drunk. This included Joe, the church handyman and school janitor, who seemed to me to be way too young to be getting as drunk as he did. I believed you had to be at least as old as my grandfather, with whom we lived, in order to get that drunk. And Joe was in his mid-twenties or early thirties at most. Nevertheless, and contrary to what the nuns of St. Albert's were teaching us about abstinence and temperance, he and the rest of the men would get plastered annually, their behavior apparently sanctioned by Mother Church since every beer they consumed contributed to the parish coffers.

All this ferment was leading up to one thing, the one thing all of us gathered in the woods were waiting for. As darkness fell and threatened to engulf the parishioners, there would come a sudden flash of light and a series of loud crackles from the edge of the woods near an abandoned field. A half-dozen Catherine wheels would explode into life, showering pinwheels of sparks and emitting ear-splitting whistles. The ground works would give way to aerial displays which garnered respectable "Ooos" and "Ahhhs," but after so much beer and dancing everyone knew what they really wanted: the grand finale, the climax of explosions and dazzling starbursts that mounted higher and higher, coming faster and faster. And when it came, the overlapping thunder of the shells and the full-throated roar of the crowd shook the woods and rattled the windows of St. Albert's—an apocalypse of thunder and fire. I can still look straight up and see the criss-crossing plumes of rocket trails, I can smell the cordite and feel the rain of tiny pellets of burnt paper on my face—charred scraps that must be caught and pocketed and carried home in secret and unwound by flashlight in my bedroom to reveal the Chinese characters written therein that must surely contain urgent messages about my importance and fate.

After one of these fests, the woods would be littered with bottles, Joe's capacity for policing the grounds having been exhausted early the previous evening. A quick scavenge would turn up empties of Gettleman's or Blatz beer with their warm, rich brown glass, dark green 7-Up bottles, and the faint celadon of a Coke. I would take shards of these to the shrine of St. Bernadette in the corner of the woods closest to the school and, kneeling there; use a favorite rock to hammer the discarded glass into multifaceted jewels, which I then arranged in geometric designs before the Blessed Virgin. Then I would press my hands together and try my best to look like St. Bernadette, though in truth there were few prayers in my head. Mostly, I was thinking up designs that I would try next time (especially if I could find one of the rare and precious Miller bottles, noted for their clear glass). Mixed with my cursory piety was a boy's sense of pleasure with private ritual, and a vague notion that somehow, by doing all of this, I was erecting a guard that might protect me the following morning when I passed by the shrine on my way to school.

My sisters and I entered the school through the back door because that was the closest. This was officially frowned upon, since students were supposed to be dropped off by their parents at the front entrance where they could benefit from the full effect of the limestone facade. But since my mother had divorced my father and my father had gotten remarried to a Lutheran, my sisters and I were not afforded that luxury. We arrived on foot, not by car, and once the weather turned, nobody, not even a nun of the teaching order of St. Francis, would ask three children to walk an additional one hundred yards to the front entrance in the piercing wind of a Wisconsin winter. When the Witch of November arrives, the first door that offers warmth is the one you take, no questions asked.

St. Albert's was built on a hill that sloped down to the woods, so the back door was also the basement door. We would have to slog across the unlit basement (which doubled as a church hall) the length of the building in our snow boots, coats, and layers of scarves and sweaters, going from near-frozen to overheated by the time we reached the front of the building. Then it was up two flights of stairs to the main entry, shedding clothing the best we could while on the march, arriving at the landing red-faced and sweaty. To our classmates just arriving in the official way, warm and dry and fresh from the admonitions and kisses of their mothers, we must have looked like pop-eyed gnomes emerging from the bowels of the earth.

My sisters and I usually arrived together, but more and more often as Kris, the oldest, approached the seventh grade, and Remy, the middle child, approached the sixth, they found arriving with their little brother, who was almost always tardy and in constant need of attention, too vexing for words. "Wait up!" I'd yell, "I have to tie my shoe!" Remy might turn around, but Kris was determined to arrive with her dignity intact and proceeded up the block. Dispirited by their abandonment, I would slow down even more until, by the time I arrived at the back door, they were already inside, across the hall, and up the stairs. Pretty soon, I got used to walking to school by myself and even grew to prefer it.

On one of these occasions, I arrived later than usual. The bell for first class had already rung, and I was crossing the darkened basement on my own, not paying much attention to where I was going. Suddenly, the door to the furnace room swung open.

This was Joe's domain. Immediately, the heat of the furnace hit me in the face, along with the sick-sweet smell of the sawdust they use to mop up vomit, and the noise of a motor thumping over and over. Joe sat on a folding chair, his legs wide apart, his hands on his thighs, seated at an angle, neither facing the furnace nor the door. He was shirtless and his chest and abdomen gleamed with sweat. His navel seemed to expand and contract as he breathed in and out. I had never seen a man without his shirt on before, not even my grandfather in the heat of summer, nor any of the drunks at the parish festivals. I don't know how long I stood there and stared, but it was long enough. Joe noticed. He twisted around and looked up at me and demanded, "What?"

What, indeed. I had no words for it. I didn't even know what I was feeling, but it pounded in my chest and bowels stronger than the thudding fireworks at the end of summer. I turned and fled.

But it did no good. More than a door had been opened.

Every day at noon, all the students of St. Albert's would line up in the upstairs corridor, ready to descend to the first floor to hear Mass in the church below. This was usually a peaceful time for me, since the nuns were particularly strict about silence in the halls, and Stephen, my nemesis, was at the head of the line, several places in front of me, and could not easily fling boogers, spit wads, or bits of pencil at me without drawing the attention of Sister Mary Agnes. Besides, he and most of the other bullies of St. Albert's would be in a hypoglycemic slump since Mass came before lunch. I could relax.

But something else disturbed my peace of mind now. Not just that vision of Joe, but another shirtless man, this one on the landing between the second and first floors, where hung an enormous cross, and on it an equally enormous Jesus. I passed by this effigy every day of my second, third, and fourth grade years and had never really noticed it. But now my eyes were opened. This was no skinny, emaciated, European Jesus. This was a muscular, healthy, all-American Joe of a Jesus, a Jesus with tits. A Jesus with biceps. Jesus with sweat and a navel and killer abs. Suddenly the Body of Christ was the body of Christ. Inescapable, human, masculine, naked. And he was everywhere: in placards in the classrooms, on tiny crucifixes in the halls, stripped to the waist on the Stations of the Cross that lined the aisles of the church. In my Confirmation Bible there was a glorious print of the Resurrected Christ draped in a dazzling sheet that looked ready to slide from his shoulder and land in a puddle before him where heavily muscled soldiers lay swooned at his feet, obviously overcome by his beauty.

Now, every day before Mass, already faint with hunger, I was transfixed at the sight of this taut, bearded young man. I passed beneath his feet, which I could have touched had I dared, on my way to a ceremony where, according to Father McGuire's Baltimore Catechism, his body would enter my body and I would become part of his.

I discovered what erections were for. However, I did my Jesuitical best to avoid damnation by divining a deeper meaning behind the threats transmitted by the teaching Sisters of St. Francis. Since I knew I must never touch myself in an impure way, I made sure I never actually touched myself at all. I scrupulously kept a cloth, usually my nightshirt, between my hand and my prepubescent cock. Occasionally this led to a kind of chafing resembling rug burn that would produce a crusty scab I would examine for days afterwards, a physical manifestation of my pride and remorse. I had turned the pale phrase "self abuse" into raw fact. I began to look at Christ on the cross in a different way, as one who understood suffering, not because of the pain inflicted on him—the nuns and priests drilled it into us that he could have stopped that in a flash—but because he chose to take the pain into himself; he was willing to pay the price for being who he was. Thus, the dark warnings of my religious mentors had taught me to eroticize and sanctify pain.

St. Albert's marched its students through the sacraments in prescribed order. In the fifth grade, my classmates and I were about to take the final step into Catholicism, the Sacrament of Confirmation. We had already gone through First Confession and First Communion together. The order of these two is very important, since the dogma we would be expected to proclaim and defend in our Confirmation required us to believe we were damned and must take steps to be forgiven in order to be loved. My first confession, undertaken in the second grade, was considered a milestone in moral development since it was evidence that I understood just how loathsome a second grader could be. Actually, this was not hard. Despite their lack of experience and skill, second graders fully understand the concepts of Absolute Evil and Absolute Justice, and how someone can end up damned for eternity by as small a thing as a dietary slip-up. Stephen, for example, believed I embodied Absolute Evil because I came from a broken home. He, of course, embodied Absolute Justice and frequently gave me a taste of it on the playground. The rightness of his actions was reinforced by the complete lack of comment on them by any of the teachers, nuns, or clergy at St. Albert's. I accepted them as well. The pummeling, the chasing by small mobs of boys, the cry of "Nigger pile!" that always ended up with me on the bottom—these seemed ritualistic, and therefore hardly personal. The fact that I was the target was beside the point. It was proper observance of form, a natural outcome of having excommunicated parents. It was not I who was evil, but the state in which I lived.

Sister Mary Agnes put an end to that. One day in early spring she said she wished to speak to me after school. Dutifully, I went. I had no idea what she wanted, but wondered if at long last my devotion to St. Bernadette and the Stations of the Cross had been noticed, and I was about to be asked to be an altar boy. (Stephen had been asked several months earlier and had already served two Masses.)

Sister had something else on her mind. She had noticed, she said, that during Mass that day, while I was kneeling in my pew supposedly at prayer, I was in fact touching myself in an impure way.

I couldn't speak. Had I actually done this? I didn't remember doing it, but it certainly was something I knew I could have been doing, especially lately.

"You are a wicked boy and you must confess it," Sister Mary Agnes said. "You must tell the priest: 'Father, I have impure thoughts and I have touched myself in an impure way.'"

I could feel my face distorting in the most intense expression of despair. The corners of my mouth were drawn so far down they actually hurt. I could feel tears streaming down my cheeks, splashing on my shirt. In my heart there was nothing but panic. How could I say these words, even in confession?

"It is a wicked thing and you are a wicked boy," Sister Mary Agnes pressed. "If you do not confess it, you are in a state of Mortal Sin and will go to Hell. Will you confess it?"

I could not speak. I jerked my head up and down. She dismissed me and sent me home. I told nobody.

Confession would be on Friday of that week, just a few days away. It felt like my life would end. Father Hennen, our pastor, had heard my first confession and given me my first communion. How would he look at me afterward? And what if it was not Father Hennen, but the new young priest who wanted us to call him Father John? Unlike Father Hennen, Father John actually smiled. He had smiled at me once. After I confessed, he would never smile at me again. He would know. All the nuns would know. Everyone would know and I would be hated by them all. Eternal damnation seemed slight by comparison.

But then I took comfort in what I had been taught about confession. That the confessional is inviolate; that the priest behind the screen is not Father Hennen or Father John, but a conduit to God; that once inside the booth, I was not this person or that person, but an anonymous sinner seeking forgiveness and wishing to avoid eternal torment; and that surely, with my sincere penitence—and it was by God sincere as I never wanted to go through this again—I would be met with loving kindness, forgiveness, discipline, and hope.

Still, my heart was thudding in my chest so fiercely on Friday I felt certain my classmates could hear it. As I knelt in the pew awaiting my turn in the booth, I felt my face grow hot and my hands and feet grow cold. When the little light above the booth went out and a girl from my class emerged, I knew I had to enter next. I didn't need to turn around to know that Sister Mary Agnes was watching.

I entered and began the usual litany of petty offenses, hoping to forestall the "Really Big One," the first truly Mortal Sin I had ever confessed. Could I back out even now? If the confessional was truly inviolate, would Sister ever know? But I was here and the time was now, so I took the plunge.

"Father, I touched myself in an impure way."

And then I waited for the sweet release of grace.

Instead, there was a sharp intake of breath on the other side of the screen, and the anonymous conduit of forgiveness, who knew neither me nor my station in life, and who acted as God's agent on Earth, said in a piercing whisper that surely could be heard clear across the church, "You again!"

In slightly lower volume he continued, railing against me for the number of times I had brought this wicked, dirty little sin to him, expecting complete forgiveness, only to return a week later with the same soil on my hands and covering my soul. He was sick of me. He was disgusted with me. He gave me a penance that would have made a martyr weep and dismissed me with the most unabsolving *te absolvo* ever uttered, then slammed shut the little screen on his side of the booth.

I staggered out and found my place in the pews. The priest I had encountered—and to this day I do not know which one it was—had just violated everything I knew about confession. He had, in my mind, committed a far greater sin than I had confessed. Not only had he not heard my confession, but he had, in a sense, told me about someone else's. And he had made it personal, very, very personal. And what was I to do with the penance? Since it was meant for someone else, would it be more of a sin to perform it and thereby steal away his absolution, or omit it and wreck the chances for mine? Whose sin was I paying for?

You might say I had my first real moral instruction that day. I learned that adults, for all their authority and certainty, can be completely wrong. They can project all the anger and fury they want at you, but that doesn't make what they say true. And I made my first real moral decision that day, too. I decided the penance I had been given was not intended for me. I examined the God in my heart, and decided I would do half of it. After all, I had whacked off a lot lately and maybe something should be paid for that, and for the knowledge that, at least in this one thing, I was not unlike other boys. Or at least one other boy. And who, I wondered, looking around surreptitiously over my folded hands between the fifty Hail Marys, could that other boy be?

I had my suspicions but never sought to confirm them. On confirmation day, we were lined up in the upstairs corridor again, this time in two rows by height. I ended up at the head of my line while Stephen was at the head of his. Just before we went down to be tested by the Bishop, Stephen reached across the gap between us with the strangest smile and shook my hand. "Good luck," he said.

I was flabbergasted. "Thanks," I said.

I looked up at my Jesus-Joe. What did this mean? I had no illusion that we were now equals. The nuns told us the Bishop would ask us thorny theological questions to see if we knew our catechism, and then, if we passed, he would slap us on the cheek to see if we were tough enough to be a soldier for Christ. The slap was much discussed among the boys. Would it hurt? Would they cry? And would the Bishop slap the girls, too, or just give then a pinch? I looked at Stephen again with new understanding. Here was a boy who actually believed the Church would let an adult male slap him in the face in public, and if he cried out, he would be ruined in the eyes of his family, his Church, and his God. He actually believed this. And I knew I believed no such thing.

"Good luck to you, too," I said. He smiled at me and seemed relieved.

In the end, the Bishop was in a hurry, there were no questions, and the "slap" was a touch on the cheek from a white-gloved hand that could scarcely be felt. The German dancers at the West-O-Rama had given each other a more heart-felt smacking.

The following fall, my mother moved my sisters and me to a small town in southern Wisconsin where she could pursue her college degree. My sister Remy wept because Mother would not take us to church on Sundays, and Remy thought that meant she would go to hell. But I had given up on damnation. I had decided to stop going to hell just because other people thought I should. My God was too busy to be interested in trapping people with their weaknesses. He wasn't even overly concerned about how boys explored their bodies, provided they didn't rub themselves raw. I am still exploring the body of Christ, the one he showed me I should love and not ignore. And I still believe in communion—that in taking in a part of another, we become one with all who live in this world and all who have partaken of it. That Body of Christ, once made sacred, cannot be profaned.

I had found my God in St. Albert's and the woods, the cross and the tree. The church I grew up in is gone, and the woods are all but gone too, its grand oaks all dead or cut down. Even the shrine to St. Bernadette is gone, demolished when the grounds became city property. You can find no trace of it, or the offerings I left there: rough jewels hammered out of broken glass.

Presión Bajo Gracia

Charlie Vazquez

Perhaps it takes horror to inspire beauty.

My Spanish-Caribbean parents were raised by strict Catholics and refused to subject my sister and I to the same superstitious tyranny that inspired them to rebel against the Holy Roman Catholic Church (by immersing themselves in the urban drug culture of New York City) in the 1960s and 1970s. Though I was spared the perceived chore of missing Sunday morning cartoons to sit on worn pews whilst absorbing the mysticism of church ritual, I was infused with Catholic esthetic through iconographic art images—to me, the Church's most profound development in its inner battle between sacredness and profanity.

This Catholic "education" was supplemented by the comedic religious outbursts of my Cuban grandmother and later, for me, the diverse canon of Catholic-inspired art centered on the male torso. My mother dutifully kept a bedroom altar of African herbs and beads, Spanish tarot cards, family photographs and glass-encased candles mixed with wrinkled images of angels and saints, such as *Las Siete Potencias (The Seven Powers).* I remember staring at the Romanesque renderings and falling into trances; my fiction still dredges visions from this potent "big bang" of religious imagery.

Spain, my family's European motherland, was an already diverse nation when she began colonizing the New World—after having been invaded and occupied by cultures as different as the Visigoths and Moors. Spanish society had always feasted upon the turbulent traffic of commerce and culture that only the Mediterranean could offer—especially as part of the multicultural Roman Empire. A musical example of this is flamenco music's scale structure and singing technique—unabashedly North African.

The Caribbean would recreate a similar crossroads dynamic based on colonization and trade. The Mediterranean boasted Phoenician, Egyptian, Judaic, Roman, Spanish, Turkish, Greek and Gallic flavors, whereas the Caribbean played host to the Old World's ocean-crossing empires, mixing them with American indigenous populations and imported African slaves—a virtual "gumbo" with a violent, oppressive and breathtaking history. Chinese workers' migration to Cuba and East Indian immigration in Guiana are severely under-reported, yet fascinatingly true. Mexico has a little-known Russian and German history. This New World "cosmopolitanism" retained much of its original Mediterranean Catholic culture—the very word "catholic" coming from the Greek word καθολικός, meaning "universal." And so, Mexico City, Havana, New Orleans, Port-au-Prince, San Juan, and Lima became the new breed of Catholic (universal) cities in the Americas.

My cosmopolitan upbringing would happen in New York City hundreds of years later, where my conscious hatred of major world religions began, like many of my mold, with the realization of my queer sexuality during my teens. The barbaric savageries of the Spanish Inquisition and the Crusades, as well as the blatant and sanctioned torture and murder of suspected "sorcerers, sodomites, and sinners" sealed the deal. Hating the Catholic Church was simple—not only for its homophobia, sexual strictures, and misogyny, but for its complicity in the brutal conquest and extermination of native peoples worldwide, its sex abuse scandals bordering on organized pedophilia, and its anti-Semitic twentieth-century war politics that did little or nothing to prevent the Holocaust.

Christianity's fixation on male energy—especially between father and son—is a haunting point of departure (or arrival) for many queer men, since so many of us are documented as having a lacking or non-existent relationship with our fathers. I was able to relate to Jesus' relationship toward an enigmatic father: loving the idea of your father, but not really knowing him. For the religious perhaps, the concept of "Father God" was a viable substitute for the lack of a proper human role model, but I didn't make that connection.

My poor relationship with my own depressive father was thus yet another reason for my aversion to Catholicism. His frequent acts of physical violence, followed by guilt-ridden outpourings and futile attempts at repentance were no moral roadmap to follow for a sensitive youth fascinated by magic and astronomy. Yet, he embodied the father image as both benevolent and violent, even if I less frequently remember my father's tender and playful aspects; his childish, country boy demeanor. Most of my memories are dominated by recollections of his wrath, destruction, and torment. Ultimately, my father's struggles with the sacred and the profane only became real when my own such struggles evolved to challenge me.

I remember asking him why he looked sad when I found him reflecting on his misery one day, storm clouds hovering around him. "God is punishing me," was all he said, his face sunken and suffering like a classical martyr. On another gloomy day, a neighborhood boy was beaten viciously, and my father took me to the scene of the virtual stoning in the basement of our apartment building. I remember watching my dad trace a cross with his fingertip, with some of the fresh blood that remained on the white wall, and mumbling Spanish prayers. I was startled by his lugubrious disposition, but it wasn't until years later that I found an explanation when I would learn that he was struggling with chronic drug addiction. Eventually, he disappeared altogether.

At the age of seventeen I left New York for Oregon and came to terms with my "sexualities"—which began as heterosexuality-turned-bisexuality, and then settled into homosexuality. My understanding of God was forged through a sexual relationship with the universe, the one he reportedly created. When I learned of Tantric yoga I knew I wasn't part of an insatiably-horny industrialist subculture—sex was a glimpse into the divine. My bacchanalian years in the Pacific Northwest were the perfect counterpoint to the strictures of Catholic dogma entrenched in my Latin-American culture, and in my family's DNA. Amidst a subculture of pagan renegade artists, I flourished. Finally in touch with nature—both inside and outside of me—I'd become the enemy of the Church.

A decade-and-a-half later, a six-month stay in Mexico changed my impressions of the Catholic Church. I heard and read stories of priests defending innocents from corrupt authorities and guerilla warriors in Chiapas—at times losing their lives in their pursuit of justice. This was a place where the Church's greatest enemies were drug gangs that turned the lives of already despairing youths completely upside down; where gang initiations often included the murder of rival youths for entry.

But what really "turned the key" and inspired me to reconsider the Church's history was my foray into Western art history studies. As I photographed a fine art collection for a friend in Baja, I became obsessed with Italian art history and read every book he had on hand, finding that any immersion in the development of Western art culture is a history lesson in Catholicism. I realized that Catholicism's symbolic struggle with its own sacredness and profanity is the fault-line that has produced some of the world's most stunning art.

To imagine a world without Michelangelo's *Piéta* or his Sistine Chapel frescoes; to suppose our existence without El Greco's *The Purification of the Temple* or any of Bernini's sculptural masterworks; to even contemplate art history without Botticelli's *Last Communion of St. Jerome* or Guernico's *The Doubting of Thomas* is to redraft the development of the Western world without The Holy Roman Catholic Church—a Jewish rebel cult turned major world theology.

In the world of Christian liturgical masterpieces, Monteverdi's *The Vespers of 1610,* any of Vivaldi's sacred works, and Purcell's *Music for the Funeral of Queen Mary* (popularized in the film *A Clockwork Orange*) are testaments to the beauty formed by Christian imagination. They are sonic tributes to the horrors inflicted upon Jesus Christ; tributes to life and death—odes to the supernatural. The conjuring and creation of transcendent exquisiteness (especially in the visual realm), which represents the love, splendor, and outrage of God, is the supreme gift of Christianity—and especially Catholicism—to the world.

And so much of it is outrageously homoerotic.

In 2005, I wrote an essay, "The Men of Oils," which took the reader through a virtual museum of masterpieces depicting stunning men in various guises—cruising the masterworks for studs. One such example of Catholicism's homoerotic portrayals of the male torso is Diego Velázquez's *The Forge of Vulcan,* where the working-class sexuality of half-dressed men surrounding a forge swells with pornographic potential. The Mediterranean skin tones and agile musculatures of the six males depicted spoke of something indescribably sensual to me. This painting, composed in Italy during Velázquez's travels, exemplifies his fascination and admiration of Italian Renaissance painting—but to me it brought to mind the Italian brothers with whom I first discovered my sexuality during my 1970s childhood.

I clearly remember their Confirmation photos wedged into the corners of their dresser mirror—all three brothers slept in the same immaculate room. My fascination began when I discovered the eldest examining his nipples—teenage hair beginning to crown them—in the dresser mirror. The gasoline really hit the fire when, noticing me frozen in my tracks, he turned to explain what he was doing. This is one such example of the "Catholic eroticism" that has always pervaded my sense of sex and art; the sacred battling the profane. The sacred friendship; my surfacing and profane desires.

Sodomite visionaries like Leonardo da Vinci, Michelangelo, and Caravaggio sought to visually convey the power and grace of God, and the muscular male torso was the centerpiece for this expression. The irony never stops. The endless catalog of art commissioned by the Catholic Church is riddled with homoerotic imagery because Catholicism, like most militaries of world history, is male-obsessed. The three aforementioned artists are just some of many who gave the Church a visual history, while also setting a coded standard for homoerotic esthetic in religious and mythological art. The queer outlaws of Italy's art revolutions refused to surrender their pagan hearts—even as their most daunting patron struggled to glorify the totalitarianism of monotheism.

Talk about a queer conspiracy.

Undoubtedly the Western world's first purveyor of virtual pornography, the Catholic Church's artistic legacy also showcases the male body as a temple of suffering and transformation—a cosmic experience. The focus on tormented masculine anatomy in Christian art—whether it be Jesus, Saint Sebastian, or Saint Lazarus—mirrored my fascination with sadomasochism and the suffering that seasons human nature. The death/ecstasy experience of the martyr (e.g., Saint Sebastian) suggests not only queer sadomasochism, but it also serves as a reminder and a historical and spiritual expression of the horrific tidal wave of pandemics such as AIDS.

For many Christians worldwide the sign of the cross is enough of a visual representation of Christ's life, but for Catholics, the cross isn't enough—the crucifix, with the anguished near-naked body of Christ nailed to the cross is as essential as the Eucharist—a visceral embodied homage to suffering; a stunning visual reminder of cataclysm.

Catholicism's struggle with the profane, in its aspiration to sacredness, began with its rejection of its pagan roots. Mythological culture was abandoned in favor of a higher source of wisdom and power—the Holy Trinity or God. Theater culture, the circus arts, and the "beast shows" of ancient Italy were seen as satanic refinements of pagan culture by the Christian clergy. Roman paganism was already moving toward the idea of monotheism when Christianity became the religion of the state, under Emperor Constantine I in AD 312 which coincidentally or not also marked the onset of the empire's decline.

Pagan (country-dweller) culture flourished in Italy before the rise of Christianity, so it's no mystery that Christianity absorbed much of its style. The (Christian) move away from nature (we are not animals), with its emphasis on the unseen, but to be feared "ideal," supplanted the former natural complex of worshipped idols. Yet Apollo, Bacchus, Venus, and Mars continued to be immortalized in popular artworks of the Italian Renaissance. Even members of the Roman aristocracy continued their devotion to these "lesser gods" despite Christianity's elevation to state religion of the empire. Mythology would endure, despite the Church's crusade to forever squash it.

Though the centralized Trinity inherited the spiritual influence formerly held by pantheons of gods and goddesses, the multiplicity of pagan "idol" adoration transferred to the body of the saint. Thus in the Caribbean, the enslaved Yoruba from West Africa were able to easily match their pantheistic "gods" with Catholic saints—the very essence of Santería (worship of saints).

Christianity's proximity to Mediterranean mysticism and mythology, especially of the Greek and Etruscan varieties, was the very curse it could not shake. In the famous Roman Lupercalia fertility rite, held on February 15th, women and men sought lashings from two boys dressed in animal skins wielding goat skin strips, their faces smeared with the blood of sacrificed goats and a dog. A haunting echo of a wilder, Earth-centered, pre-Christian world, this popular rite lasted well into the fifth century, while the holiday itself was eventually assimilated and subsumed into Saint Valentine's Day.

Catholicism's inheritance of magical imagery is so perversely enormous that its mission over the millennia to squash pagan cultures seems comedic. Angels (messengers), prevalent creatures in Christian folklore and art, are a direct link to legendary man-beast combinations representing animal impulses—such as the famed Minotaur, Centaur and Pan, some of whom (in the case of the Minotaur) were created by acts of bestiality.

Catholic Mass itself is loaded with pagan ritual.

The Eucharist is an obvious vestige of Catholicism's pagan roots. It's the one aspect of church ritual that I identify with the sensuality of vampirism, a myth cultivated over time with obviously cannibalistic roots. And this relationship between predator and prey was assimilated by the Church; the consumption of "blood and flesh" empowers the faithful—much as warriors of yore would consume the blood and entrails of a mortal enemy to absorb their power.

"Whoever eats My flesh and drinks My blood has eternal life, and I will raise him up at the last day. For My flesh is food indeed, and My blood is drink indeed. He who eats My flesh and drinks My blood abides in Me, and I in him. As the living Father sent Me, and I live because of the Father, so he who feeds on Me will live because of Me." (John 6:54-57)

The essential power of water as a cleansing element is certainly no Christian invention. Water and river gods and goddesses date back to the beginning of humankind's mythological and demonological history—their supremacy as crucial as the presence of drinkable water for our livelihood. Baptismal water cleansing evolved from Earth-cult water worship, derived of nature magic systems.

Frankincense and myrrh from the Arabian Peninsula had likewise been used for spiritual purposes long before Christianity's development. Catholics use this incense to symbolize the Spirit touching all and the ascent of prayers to heaven—even to purify the dead before burial, another shamanistic pre-Christian behavior.

Reliquaries, vessels containing pieces of skull and/or bone fragments of famous saints and holy figures, are a link to rites of sorcery—pieces of the deceased are believed to contain miraculous powers of healing. Anointing of the sick with holy oils also points to Jesus' reputation as a supreme magician—this practice mimics his shamanistic powers of healing and miracle-performing. Jesus' legend is in fact riddled with shamanism, the very kind of sorcery the Church has continually tried to suppress outside of its walls, while mimicking it within them.

Just as the National Cathedral in the heart of Mexico City was built over (and with) the ruins of destroyed Aztec temples, Catholicism's pagan history is its very fiber—which is also why it's been the one major world religion that interfaces with animist belief systems worldwide more easily than its competition. Its visual representation of "divine figures and symbols" sets it apart from Judaism and Islam, which do not represent divinities graphically.

Its ability to fuse with animist religions won it easier converts, as in the *cabildos* implemented by the Spanish in Cuba to give African slaves a forum in which to express their "African-ness"—a time of cultural reflection, as well as the wellspring for Santería. (Brazil's famous *carnaval* celebrations are a related result of this church-implemented policy). Catholicism melded with indigenous "flavors" to create *pastiches* of Catholic subcultures around the globe—most notably in the Americas, the Philippines, the Caribbean—and even East Timor in Southeast Asia. Holy images were allowed to portray indigenous facial features and skin color to more exactly appeal to the people of the region. African depictions of the saints are popular in Rwanda and the Caribbean, and Korean versions of Jesus exist in the Far East.

Whereas later Christian sects would become absorbed in the words of the faith as written in The Holy Bible, the Catholic Church maintained a mystical and nonverbal edge with its proliferation of dazzling imagery and iconography as a means to circumvent illiteracy and transcend diverse languages in the lands of its conquests. Pope Gregory the Great, a liturgical hero of Catholicism and whom the Gregorian chants are named for, himself said:

"For painting is used in Churches so that those who cannot read or write may at least read on the walls by seeing there what they cannot read in books." Pope Gregory the Great, to Bishop Serenus of Marseilles, 6th Century.

The supernatural landscapes and dramatic staging of the medieval and renaissance Catholic art canon illustrate—through grief, gore, wonder, imagination, and mystery—the tribulations and ecstasies of the theater of human experience. Before the modernization of theater and the invention of cinema—long before daguerrotypes captured actual human form and launched the realism of photography, the world of painting was the looking glass that brought to life both dreamy and monstrous figures—in the case of Catholicism, a catalog of mother's anguish, infantile tenderness, thunderous rage, and gruesome torture.

This precious wonderland of otherworldly masterpieces is the greatest endowment Catholicism has bestowed upon future generations. It is a glowing tribute to what religion has sought to capture—the believer's mystical relationship with the universe and God. It is also a legacy spearheaded by homoerotic pioneers like the temperamental Michelangelo and murderous Caravaggio—a fantasy plane of near-pornographic sensuality. It is a parallel universe depicting the trauma of Jesus and others—often from the perspectives of struggling, queer artist outlaws. Swirling with the hope and suffering of mankind, bursting in jewel tones and grieving in storm-cloud shadows—leaving nothing out—it is, to me, a cauldron of eternal fascination and a landscape of carnal desire.

PRIESTS

Father Tongue

Thomas Burke

Though I am not sure Holy Mother Church intended, she taught me being gay was all right. Catholicism informed me that I had history as a gay person. The religion of my childhood led me to a revered literary canon to which all gay writers are inheritors. The Church taught me that males could live together in a loving and intellectually vibrant community.

I attended a Catholic boys boarding school of the sort that used to be more common in America. *Scholae Praeparatoriae,* prep schools like mine, were on the grounds of monasteries. These schools were staffed by overly educated cloisters of priests. Though it was at my *schola praeparatoria* that I got a real hard-on for Latin, the churchly language had always been in my consciousness.

My father's favorite lullaby was a deep and vigorously chanted, "*Tantum ergo sacramentum.*" I am just the right age to have briefly known Latin as the language spoken at church. At home, along with the lullaby, Dad used Latin fluently. He cursed in it. My father wanted his six children to speak Latin at dinner. My mother, an ascendant Irish American, thought French at the table would be nicer. For dinner time, we slothful six compromised on American, with the occasional digression to both English and French pig Latin. "Ass-pay le eurre-bay," would get the butter heading your way.

The Latin language is inextricably male for me. Roman literature is full of homosexuality. My school texts tried to explain away, or outright ignore, the homosexuality inherent in Horace, Plautus, or Virgil. But there it was. Among the odes and eclogues of the sacred language of my religion were men who found men beautiful, just like I did. Through Latin I came to a deeper understanding of the beauty of language. I wanted to be a part of that beauty. I wanted to write, to join the history.

The old bromide is true: the study of Latin gives one a greater understanding of English, of how language and the human mind function together. Latin, with its inflected nouns, made me understand case in a way that English never had. That voice—active or passive—can affect case and that verbs have mood is delicious; think of the possibilities for sex talk among the Romans. How words truly fit and work, in any language, came home to me through my love affair with Latin.

In the second grade I learned all the Latin prayers an altar boy should know. *"Misereatur tui omnipotens Deus,"* I could intone gravely at the age of seven. Chanted, spoken, or read, by third grade I was hooked on the masculine musk of *latinam linguam.*

In high school I fell in love with the Latin teachers. At *schola praeparatoria* we also studied classical Greek and classical Hebrew (to better know the Bible), but it was churchly Latin that always called to me. Our black-robed masters told us Latin was our *Sermo Patrius,* our Father Tongue. We all had a mother tongue (presumably English), but now we would learn what was our birthright as Catholic males, our *Sermo Patrius.*

Latin is yet present in my life. I go back to the *Eclogues* of Virgil. This summer I sought out Horace's *Odes.* The comedies of Plautus can still get a laugh from me. Literature that stands up to rereading both returns us to our past and takes us to surprising new places.

I reread the *Odes* in 1990 with my *schola* friend Darius, as he lay dying of AIDS. We took turns speaking them aloud. Among the odes we found words to bring alive what little had been left unsaid between us. One night this past summer my eighty-five-year-old father and I, sitting in his tiny, second-floor den, read some Horace from an edition that had belonged to his uncle. The tissue-thin nineteenth century paper made me think of prayer books. We laughed and plodded through. I told Dad about reading Horace with Darius as he was dying. Dad and I cried for Darius, dead these sixteen years. We had never cried for Darius together. *Horatio gratias.*

My father still drops me the occasional note with a few lines of Latin mingling fluidly with his English prose. A sleepy old lion, my father's once strong body still radiates a masculine physicality. His is a masculinity that does not fear intellect. It is a kind of masculinity we both learned among the black-robed masters of our youths.

The decidedly Romish sound of men chanting can spirit me to the sacred space and time of my first true boy-on-boy kiss—it was with Darius in 1971—we were fourteen and Third Formers. This neo-British expression for freshmen aped the parlance of WASP prep schools from which our *schola praeparatoria* was separate, but equal. On a hot, September night Darius and I headed to the cool marbled tomb that was the chapel. For our first date we toured the elegant little Romanesque building like pilgrims.

Some of the young novices were in the choir loft. They were practicing a chanted *saecula saeculorum* from an antiphon. The loft was high up, hidden from the rest of the chapel. It sounded like the song of heaven. Latin chant and the touch of a man's lips are forever married for me.

Earlier that day Darius had performed well in Latin class. He knew how to decline first declension nouns. Father Southwell, our Latin teacher, was clearly impressed. The priest had begun class with what would become a welcome phrase, a signal to a mystery both erotic and intellectual.

"Adulescentuli," Father Southwell said.

He called us by this Latin word, roughly meaning lads.

"We'll have class in the natatorium today."

The natatorium, a good Latin-based English word, was the indoor swimming pool. Built around the time of the First World War the pool was in a free-standing, red brick cottage. Its walls were punctured by evenly spaced floor-to-ceiling Palladian windows.

Many Latin classes were held there. Humidity, full of the ripening scent of us boys, hung languidly in the natatorium air.

Father Southwell was one of a trivium of priests who would teach me Latin at *schola praeparatoria*. These three men held doctorates in classical languages; they were teaching, in a high school, in the hinterlands. Part of that once huge population of American religious, these scholars had been the best and brightest Catholic boys—they had grown up into that once exalted Catholic social achievement: a priest. My teachers could have been on the faculties of universities, but I think they were happy among the ephebes of our little Arcadia.

Two of the trio, Father Southwell and Father Hopkins, were in their late twenties, certainly no more than thirty. They were both tall and gloriously hairy. Southwell was muscular and thick; hair climbed up his back and over his Roman collar. He was the scholar-athlete, frequently organizing pick up matches of what he called medicine ball. He claimed the Romans played the game. It seemed a form of Rugby with lots of scrummy moshing; that was the part I liked best. A thin and bearded aesthete, Father Hopkins looked like a young Lytton Strachey in a cassock. Though clearly different in personality the two men delighted in one another's company. Hopkins rarely joined a game of medicine ball; he was not a vigorous athlete. Southwell relished Hopkins's quick and brilliant tongue.

Famous for rigor and creativity in teaching, Hopkins assigned a writing project, in Latin. We were to compose an original, five-page piece of prose, typed on onion skin, I wrote a short story about a beauty contest, of gladiators. It was all very butchly comic, to be sure. I borrowed *Miles Gloriosus* from Plautus for my beauty contest Master of Ceremonies and stock stooge. Proudly reading it to my friends in the dorm, I truly did not know how gay it was.

Hopkins gave me an A. There was no other comment on the paper.

The third member of the teaching trivium was the nearly seventy–year-old Father Campion. The two younger men showed Campion great respect. They were protective of him. We boys loved the rough and tumble of Southwell and the wicked—even arch—humor of Hopkins. We might have dismissed Campion in our youthful boisterousness had we not witnessed the example of love and care the two younger men showed for the older man. Campion moved slowly; his voice was no longer strong. He was brilliant and kind, once one got to know him.

In Fifth Form, our junior year, the two younger priests engineered a small group of us to be adopted as pets by Father Campion. One afternoon a week, we "pets" were excused from compulsory sports and gathering under a tree, by a pond—truly—Father Campion would have us work on sight translations—no notes, glossaries, or dictionaries. We strove at the real meaning, the feel and idiosyncrasies of the art of translation. We acolytes lounged on the ground. Father Campion reigned from a limestone bench.

One soft, spring afternoon Darius had brought a collection of Virgil that he'd found in the school library. Some of the library's books were in a format of Latin text on one page with the English translation on the facing page. We had discovered the best books were those with no English translations; no English was a good indication that something spicy was between the covers. A comparison of a Latin-only edition of Horace's *Satires* with a version containing both the Latin with English translations revealed to us that large passages in the bilingual edition had been left untranslated into English; the untranslated parts were full of sexual innuendo: homo, bi, and hetero. This knowledge made purists of us when in search of library books.

Darius's chosen collection contained not Virgil's *Aeneid* (we had slogged through that in Latin II), rather, the *Eclogues*. Frequently called pastoral poems, the *Eclogues* are indeed that, but some are also love poems, love poems by a young man about young men.

Darius arrived at Eclogue II, perhaps the gayest of Virgil's poems.

"For beautiful young Alexis, young Corydon burned," Darius translated slowly.

Darius's word choice was rather different than Dryden's standard translation of 1697 that I would later come to know.

Father Campion nodded encouragement.

Darius paused.

I knew Darius was both exhilarated and nervous.

"Father," he said again pausing.

Darius was trying to get at the true meaning. He was relating to the true meaning and that scared him.

"Yes?" Father Campion said.

"Well," Darius continued, slowly. "This shepherd boy, Corydon, seems to be in love with this boy Alexis."

"Yes," Father Campion said, "that's exactly correct."

"Well, Father, is that okay, boys loving boys?"

"It's literature," Father Campion said. "Great literature."

Freshman year, during our first natatorium Latin class, I stood alternately luxuriating in and being embarrassed by my nakedness. Swimming, and we seemed to swim a lot, was always done nude. I knew the drill. My elder brother had gone to the school. The place was an entirely male environment: male students, male teachers, even a male nurse to take care of us. We were an American Mount Athos. The summer before freshman year I had grown to a height of six feet. I weighed barely one hundred pounds and now had bushes of pubic and underarm hair, of which I was quite proud.

"Um, Darius," I said, "you have to be naked to go in the pool."

Doffed slacks, blazers, and underpants lay all about. Darius waited near me. It was at least 90 degrees that afternoon. He shivered slightly, and still wore his white under shorts. Dark curly hair stuck out of and over his shorts.

"I'll just keep these on," Darius said.

"Adelescentulus," Father Southwell shouted, pointing at Darius. "Strip."

Southwell, who was not going in the pool, but would be sitting fully dressed on the diving board for class, remained in his cassock. He began to arrange himself on the diving board at the deep end of the pool. His cassock draped over the sides of the board.

"The Romans," Southwell continued, "didn't bathe in their shorts, and neither shall we."

Darius complied.

Since Southwell was at the deep end of the pool to be near him we had to tread water for the duration of the class.

"AMO

"AMAS

"AMAT

"AMAMUS

"AMATIS

"AMANT."

We yelled in response to the young priest's drilled questions.

Imagine Southwell's view: twelve teenage dicks bobbing up and down as we treaded water and shouted out our conjugations and declensions.

We boys loved those class sessions. Being in the pool made us feel as though we were getting away with something. Being naked in the water appealed to all of us on a primal level. The pool facilitated kinesthetic learning. Movement helped me remember grammar rules. Movement, and the fact that certain verb forms will be forever associated in my mind with twelve bobbing, wet dicks, helped me learn.

Today this kind of activity would never be allowed in any school. At best it would seem lascivious in an instructor; at worst it would be viewed as child abuse.

Have I said that we boys loved those natatorium classes?

Recently out of college and far afield from *schola praeparatoria,* I was living in Paris. I reveled in being foreign and gay. Two layers of my identity, gay and Catholic, gave me entrees into other cultures. I met French people easily because I went out to gay clubs. Boys looking for boys operate in the same way, no matter the country. When I felt homesick I would go to Mass at the Seventeenth Century parish church down the street from my apartment. All the prayers were in French, but everything else was the same, intuitive. Stand. Sit. Kneel. The parish priest was a charming, puffy, old queen who always affected delight in seeing me.

It was through the parish priest that I met an elegant gay man of indeterminate middle European origins. He called himself Charles, pronounced à la Française. In his apartment hung a big-dicked Mapplethorpe. I told Charles that I was going to Budapest for a visit. He gave me the name of someone and said, "Call him. He knows all the gay people in Budapest."

It was 1980 and Hungary was still a part of the Soviet Empire. Budapest looked as London must have in the years just following World War II. Crumbling Baroque jewels stood next to vacant rubble-strewn lots. Prewar street cars rattled along the gray boulevards.

I rented a room in a flat from a man who was on the state approved tourist agency list. My room was right off the entry hall and it was clear I would not gain entry to the rest of the flat. I could not tell if he lived alone, or if there were swarms of people on the other side of the door. My host was older, elegant, and austere. I attributed his reserve and distance to the waning Cold War.

He spoke no English. I spoke no Hungarian. Somehow he communicated that I was not to use the telephone that was in plain sight on a table in the entry hall.

I found a phone in a shop down the street. It felt like a spy novel. I had been given a password from my friend Charles in Paris.

A man's voice answered the phone.

"Vous parlez Français?" I said.

"Oui."

"Je suis un ami de Charles, à Paris."

There was a pause on the line.

"Pamplemousse," I said.

Grapefruit. The password was grapefruit.

I was invited to a party outside the city. Someone, not the man on the phone, would pick me up in a car. I was told on what corner to wait. The password would be used again. The skullduggery of it all appealed to me immensely.

A dusty white box of an East German manufactured car—a Trabant—pulled up on the appointed corner. Five men were stuffed into the tiny car.

The driver rolled down the window and we grapefruited each other. A back door opened and one of the guys motioned that I should sit on his lap. Quickly it became clear that among the six of us there was not really a common language. Grapefruit was the extent of their French vocabulary. They seemed nervous. With bits of German and English (and the surreptitious probing of my crotch by the guy on whose lap I sat) we established that we were all, indeed, gay. They relaxed, a little, after that.

I suppose I should have been scared. Behind the Iron Curtain, in a car among five strangers with whom I could not communicate, headed out into the dark of night: I was high on the experience.

After about an hour's ride the stuffed little Trabant pulled into a farmer's field. In the dim of the headlights I could see at least thirty other Trabant-like cars parked on the grass. At the far end of the field was a barn.

Two very large, very handsome men stood guard at the entrance to the barn. My new friends knew the men. Even without speaking Hungarian I could tell I was being vouched for.

The barn had been transformed into an ersatz gay disco. A dance floor, already full of shirtless guys in tight Levis 501 blue jeans, throbbed to a sound system wailing Grace Jones. People were dancing, drinking, and generally rubbing up against one another.

My Trabant friends introduced me around. Everyone seemed to know everyone. Again language was a problem. We were all very polite: nodding and smiling. Most Hungarians spoke Russian and German, but not English or French.

I worked especially hard to pronounce the name of one young man. There had been a charge between us when we shook hands. I knew he felt it.

"Gabor," he eased out the two syllables of his name.

"Gabor," I said slowly.

He nodded

"Tamás," I heard him pronounce my name.

The music was so loud we didn't say much else.

With dark hair, dark eyes, and a patch of chest hair peeking out from his v-neck sweater, Gabor reminded me of Darius. He pointed to his ears, shrugged, and then motioned that we should go outside.

A bench ran along the outside wall of the barn. It was warm from the heat of all the men dancing inside.

"English?" I asked, now that we could hear.

Hungarians assumed foreigners could not speak their language, so it was safe to begin inquiries from the get go.

Gabor shook his head no.

"Deutsche?" he asked.

"Nein," I said, and then asked, "Français?"

Gabor smiled. He shook his head 'no' in a way that said he didn't care. He was happy just to sit together.

I returned the smile and the sentiment.

He reached for my hand and held it. We sat looking at the sky and occasionally smiling.

After about a quarter of an hour, Gabor turned to me.

"Latina lingua?" he asked.

"Cetrte," I replied.

Gabor had studied Latin.

In Soviet-era Hungary the state had taken over all schools, except for a few Catholic seminaries. Gabor had gone to a high school operated by one of the seminaries. It had been a form of protest by his parents, sending him to the school. At Gabor's *schola* he got a classical education that a state school would never have provided, and he learned Latin.

Fathers Campion, Southwell, and Hopkins had always said that Latin was a language to be spoken.

In halting Latin we began to converse. Gabor told me that most, but not all, of the people at the barn were gay. Everyone was an artist of some kind: painters, filmmakers, writers. Most had made a bargain with the state. If the artists were discreet they got nice apartments or studios. The state would support their work if it was not blatantly political. The caveat was they could not travel abroad. An exit visa was prelude to exile. If they left it was likely their relatives in Hungary would lose jobs, choice housing, or positions in universities.

Gabor would have left already if not for his family.

Back inside the barn I began to meet Gabor's friends. They were amused to find out that he and I could speak Latin.

On the dance floor we whispered Latin sweet nothings. The language we used was very formal. There was no slang, nothing rapid fire. Our communication was careful and full of poetry. That's the Latin we knew.

I asked him if he wanted to spend the night with me. He wanted to, we both wanted to, but he wasn't sure if it was a good idea. It might not be safe for either Gabor, or my host.

As we stood by the bar talking with a group of Gabor's friends I noticed two older men walking toward us. The younger guys became more formal. They stood up straighter. One even put his sweat-soaked T-shirt back on.

"The Prince-Cardinal is coming over here," Gabor said.

It took me a minute to translate Prince-Cardinal to myself.

"A real Cardinal," I asked, "from the Church?"

"No," Gabor said and laughed. "His name is Jozsi. He is a Papa to all of us. He takes care of us, lets us stay in his flat sometimes. He feeds us. He let us know that there were people like us, gay people, in Hungary. He's very brave and very funny."

"Why do you call him Prince-Cardinal?"

"When he was young he was the secretary to the real Cardinal in Budapest. Jozsi was a priest, but he gave all that up years ago. He can still be very Austro-Hungarian, very correct, when he likes."

When I turned to be presented to the Prince-Cardinal I found myself shaking hands with the man in whose flat I had rented a room.

We were both shocked.

The next morning Jozsi fixed breakfast for Gabor, himself and me.

When we came back to Joszi's after the party I got beyond the big door in the entry hall, into the rest of the flat. There were no swarms of people, only a few rooms. He had a kitchen, a closet of a bedroom, and one other large room with windows looking over the hills toward Buda Castle. The big room was filled with books. A phonograph that would have been at home in my grandparents' neo-Victorian living room had pride of place along one wall.

Literature and music were Joszi's forbidden pleasures. He had books in French, English, German, and Latin. On his shelf was what looked like a first edition of *The Great Gatsby.* Now that he knew I was safe, one of the family, Joszi admitted to being a polyglot. He truly spoke Latin, a remnant from his days as a priest. He also knew French and English. Among the three of us conversation flowed more easily, with Latin still our primary common tongue.

On the ancient phonograph Joszi played a scratchy LP of a Latin Mass chanted by a choir of monks. I waited for my favorite moment: the monks would chant the words *saecula saeculorum.* No matter who composes the chant, those Latin syllables are always the most beautiful. The "o" in the *saeculorem* is always stretched by ecstatic melisma. It washes over me. The phrase, *saecula saeculorum,* sometimes *per omnia saecula saeculorum,* used to be translated as, "world without end"; increasingly it comes across in English as, "forever and ever." *Saecula saeculorum* is the Gregorian chant prelude to the Gregorian money-shot of the Great Amen. The pre-ejaculate joy of *saecula saeculorum* (more literally translated as: from or into the generation of the generations, from or into the century of the centuries) fills me up and takes me away more than any of the Great Amens can.

The young novices, with Darius and me below them in the chapel, were practicing *saecula saeculorun,* world without end, that night in 1971. It was the soundtrack of my first kiss.

I told Gabor and Jozsi the story of Darius and me, in a side chapel, sweetly kissing for an hour. From far off we heard, *"saecula saeculorum,"* over and over. We thought we heard angels.

"That reminds me of when I was at school," Joszi said. "I remember asking the rhetoric master, a sturdy Austrian Cistercian, about all the men loving men in Latin and Greek literature . . . ."

"It's all pre-Christian," Gabor and I said at the same time, and laughed. Latin masters in Hungary and America, it seemed, employed the same literary theory for any uncomfortable truths in the canon.

Joszi turned to Gabor and asked, "What made you ask Tamás if he spoke Latin?"

"It was his hands," Gabor said. "And I could see the hair on his arms. It made me think of a priest I liked at school. This priest always called Latin our *Sermo Patrius*. So I tried it."

The study of Latin and Greek were once components of a standard non-Catholic American college prep track. By the time I was in high school, Latin and Greek had been cast aside from most American—Catholic and non-Catholic—high school curriculums. Latin had survived at the *scholae praeparatoriae* because it was the language of the Church. As Latin receded from the Church, so too did it from schools and the culture. A literary interest in Latin now borders on the foppish.

I wish I had studied more Greek. The homo-lit in Greek, so the gay critics argue, is the genuine article. Roman literature, they say, is all derivative of the Greeks. Unfortunately, the Greek language didn't have the context for me that Latin did. Greek always seemed "other" to me. Latin was never other; it was a natural fit.

Fathers Campion, Southwell, and Hopkins, in the hyperathletic environment that was *schola praeparatoria,* saw us lads naked with great frequency. While the atmosphere in the field house, the dorms, and the natatorium could definitely be homoerotic, those particular priests never laid hands on us. We boys were busy with each other.

The three were fine and loving men. Eccentric, in the best sense, by their example I saw an alternative to a heteronormative life. Here were men who were educated, revered in their culture, and living well outside a heterosexual marriage relationship. They passed on to me my Father Tongue, my *Sermo Patrius*. They made real the bond I have—through the century of the centuries, world without end, *in saecula saeculorum*—with all the gay writers and thinkers who have read and held dear Roman Literature.

I am grateful to have come under the care of these black-robed *magistri* when I was young.

Priests

Ramón García

Priests were a natural part of the social fauna, in both Coalcoman and Modesto. They were men, but not entirely, their maleness was shrouded in a surplus of mystery, formality, and authority. To my adolescent mind, half of who they were was either obscured in some unquestioned privacy, or just missing. The lives of the men around me, the uncles, fathers, and *compadres,* were evident and clear—work, and more work, providing for their families. Their lives set all they were before you. I thought nothing of it. But the priests lived in some other male realm, where silence and solitude reigned.

Padre Rayas was a friend of my parents in Coalcoman. He took me to a ventriloquist show that provided entertainment for the children of the pueblo. I remember various ventriloquists, their dummies intrigued me, the way their stiff mouths in their wooden, poker-faced heads moved to expression; I watched to see if I could catch the ventriloquist's mouth moving with the words the dummy's mouth was uttering. Padre Rayas was friends with one of the ventriloquists. Like the priesthood, the art of ventriloquism seemed like a calling, a strange male dedication, an aberration of manhood.

I went to a restaurant with Padre Rayas and his ventriloquist friend. They ordered beers, they talked and laughed, they could have known each other for a long time, childhood friends, perhaps. Or what they shared could have been a fresh intimacy, a new friendship without years of history. Their conversations were no different than anybody else's. I remember they talked about their families, their brothers and sisters, their parents—Padre Raya's parents lived in Guadalajara. It was strange, they suddenly became men like any other men in town. And like many ordinary men who had not devoted their lives to any special calling, Padre Rayas drank too much; at home my parents joked about it, about how he liked the communion wine more than he should. "It must cause him problems," I remember my mother saying compassionately. My father speculated, "Maybe not; maybe all the *padres* drink now and then; maybe they need it; they don't have any other excitement in their lives."

In Coalcoman, we lived under the image of Christ crucified, the bloodied God on the cross. The early nineteenth-century cathedral housed a crucifix with a realistic sculpture of Christ's body hanging on it. There was also a life-size rendering of a bloodied Christ laid out in a shroud inside of a glass coffin. Believers reverentially touched the glass and made the sign of the cross. During mass on Sunday, sitting on a bench next to mother, looking up at the saints and the candles and the looming body of Christ, I contemplated Christ's starkly realistic wounds. They were the lacerations of the victim, the violated. Christ's body was lean and muscular, but marked by all the suffering and violence we read about in catechism. The loincloth barely covered the fact of his unspoken maleness. I stared at Christ's face, at the sensual expression of agony and betrayal, the crown of thorns streaking the temples and cheeks with blood. The sculptures of Christ always had uncannily realistic eyes, unlike dolls and dummies, and more like those of taxidermied animals, like the tiger and deer heads *tio* Juan had hanging in his study. To look at the eyes, one almost expected them to move, to look back in turn; or, one felt intrusive, almost ashamed, as if voyeuristically looking into someone else's suffering.

I sat daydreaming while the priest said mass; through parables he expressed the lessons connected to some story or idea in the Bible (I hardly listened to what he said, it was meant for the grown-ups anyway). Still, in my young mind, I contemplated the terrible crime committed in those New Testament stories that we studied in catechism class before mass. The dramatic injustice of Christ's martyrdom and the necessity of his suffering for humanity's salvation resulted in making him God, and after thousands of years we, Mexicans in Modesto, were still gathering in his honor and the promised glory of what had been prophesized. There were no more bloodied Christs locked up in glass coffins at Saint Stanislaus in Modesto, and the Christ nailed to the cross was a little less brutally wounded, the air of religion a bit less heavy than in Mexico, though the mass, the prayers and the songs were the same.

The *Virgen de Guadalupe* was the invariably identical image inside of St. Stanislaus as anywhere in Mexico. At home, there was a crucifix in every bedroom, a framed picture of the *Virgen de Guadalupe* in my parents' bedroom. These are the props of our religious beliefs, figures that ground and sustain a sense of permanency and stability in lives that have been deracinated from one world into another.

On Sundays, mass hangs over the morning hours. The shower never seems to stop running, we must get dressed, look presentable, and then the inevitable argument because Dad doesn't want to accompany us. Instead, he stays home to watch the soccer game on the Spanish language TV station. "What kind of example are you setting for your children," Mother would scold him. But he would make some lame excuse; he was tired, his back hurt; anything to end mother's nagging. I didn't think anything of it, it was so like Dad, he didn't really do anything with us. Besides, I understood how boring it was for him. I sensed he was easily bored, it was something I could understand, a trait we had in common. Nonetheless, Dad did go to mass on some special occasions—midnight Christmas mass, and mass for Easter Sunday and Thanksgiving. I remember Dad at one Good Friday mass, the longest mass of the year, which would last for hours as the padre did the stations of the cross. Dad was visibly bored, anxious, and then he started to fall asleep. Mom took mass seriously, it was her time to pray, to feel religion, and she angrily poked Dad to wake him, and my older brother and I laughed.

At another mass during Holy Week, the priests at Saint Stanislaus washed people's feet. Tubs of holy water were placed below small benches near the altars. People would line up to sit on the benches and have their feet washed with a white towel and then wiped clean with a dry one. Then the priest would bend to kiss the feet. There was something sad and creepy about the whole thing, though I understood it as a reenactment of what Christ had done, a simulation of his humility and love for his people. I was glad mother never participated or asked us to get in line to have our feet washed. During communion, a priest held a huge crucifix while another priest handed out the communion wafer. The crucifix had a miniature version of the sculptures of Christ crucified, and congregants bent their heads to kiss its feet. Then the Father would wipe Christ's feet with a handkerchief after each kiss, and another priest or some altar boy offered a chalice of red wine to drink from, after which the rim of the chalice was wiped with a handkerchief. We knew it was a special occasion because it was the only time of the year wine was offered, because Christ had also offered his apostles wine, which was supposed to be his living blood. We knew it was meaningful because even the children were permitted a sip of the wine.

Dad rarely went to Holy Week mass. Though he never said so, I could tell he found the public washing of feet distasteful and burdensome. I dreaded the exceedingly long Good Friday mass, with the tedious sermonizing at every station of Christ's passion, and Holy week mass, and the weird washing of feet, with its inescapable morbid solemnity.

In the extended family there was a vague unspoken hope that perhaps I would become a priest. There were no priests in the entire family, just as there were no military men of any sort, in Mexico or the United States. I was quiet and pious and good, and so the priesthood seemed like a good fit for me. I didn't think much about it. I knew I wouldn't be forced into it, that I had a choice to pursue another route if I wanted.

When the family moved into the house on Renee Drive, Mom invited a priest from St. Stanislaus to come and bless it. At the door my mother told me to kiss his hand. I was surprised and disgusted in the face of another gross ritual I didn't know about—how many were there? Although I didn't want to feel my lips on the old man's hand, I did what I was told. I secretly felt some anger about it, half directed at my mother who had forced me to do such a creepy thing. The sad solemnity and the authority of the priests had begun to seem questionable, unpleasant, and something in my teenage recklessness wanted nothing to do with them. The idea of becoming a priest had become grotesque. Their isolation and servitude seemed sad, and even though I had no sexual experience, their vow of chastity seemed unnecessary and absurd. I would not be a priest, or a dentist like the cousins in Mexico, as Mom and Dad had hoped. There was nothing I could imagine myself doing.

Chain of Fools

Kevin Killian

Again I approach the Church, St. Joseph's at Howard and Tenth, south of Market in San Francisco. It's a disconcerting structure, in late Mission style, but capped with two gold-domed towers out of some Russian Orthodox dream. I'm following two uniformed cops, in the late afternoon this October, we're followed by the sun as we mount the steps to the big brass doors and enter into the darkness of the nave. I see the pastor, Filipino, short and shambling, approach us from the altar, where two nuns remain, arranging fall flowers around the vestibule. I fall back while the cops detain the priest. They're passing him a sheaf of legal papers regarding the closing of the Church, which has been damaged beyond repair by the earthquake of '89. Anger crosses the priest's handsome face, then he shakes the hands of the two policemen; all shrug as if to say, *shit happens.* I glance up at the enormous crucifix where the image of Christ is sprawled from the ugly nails. His slender body, a rag floating over his dick. His face, white in the darkened upper reaches of the Church. His eyes closed, yet bulging with pain. Again I bend my knee and bow, the body's habitual response. Across my face and upper torso I trace the sign of the cross, the marks of this disputed passage. I'm dreaming again—again the dreaming self asserts its mastery over all of time, all of space.

Late in the 1960s Mom and Dad enrolled me in a high school for boys, staffed by Franciscans. I was a scrawny, petulant kid with an exhibitionist streak that must have screamed trouble in every decibel known to God or man. My parents had tried to bring me up Catholic,

---

"Chain of Fools" was first published in *Wrestling With the Angel: Faith and Religion in the Lives of Gay Men,* ed. Brian Bouldrey (NY: Riverhead Books), 1995; and then in the collection *Little Men* by Kevin Killian (West Stockbridge, MA: Hard Press), 1996.

but as I see myself today, I was really a pagan, with no God but experience, and no altar but my own confusing body. In a shadowy antebellum building high on a hill above us, the monks rang bells, said office, ate meals in the refectory, drank cases of beer. In the halls of St. A—, bustling with boys, I felt like the narrator in Ed White's *Forgetting Elena,* marooned in a society I could hardly understand except by dumb imitation. In every room a crucifix transfixed me with shame: I felt deeply compromised by my own falsity. My self was a lie, a sham, next to the essentialism of Christ, He who managed to maintain not only a human life but a divine one too. He *was* God, the Second Person of the Trinity.

But I talked a good game, as any bright student can, and did my best to get out of my schoolwork, so I'd have more time to develop my homosexuality. I spent a year in French class doing independent study, reading *Gone with the Wind* in French, while the other students around me mumbled *"Je ne parle pas"* to an implacable friar. Presently I was able to convince the history teacher that reading *Gone with the Wind* in French should satisfy his requirements too. Then I could go home and confront my appalled parents by saying, "This is something I have to read for school."

Later on, when I was a senior and drunk all the time, a friend and I invented an opera, a collaboration between Flaubert and Debussy, set in outer space and ancient Rome, that we called *Fenestella.* George Grey and I flogged this opera through French class, music class, world literature, etc. We recounted its storyline, acted out its parts, noted the influence of *Fenestella* on Stravinsky, Gide, etc, you name it. Our teachers slowly tired of *Fenestella,* but we never did. The heroine was an immortal bird—a kind of pigeon—sent by St. Valentine out into Jupiter to conquer space in the name of love—on the way to Jupiter she sings the immortal "Clair de Lune." I must have thought I too was some kind of immortal bird, like *Fenestella,* like Shelley's skylark. None of our teachers pointed out the unlikelihood of Flaubert (d. 1880) and Debussy (b. 1862) collaborating on anything elaborate. We had them quarrelling, reuniting, duelling, taking bows at La Scala, arguing about everything from *le mot juste* to the *Cathedrale Engloutée.* Nobody said a word, just gave us A's, praised us to the skies.

I had no respect for most of these dopes. In later life I was to pay the piper by dallying with several teens who had no respect for me.

Nothing's worse than that upturned, scornful face that throws off youth's arrogance like laser rays. When I was sixteen I had the world by the tail. But in another light the world had already made me what I was, a blind, struggling creature like a mole, nosing through dirt to find its light and food.

In religion class Brother Padraic had us bring in pop records which we would play, then analyze like poetry. It was a conceit of the era, that rock was a kind of poetry and a way to reach kids. Other boys, I remember, brought in "poetic" records like "All Along the Watchtower," "At the Zoo," "Chimes of Freedom." The more daring played drug songs—"Sister Ray," "Eight Miles High," "Sunshine Superman," or the vaguely scandalous "Let's Spend the Night Together." When it was my turn I brandished my favorite original cast album—*My Fair Lady*—and played "Wouldn't It be Loverly." "Now, that's poetry," I would say expansively, mincing from one black tile to a red tile, then sideways to a white tile, arms stretched out appealingly. After the bell rang a tall man dressed in black stepped out of the shadows between lockers and said, "Have you considered psychological counseling?" I should have been mortified, but I shook my head like a friendly pup and, with purposeful tread, followed him to his office. Then the office got too small for his needs and he drove me to what I soon came to think of as *our place,* down by the river, down by the weeds and water birds.

Getting in and out of a VW bug in those long, black robes must have been a bitch. Funny I didn't think of that till later. It happened in front of my eyes but I didn't really notice. I was too—oh, what's the word—ensorcelled. He—Brother Jim—wasn't exactly good-looking, but he had something that made up for any defect: he'd taken that precious vow of celibacy, though not, he confided, with his dick. First I felt for it through the robes, then found a deep slit pocket I was afraid to slip my hand into. Then he laughed and lifted the robe over his legs and over most of the steering wheel. And down by the gas pedal and the clutch he deposited these awful Bermuda shorts and evocative sandals. And his underwear. His black robe made a vast tent, a dark tent I wanted to wrap myself up in and hide in forever, with only his two bent legs and his shadowy sex for company. So I sucked him and sucked him, Brother Jim.

"Why don't you turn around?" he asked. "Pull those pants all the way down, I like to see beautiful bodies." He made my knees wobble as he licked behind them. Wobble, like I couldn't stand up. On the wind, the scents of sand cherry and silverweed, the brackish river. The squawk of a gull. Scents that burned as they moved across my face, like incense. After a while he told me how lonely his life was, that only a few of the other monks were queers, there was no one to talk to. "You can talk to me," I told him, moved. Every semester he and the few other queer monks judged the new students like Paris awarding the golden apple. Some of us had the staggering big-lipped beauty that April's made from; some of us were rejected out-of-hand, and some of us, like me, seemed available. Then they waited till they felt like it, till they felt like trying one of us out.

He made me feel his . . . dilemma, would you call it? Boys, after all, are tricky because they change from week to week. You might fancy a fresh complexion: act right away, for in a month that spotless face will have grown spotted, or bearded, or dull. You might reject me because I have no basket, well, too bad, because by Christmas I'll be sporting these new genitals Santa brought me, big, bad, and boisterous. This was Jim's dilemma—when you're waiting for a perfect boy, life's tough. So they traded us, more or less. Always hoping to trade up, I guess. "Don't trade me," I pleaded with him. "Oh never," he said, tracing the nape of my neck absently, while on the other side of the windshield darkness fell on a grove filled with oaks and wild hawthorn. "Never, never, never."

I wanted to know their names—who was queer, which of them—I *had* to know. He wouldn't say. *I* named names. How about the flamboyant arts teacher who insisted on us wearing tights, even when playing Arthur Miller? No. None of the effeminate monks, he told me, were gay. "They just play at it," he sneered. How about the gruff math teacher who had been the protegé of Alan Turing and John van Neumann? If you answered wrong in class he'd summon you to his desk, bend you over his knee, and spank you. If you were especially dense you'd have to go to his disordered room in the evening and he'd penetrate you with an oily finger, sometimes two. "No," said Brother Jim, my new boyfriend. "Don't be absurd. None of those fellows are fags. You'd never guess unless I tell you." I told him I didn't really want to know, a lie, I told him I'd never done this with a man, a lie, I told him I would never tell another about the love that passed between us, a lie. And all these lies I paid for when June began and Jim got himself transferred to Virginia. But then another teacher stopped me in the hall. "Jim told me about your problem," he said, his glasses frosty, opaque. This was Brother Anselm. "He says you feel itchy round the groin area."

He's the one who took me to see *The Fantasticks* in Greenwich Village and bought me the record, "Try to Remember." If you're reading this, Anselm, try to remember that time in September when life was long and days were fucking mellow. As for you, Brother Jim, whatever happened to "never?" You said you'd "never" trade me, but when I turned seventeen I was yesterday's papers. Thus I came to hate aging, to the point that even today I still pride myself on my "young attitude." Pathetic. I remember that our most famous alumnus was Billy Hayes, whose story was later made into a sensational film called *Midnight Express.* At that time he was mired in a Turkish prison for drug smuggling. We students had to raise funds for his legal defense, or for extra-legal terrorist acts designed to break him out. Students from *other* schools went door-to-door in elegant neighborhoods, selling chocolate bars to send their track teams to big meets, but we had to go around with jingling cans, asking for money for "The Billy Hayes Fund," and you know something, people gave! They didn't even want to know what it was, good thing too. Later when the film came out its vampy, homoerotics gave me a chill. Later still, its leading man, Brad Davis, played *Querelle* in Fassbinder's film of the Genet novel. And even later still Davis died of AIDS and I conflated all these men into one unruly figure with a queer complaint against God.

Standing on the desert's edge, a man at the horizon, shaking a fist against an implacable, empty sky.

At first I resented Jim and Anselm and the rest, their careless handling of this precious package—me. But after awhile I grew fond of them, even as they passed me around like a plate of canapes at a cocktail party. Anybody would have, especially a young person like myself who thought he was "different." I watch the E Channel and see all these parents of boys, parents who are suing Michael Jackson, and I want to tell them, your boys are saying two things, one out of each side of their mouths, or maybe three things, one of them being, "Let me go back to Neverland Ranch where at least I was *appreciated*."

Unlike Michael Jackson, the religious staff of St. A—wore ropes around their waists to remind themselves, and us, of the constant poverty of St. Francis of Assisi. One of them quoted St. Therese to me, to illustrate his humility: "I am the zero which, by itself, is of no value but put after a unit becomes useful." I pulled the rope from around his waist, teasing him. I took one home as a souvenir. These fat, long ropes, wheaten color, thick as my penis and almost as sinuous. I believed in those ropes. I said to myself, why don't *you* become a monk, think of all the side benefits? I walked down to the grove of trees by the river's edge one April afternoon, thinking these grand thoughts of joining the seminary. Beneath my feet small pink flowers, a carpet of wood sorrel or wild hepatica, leading down to a marshy space tall with field horsetail, up to my waist. "God," I called out, "give me a sign I'm doing the right thing." I felt guilty that I had sinned in a car, guilty and stained, like a slide in a crime lab. I waited for His sign, but zilch. Above me a pair of laughing gulls, orange beaks, black heads, disappeared into the sun. *Is that my sign?* thought I, crestfallen. *How oblique.* But right around that time I began to realize that there was something stronger than a Franciscan brother.

They used to say that marijuana leads to heroin,. I don't know about that, but after awhile friars just don't cut it, you want something stronger, something that'll really *take you there.* You want a priest. Ever see *The Thorn Birds,* the way Rachel Ward longs for Richard Chamberlain? Or Preminger's *The Cardinal,* with Romy Schneider yearning for some other gay guy, it's a thrill to think, y'know, with a little luck, this man licking my cock could turn out to be the Prince of the Whole Church, the Supreme Pontiff, in ten or fifteen years and right now, you can almost see his soul shining right through his thinning blond hair, already he's godly—again the dreaming self rises above the squalid air of the black back room, the hush of the confessional, breaking free into a world of pleasure and Eros and hope, all I continue to pray for and more. Out in the snowy East of Long Island I bent over Frank O'Hara's grave and traced his words with my tongue, the words carved into his stone there: "Grace to be born and to live as variously as possible." Another lapsed Catholic trying to align the divine with the human.

And because I was so willful, I made spoiling priests a kind of game, like Sadie Thompson does in *Rain.* Under those robes of black, I would think, are the white limbs of strong men. I trailed one priest, Fr. Carney, from assignment to assignment. I was his youth liaison—encouraged to inform on my peers' drug habits, I had first to increase my own. You have to be a little hard, a little speedy, to become what we then called a "narc." He also got me to bring along other youths to retreats staged at isolated Long Island mother houses. When I graduated from St. A—I continued to traipse after Fr. Carney, like Marlene Dietrich slinging her heels over her shoulder to brave the desert at the end of *Morocco,* all for Gary Cooper's ass. "You don't have to call me Father Carney," he would say to me. "Call me Paul." I felt like king of the hill, top of the heap. Oh, Paul, I would say, why am I being treated so well? "Because you are who you are," he told me. "You are someone special. You are Kevin Killian."

I grew more and more spoiled, and he must have enjoyed my ripeness, up to a point; and then he left me, in this valley of tears. I remember standing in his room watching the cold, green spectacle of Long Island Sound, leaves of yellow acacia tapping into the window, with this pair of black gym shorts pulled down just under my buttocks, and thinking to myself, I'll bring him back to me with my hot skin and my healthy boy-type sweat. And him, Paul, slouched on his king-size bed, turned away from me, bored, extinguished, his breviary pulled next to him like a teddy bear. "There's a list on my desk," he said. "Some of them may be calling you." So when I pulled up my pants I'd have this list to turn to, the names of other priests, *next!*—like one of those chain letters, filled with the names of strangers, to whom you have to send five dollars each or Mother will go blind. "You're trading me too," I said, before the door hit me on the ass. Thump.

So the next guy called me, Father some-Polish-name, and he turned out to be—*really into the rosary.* Around this time I got to thinking that despite what they told me, I was not someone special after all.

These men were connoisseurs all right. They pulled out my cork and took turns sniffing it. Meanwhile the *sommelier* stood by, a smile in his eyes, attentive, alert. Disillusioned, dejected, I began to read the whims of these men not as isolated quirks, but as signs of a larger system, one in which pleasure, desire endlessly fulfilled, *jouissance,* are given more value. Within the Church's apparently ascetic structure, the pursuit of pleasure has been more or less internalized. By and large, the pursuit (of violence, danger, beauty) *is* the structure. I had to hand it to them! Under their black robes those long legs were born to *can-can.* Pleasure, in a suburbia that understood only growth and money. Aretha Franklin said it best, singing on the radio while I moped from man to man. *"Chain-chain-chain,"* she chanted. *"Chain of fools."*

I met Dorothy Day in a private home in Brooklyn, when Father Paul took me to meet her. She was seventy then, and had been a legend for forty years, both in and out of the Church, for her activism, her sanctity, her saltiness. I had read all about her in *Time* magazine. She sat on a huge sofa almost dwarfed by these big Mario Buatta-style throw pillows, gold and pink and red. Her hands were folded neatly in her lap, as though she were groggy. "The way to get closer to Christ," she asserted, "is through work." Father Paul argued mildly—"what about the Golden Rule? Isn't love the answer?" "No," she responded sharply—"work, not love." Last night on TV I rewatched *The Trouble with Angels,* in which mischievous Hayley Mills raises holy hell at a Long Island girls school, till she meets her match in imperious, suave Mother Superior Rosalind Russell. At the denouement she tells her plain girlfriend that she won't be going to Bryn Mawr or even back to England. She's decided to "stay on," become a nun, clip her own wings. I remember again wavering on the brink, of becoming a priest, saying to myself, why don't you do the—*Hayley Mills thing?* Saying it to myself from the back row of this cobwebbed movie house in a poky town on the North Shore of Long Island, fingering the beer between my legs, all alone in the dark.

Now I'm all grown, Dorothy Day is dead, and when I open *Time* magazine I read about altar boys and seminarians suing priests. One quarter of all pedophile priests, they say, live in New Mexico. I have no interest in pursuing my "case" in a tribunal, but I'd like to view such a trial—maybe on Court TV? Or sit in the public gallery, next to John Waters, while my teachers take the stand and confess under pressure or Prozac. I'd get out a little sketchpad and charcoal and draw their faces, older now, confused and guilty, and perhaps a little crazy. Then their accusers would come to the stand, confused, guilty, crazy, and I could draw in my own eyes into their various faces, into the faces of my pals and brothers.

Oh how I envied them their privilege, their unflappable ease, the queers of the Church. If they were as lonely as they claimed, weren't there enough of them? If their love lives were dangerous, surely they would always be protected by the hierarchy that enfolded them. I remember one monk who had been sent away years before to a special retreat in Taos and he said, *I didn't want to have to come back and see any boys. But then I wanted to come back, it must have been to meet you, Kevin.* And I pictured this empty desert sky with nothing in it but one of Georgia O'Keeffe's cow skulls staring at me through time. My face broke into a smile and I said, "That is so sweet."

I broke with the Church over its policies on abortion, women's rights, gay rights, just like you did. Perhaps its hypocrisy angered you, but that's just human nature, no? What scared me was its monolithic structure. It's too big either to fight or hide within, like the disconcerting house of the Addams Family. I tried to talk to It, but It just sat there, a big unresponsive sack of white sugar. So good-bye. And yet I suppose I'm a far better Catholic now than then. I dream of this god who took on the clothes of man and then stepped forward to strip them off at the moment of humiliation. This renunciation for a greater good remains with me an ideal of society and heaven. I try to get closer to Christ through work. I tried love for a long time but it only lengthened the distance between Him and me.

So I try to call the number of St. A—to see where the twentieth high school reunion will be. That's when I find out the school's now defunct, for the usual reasons: indifference, inflation, acedia. I continue to see the Church as the house of Eros, a place of pleasure and fun, and I continue to regard men in religious costume as possible sex partners, yearning to break free. Such was my training, my ritual life. I can't shake it off, I'm not a snake who can shed its skin. Every time I pass a crucifix I wonder, *What if it had been me up there instead—could I have said: Father, forgive them, for they know not what they do?* I don't think I'm so special, not anymore. At the Church here in San Francisco, I bow down and make the sign of the cross, the logo of the Church, an imprint deep within forcing me to replicate it. Up, down, left, right, the hand that seeks, then pulls away frustrated. The hand tightens, becomes a fist, the fist is raised to the sky, on the desert's edge, angry and queer. Inside the Church burns incense, tricky and deep-penetrating, strong, perdurable, like the smells of sand cherry, silverweed, trillium.

Lesbian Catechism: Samplings from a Life

Mary Beth Caschetta

I spent my life wanting to become a nun, but somehow ended up a lesbian. I wish I'd had formal instruction. Instead, I made the rules up as I went along, writing them down, as I had somehow also ended up a writer. These are excerpts from my catechism, profession of my own personal lesbian faith.

PROFESSION OF FAITH

The face of Jesus appeared to me once in a glass of orange juice. Maybe it was the pulp, but by the age of seven I was already damaged and hypervigilant, one of God's faithful servants by my own design. A few years later, I had a second vision: the vague outline of a skinny Christ, arms stretched out on a cross– this time, in a spot of rust on the hood of Steven DaSilva's car.

Although for years, I searched for someone to tell, I decided to keep the visions to myself. I guess I thought a miracle might follow and shed some light. On both occasions, though, what came next was fairly inconclusive. My brother drank the holy juice which I'd carefully placed on the top shelf of the refrigerator for further consideration, and Steven DaSilva, the neighborhood rebel, crashed his dark gray Mustang, burning to death and taking with him to Heaven the rusty crucifix and three of his high-school buddies.

Steven DaSilva was the first boy I ever knew who died—the first person—and for a few years, the thought of his mortal body floating out a windshield brought me to my knees. I might have mentioned that rusty Jesus to someone, I knew. I might have saved his life. Too late for salvation, I repented with vigor.

As a child, I'd prayed nearly all the time for redemption, but without any real cause or direction. Before my negligence about the rusty Jesus, I was merely a sinner because we were all sinners. In part, until Steven died, I experienced religion as an empty shell, reading the Bible from cover to cover like a trashy novel about people with enviable lives, deserving of punishment and forgiveness. In a way, the Good News cultivated my first appreciation for a good plot—the beginning of my conscious life as a writer. I also paid attention to character. I could name the disciples by heart—even the minor ones—and fostered an uncanny ability to distinguish among the Gospels of Matthew, Mark, Luke, and John according to writing style. In short, I was a strange, fanatical kid, in search of mercy as much as a good story line.

We heard about it on the radio: how Steven had wrapped the car around a telephone pole. "That kid was a hoodlum," my father said, breaking into his runny eggs. "Probably driving drunk with those derelict friends of his."

It was a well-known fact at the time (to everyone but me) that Steven DaSilva's father, a dentist, had connections to the Mafia. I found out about Mr. DaSilva years later, after college, when a childhood friend let it slip that an organized crime crack down was the reason the DaSilva's moved away in such a big hurry.

"Jesus, how could you not have known?" my friend said. "You were Maria DaSilva's best friend. I thought you knew."

Maria, tiny and wild-eyed, was younger than me by four months. She ran around topless, dropping her panties for any boy who wanted a glimpse. Once in her basement while playing "Hug Like a Husband," she bit my shoulder so hard that I bled on her mother's coffee-colored carpet.

Later when I was allowed to play with her again, she explained. "I didn't mean to hurt you. It just came over me, like God pressing down. Like love."

I touched the place where her teeth had made their mark. "No more biting," I warned, secretly flattered. "I don't care *who* presses on you."

For obvious reasons, I rarely got to play next door. In fact, in all the years Maria was my best friend, I never slept over and only ate dinner there once.

A few weeks after Steven had died in the miracle car, I remember the shades were still drawn. It was a Thursday afternoon, quiet and gray, a few days after the first big thaw of early spring. Mr. DaSilva arrived home with fresh bread from an Italian bakery, as if it were Sunday. But before we had a chance to slip off the warm white bag and sneak a bite, Maria's mother got mad at her father for making a snide remark about her cooking, and she turned a bowl of salad over onto her husband's head.

"Son of a bitch," she said. "You're not the King of this household."

I was shocked. At my house, my father was the King of everything, and we knew better than to challenge him.

I felt Maria hold her breath with me. We waited for a fiery response, but Mr. DaSilva had his own style. He was soft and clear-eyed. He just sat there brushing tomato and vinegar off his shirt, but for some reason left the bowl on his head.

Maria and I looked down at our plates, as if we were nearing the part in a scary movie where the music indicated something terrible was coming to make us scream.

Nothing happened.

"Aren't you mad at all?" Maria whispered to her father.

The question must have seemed funny to Mr. DaSilva, who started to laugh and placed his hand softly on his daughter's head, the way priests sometimes did when they blessed a bald baby during Communion. I always figured they knew something I didn't, like how a gentle touch could actually ease the pain and defeat of that bald baby's struggle to grow up.

Finally, Mrs. DaSilva returned from the bedroom, where—from the look of things—she'd been crying.

"Take the bowl off your head," she barked, but her voice was no longer a threat.

Refusing to look at Mr. DaSilva, she served us garlic-roasted chicken with string beans and red potatoes. We ate in silence until Mr. DaSilva started laughing. First quietly to himself, and then with his head slung back as if inviting everyone to join him. Tears rolled down his cheeks which made Maria giggle nervously. And even Mrs. DaSilva coughed up a chuckle despite herself.

By thc time dessert rolled around, we were acting like the salad bowl was the most hilarious thing that had ever happened. Maybe, at that particular moment, it was.

SACRAMENTS

By the time puberty rolled around, I planned on joining a convent. I'd spent months imagining myself in a little stone chamber with stern, dowdy women who believed in the merits of study and silence, and who might someday kiss me in the passionate name of the Lord.

Instead, I went to Vassar.

There, I learned a vocabulary that helped my life make more sense: depression, scholarship, homosexuality, desperation.

There were interesting texts to replace the old familiar one about Jesus and his cross—complex stories by Milton and Shakespeare, Bronte and Tolstoy, Virginia Woolf. Luce Irigaray, Francis Bacon, Margery Kempe. New characters to envy, new writing styles to emulate.

At first, I thought I wanted to be a writer, and when that wore off, I knew I wanted to write. Except for a few poetry contests, I'd always been careful to keep my writing private. I carried around small piles of bad poems and a novel I once wrote in a thick spiral notebook about a gynecologist who kept jars of dead babies in the basement. My father was a gynecologist.

By sophomore year, I'd taken workshops with hundreds of other students, contributed to a literary magazine that published twice a year, and filled my semesters with courses dedicated to fiction-writing causes, taught by real fiction writers. Once, Grace Paley workshopped a new novel I was writing about an Italian-American woman who ran away from her husband and children and returned to Italy to kill her father for sins committed during her childhood. My father was not from Italy, but this, after all, was an attempt at fiction. It was stagnant and stale, but everyone praised it anyway. Only later did my writing teacher come clean: "Listen, everyone gets to write one bad novel. Consider yourself lucky. You got it over with while you are still young enough to bounce back."

Perhaps in a small way, going public with my writing replaced my childhood need for secrets and God. Or perhaps for revenge. Either way, I began to write the way I used to pray—constantly and passionately, hoping eventually I'd be deserving of a forgiving reader.

In the meantime, everywhere I turned, it seemed, there were people standing around eager to encourage me to write. This was new, and I was tempted to correct them: "My brothers are good at things, not me." Slowly, though, it dawned on me that God and my belief in God wasn't what defined me. Praying all the time wasn't going to make me a feminist which was what I newly wanted to become. I ditched the Catholic group on campus which had comprised my early campus social life, and began hanging out with secular kids.

By then, the very notion of a paternal divinity had become restrictive, a relic from my past. Not a symbol of my future.

After an incident with a visiting priest from Rome, who tried to seduce me and my roommate at an off-campus rectory one Saturday afternoon, I became an atheist by default. We'd volunteered to help him get oriented on campus, when he came up with some excuse to drive us back to his place, a few miles out past Vassar Farm. At the rectory, he built a fire in the fireplace and offered us a drink, suggesting that he'd like for us to rub one another's backs, while he drank wine and watched. He claimed that whenever two or more were gathered in His name—rubbing backs, apparently—he could feel the hand of God pressing on his heart.

"An adult form of faith," he said, holding up a bottle of Merlot. "Or I can draw you a warm bath. Would you like that?"

My roommate and I sat on a little wooden bench in the foyer of the grand old house, staring up at the priest who was still in his robes from Mass.

He was smiling, white teeth against olive skin.

"No," my roommate said quietly, snow melting in a puddle at her feet.

"You gotta be kidding, right?" I asked the guy. "I mean, do we look stupid to you?"

My roommate shook her head like a cartoon character.

Something about the look in her eyes made me burst out cackling, a release, I guess, of fear and indignation.

"Beautiful laughter," the priest said, lifting his wine bottle higher in the air. "Also a form of prayer."

For some reason, I couldn't stop myself from laughing and slapping the priest on the back, as if we were sharing a really good joke. The sound of my laughter was like a tiny howling which continued for a minute or so, until my stomach began to hurt.

"C'mon," my roommate whispered, grabbing my hand. "Let's get out of here."

It was a long walk back to campus. In the dusk and the cold, nothing about the incident felt funny anymore.

"Maybe it's because he's European," my roommate said, meaning, I guessed, Italian.

"Or maybe just an asshole," I said. Halfway home, as it started to snow. "The church is filled with hypocrites."

"With humans, anyway," my roommate said, not looking me in the eye.

Wet snow slung down on us, giving me the idea that emptying my backpack would lighten my load, get us home faster. "I'm not going back to church," I said, leaving my faith on the side of the road with my half-eaten lunch, but my roommate didn't comment.

I remember that moment vividly and often: how the weight of my words made me cold inside, as if an important decision were being made. Or maybe that's the way you always feel when you step over the perilous line separating conviction from doubt. I can still see us, walking home, arm in arm, escapees from a tainted baptism, flakes of snow melting all around us.

About halfway to campus, she was the one who suggested we repress the whole thing, and we did manage to disremember until spring semester, when another freshman who sang and played guitar at Saturday Mass went public with her charges.

Assault, we heard, and *endangering a minor.*

"My feet are frozen," I complained after it had been snowing long enough to seep through my sneakers. "I can't take another step."

"See that light up there?" My roommate pointed due north. "That's the campus."

Less than a few yards, I could see the outline of the place we suddenly came to think of as home. I was wearing one of her mittens and had started to think about crying.

"Come on," she said grabbing my hands. "We can run the rest of the way."

A LIFE OF FAITH

For years, my mother dragged me off to the back pews of dark churches to watch perfect strangers get married.

"Someday that'll be you," she whispered, pinching me.

I was supposed to want to be the bride but pictured myself more the priest, holy and disinterested. I liked his crisp white collar, asexual demeanor, and his purported closeness with God, but by then I'd learned to keep my mouth shut. My mother was typically Italian, obsessed with marrying me off, and someone for whom weddings were the ultimate sport. There was no room in her agenda for fantasies of the priesthood. She trained me hard: double sessions, field trips to St. Anthony's, St. Michael's, St. John's.

Each time a new bride stood at the ready, my mother cried into a wadded Kleenex. "So beautiful," she said.

It wasn't true: some brides were scrawny, with beaky noses. Some were heavy, with wire-like curls sprayed into a nest. Other brides were just plain homely in a way that makes me think of specific towns in western New York, as if a particular brand of unattractive Italian woman was left behind on the Genesee River, while the pretty got to forge onward to Canada.

Still my mother could detect beauty in any girl about to be given away to a man. And we both knew that it was me she saw in that long white dress with matching veil and shoes. Not a stranger, but her daughter. Me, flanked by a lineup of broad-shouldered attendants clad in taffeta, and men in rented shoes.

In Italy, as in my corner of Rochester, New York, wedding receptions were a birthright: soggy macaroni and chicken thighs. Music played by a DJ, and an open bar.

My mother couldn't wait to show me off to the crowd of whiskery *gumbas*, my great aunts, who magically appeared at every reception. "*That's* who knows about marriage," my mother said, when the old women from Calabria stood *en masse* to dance the tarantella. This was their blessing on every bride, their warning for every groom, the promise of what awaits him. Watching from a distance, I could feel the weight of their swollen stomping feet, their arthritic clapping hands.

Long ago, they let me in on the secret of matrimony: that a man (my father, say, or one of my brothers) could be so *stoonad* (stupid) as to believe he is king, when everyone knows that women rule. Italian women.

The youngest of four, the only girl in our family, I nodded and smiled, as if I were interested.

Aunt Peppie pointed a gnarled finger, "You too."

I believed her. I'd seen her perform magic: she and her sisters, my grandmother included, could make headaches go away by dripping oil into water and saying *mal'occhio,* the evil eye. (*Mumbo-jumbo,* my father called it.) Any one of them could snap a rabbit's neck in half, skin it, and fry it with greens. Probably they were witches—Italian witches, of course, the good kind. Any prediction they made was likely to come true.

Unable to shake off Aunt Peppie's words as I walked the hallways of junior high, I found myself agreeing to go out with a boy who'd been pursuing me since seventh grade. Not Italian. It might not actually matter, I decided, since for years I'd resigned myself to an eerie certainty that nuptials (like train wrecks and cancer) were what awaited other people—my cousins, my brothers—not me.

Imagine my surprise, twenty-five years later, when Massachusetts, a state in which I am living by utter chance, makes it legal for people like me to marry.

"Are you sure?" I ask my partner Meryl. We watch the news on New England Cable. "Do you think it's really going to happen?"

I never figured on becoming a modern bride.

PRAYER

On May 17, 2004, a raw morning in Cape Cod, Massachusetts, Meryl and I stood waiting to fill out some paperwork. It was the first day queers could legally marry, and we had one of the first appointments. A line was already forming behind us, couples standing shoulder to shoulder on the steps of the town hall.

By 9:00 a.m., the streets were filled. Hundreds of onlookers watched and waited, cheering. People threw confetti, took photographs. Some carried signs; others handed out roses to every bride, male or female. Volunteers from the Human Rights Campaign cut wedding cake for any two waving a license to marry. The festive atmosphere harkened back to earlier days: the first Gay Pride parades in New York City, the Marches on Washington, the 1980s, the 1990s. Though now we were decades from our youth; our friends no longer dying in droves.

"This one's pretty," my mother had said about Meryl. She liked her on first sight, because of Meryl's good looks and her own vanity. Still she had come a long way since the days of hysterical crying, breast-beating, throwing herself at me; my mother hadn't cornered me in a kitchen or attacked my short hair in years. We were in easy daily contact, thanks to the computer my brothers and I had given her for her seventieth birthday. And while she might have said a secret novena now and then, petitioning the Virgin on my behalf, she seemed okay with my current situation.

Handing over our paperwork, we raced up the Cape to Orleans District Court, where we paid for our waiver of the three-day waiting period, an arcane holdover from the days of syphilis and shotgun weddings, when a few days of clarity might have made a difference. Formerly $65, this waiver suddenly cost $195, the special homosexual rate. Greeting us in chambers was Judge Welch, a small, worn New Englander in formal robes, whose father, like his father before him, had been a judge.

His office was dark and smelled of cherry tobacco. "I'm pleased to take part in this special day." His eyes twinkled. He pressed our hands into his small but binding grip. "You love each other a lot."

We held our breaths. There we were: among the first gay people to marry in the United States of America, in the first state to go legal, on the fiftieth anniversary of Brown v. the Board of Education.

"A fine day for civil rights!" the judge said breaking into a smile.

Returning to Provincetown for our final license, we were greeted by an army of television cameras. Over the past few weeks we'd turned down media requests from *Newsday* to TV Japan, politely declining reporters who wanted to follow us around to document our wedding day. We were camera-shy. Still, the local news caught our happy moment. (The reel later ran in a continuous loop on the *New York Times* website.) We headed for home.

At four o'clock, we were married in our living room, not by a priest or a rabbi. Instead we chose someone we had only just met. Angry Republican Governor Mitt Romney had made sure that friends of gay people were not swiftly deputized and pressed into service, so we hired instead a lovely, elderly, lesbian African-American minister who walked with a cane. She spoke solemnly of candles and circles and unions and avoided evoking the God of our childhoods. And yet it felt suddenly spiritual, even religious, to participate in an institution, a sacrament technically, which was designed for my exclusion.

Flown in from New York, Meryl's gay brother stood as our witness, ring-bearer, and flower boy. Her sister called a few moments after we'd taken our vows; my new father-in-law and his wife phoned that evening. Meryl's mother sent flowers.

From my family, there was only eerie silence. By May 17, well through the following Sunday, when our marriage was announced in the *New York Times,* I'd still heard nothing from my family.

I could feel my mother's long-suffering grief, feel the weight of her prayers on my shoulders.

All my life, I'd struggled against absorbing her quiet devastation over who I turned out to be. Surrounded by my dearest and queerest friends, I felt happy in life at long last: lucky and proud. I wished I could somehow show my mother that I was not so different from who I used to be.

At the wedding, of course, none of it mattered. Not even my mother.

"Do you take this woman?" the minister asked, making me want to believe in God again.

And I did.

Completely and happily, I did.

Fully Human, Fully Alive

Salvatore Sapienza

In *Fully Human, Fully Alive,* gay writer and former Catholic brother, Salvatore Sapienza, reminisces about his friendship with Father Mychal Judge, a Roman Catholic Franciscan priest. During his forty years as a priest, Father Judge ministered to people with AIDS and was a long-term member of Dignity, a gay Catholic group. His last assignment was as Chaplain of the Fire Department of New York City. On the morning of September 11, 2001, Father Judge rushed to the World Trade Center, where he was among the first victims killed when the towers collapsed. A photograph of Father Judge's body being carried from the rubble has become one of the most famous images of that day. Since his death, there has been a growing movement to have Father Judge canonized as the first openly gay saint in the Catholic Church.

Walking to the subway station after an AA meeting in Manhattan, Father Mychal Judge, a Franciscan priest fully attired in his hooded brown monk's habit, turned to a young gay man he met at the meeting and exclaimed, "Isn't God wonderful!" When the young man asked the priest why, Father Mychal responded, "Look at all the beautiful men out on a Friday night."

What may sound like the introduction to another sordid story about the secret sexual lives of Catholic priests is anything but, for this is the tale of a man who took his vow of celibacy very seriously, yet still celebrated his sexuality openly. A man of God, but still just a man.

Although most would come to know him following his death on September 11, 2001, Father Mychal Judge entered my life in the late 1980s, a time when the Catholic Church was beginning its regression back to its pre-Vatican II era of fear and repression. Up until then, my life as a gay Catholic was exceedingly smooth-going, if not downright idyllic.

I was extremely lucky (Mychal would later tell me I was fated) to come of age during a very short window of time in the Catholic Church where "God Don't Make Junk" was becoming the company's new motto. The young nuns, priests, and brothers who taught me were products of the "peace and love" 1960s. They wore bell-bottoms and Birkenstocks under their habits and sang joyful Kumbaya-like folk songs about loving one another. The catechism taught for decades was replaced with "The Good News." This contrasted sharply with the pre-Vatican II era church of my parents' generation, where priests said mass in Latin with their backs to the congregation and morose hymns were sung about fearing the Lord's wrath.

On the walls of my Catholic elementary school, for example, all the spooky looking pictures of Jesus with the sacred heart bursting out of his chest were replaced with newer portraits of a more approachable, smiling, handsome Jesus. This figure was not some untouchable icon to be feared. Rather, I remember praying to this image and finding comfort. As a sensitive, artistic kid growing up in a tough, Italian working-class Queens neighborhood, I often found solace picturing myself being held in the arms of this gentle man whom I was told loved me unconditionally.

It was also at grade school where a very cool young nun—who wore lipstick!—named Sister Eileen first noticed my interest in other boys. While the rest of the sixth-grade boys showed off their athletic prowess during gym class, I hid behind the bleachers drawing them—okay, mostly one of them: my crush, Pauly Noto—in my sketchbook. Finding me there one day, Sister Eileen reached down and took the book from my hands. I feared she might reprimand me or, worse yet, force me to join the other boys in sports. Instead, as she flipped through the drawings, she smiled and said admiringly, "You have a good eye for the male form." And then, handing the book back to me, Sister Eileen added, "That's a gift. Don't hide your light under a bushel basket."

A few years later, at the all boys Catholic high school I attended, Brother Thomas, my history teacher, asked for my help in creating a display in commemoration of the school's twenty-fifth anniversary for the bulletin board case outside the main office. As we worked after school every day for a week on the project, I came to know him as a person, rather than simply an authority figure in religious garb. He later became the first person to whom I confided I was gay. He didn't tell me it was just a phase all boys went through, nor did he tell me I was going to hell. Rather, he gave me a copy of John Reid's book, *The Best Little Boy in the World,* in which he inscribed, "You are God's perfect creation."

I hear horror stories from strangers, colleagues, and friends—both gay and straight—about their growing up Catholic. Stories of ruler-wielding nuns and predatory priests. Guilt, oppression, and shame are the keywords they use in describing their experiences in the Church. I have no such tales to tell, and maybe that's why as a gay man, I find myself apologizing for having come through my twelve years of Catholic schooling not just unscathed, but uplifted, and inspired, whereas most of my gay brethren were not as fortunate. I never really struggled thinking that being gay was wrong or sinful, as I had been raised in a church which taught me that I was perfect just how God made me.

It was because of people like Sister Eileen and Brother Thomas that I decided to enter religious life myself after graduating from college and living as an openly gay man in Manhattan in the 1980s. Like their calling in the sixties, I too felt the urge to live counter-culturally in response to the changing climate of the times. The "greed is good"-yuppie movement and the sexual promiscuity of the gay club scene clashed with the ideals I had for myself and for my generation, and I hoped my commitment to poverty, chastity, and obedience would serve as an inspiration to a world obsessed with money, sex, and power.

During my years of religious training in the novitiate, we were encouraged to read *Fully Alive, Fully Human,* a book written by the Jesuit priest, John Powell. In it, he wrote: "We are not prisoners of the past, but pioneers of an exciting future." Unlike the previous generation of clergy who suffered through and repressed their sexuality for the sake of the Kingdom, we novices learned that we could be sexual and celibate. We were reminded time and time again that Jesus—although fully God—was also fully a man with all of his human desires intact. Although we were to lead a chaste life, we were warned not to become asexual beings. And, indeed, I was welcomed into religious life in the Catholic Church as an out gay man by my superiors and religious community.

Which brings me back to Father Mychal Judge and his admiration of all the beautiful men walking the streets of Manhattan that Friday night. His declaration was a joyful expression of his God-given gift of sexuality. This was a celebration of a celibate life lived happily and fully.

Ironically, it was the burgeoning AIDS crisis—a time of great death—that brought me together with this man so full of life. The Catholic Church that I had been brought up in, which had shown me so much acceptance—the very church to which I had just committed my life—was beginning to revert back to its former, judgmental self. It coincided with the commencement of AIDS and it seemed to happen overnight, though in retrospect, it had been on a slow boil for quite awhile.

At a time when the Church should have come roaring into action—for this is where Jesus would surely have been with the outcasts and the sick—church leaders, instead, chose judgment over love. This was especially true in New York City, one of the places hardest hit with the virus, where Cardinal John O'Connor became the face of hate to the gay community.

While most Catholic clergy members kept their distance, Father Mychal took it upon himself to address the needs of the gay community at this time of crisis. He formed Saint Francis AIDS Ministry, one of the first Catholic AIDS organizations in the country. He, along with myself and three other professed religious men, began to minister to people with AIDS in area hospitals, where we were often met with distrust and sometimes outright hostility from those we visited.

Their reactions were understandable, for the Church had become the enemy. Among many other offenses to the gay community, Cardinal O'Connor had banned the gay Catholic group, Dignity—of which Mychal was a member—from meeting in any of the diocese's parishes, and he also supported efforts to keep gays from marching in the Saint Patrick's Day Parade.

Hearing the criticisms of the Church from those to whom I ministered, I began to question my calling, and I found myself becoming anxious each time I entered a patient's hospital room for the first time. Although a member of the gay community, I was also a representative of the Catholic Church. I had one foot in each camp, and both sides seemed to question where my true allegiance lay. Even I was becoming unsure. I told Mychal that I felt like I was leading only half a life, to which he responded, quoting from Scripture, "I came that you might have life, and have it to the full."

I knew I couldn't be all things to all people, but Mychal Judge somehow could. Whether sitting on a cot talking to a destitute man in a homeless shelter, shooting the breeze with a bunch of macho firefighters at a New York City firehouse, or schmoozing with some rich society matrons at a swanky benefit, Mychal had the amazing ability to socialize and empathize with everyone he met.

One of the aforementioned wealthy parishioners volunteered the use of her beach house on the Jersey shore for a week's retreat for our AIDS ministry, so the five of us could get away, renew ourselves, and reflect on the work we were doing.

Knowing my frustrations about the ministry and my doubts about my vocation, Father Judge took me on a long walk along the beach one day that week. After walking in silence for quite awhile just listening to the waves crashing onto the shore, Mychal put his arm around my shoulder and said, "Who better than you?"

"What do you mean?" I asked.

"Let's pretend you're God, okay?" he explained. "You've got these two groups at war with one another, so you need to hire a peacemaker that understands both sides, right? Well, who better than you?"

And then he grabbed both my hands in his and prayed aloud the prayer of Saint Francis, the namesake of our AIDS Ministry: "Lord, make us an instrument of your peace. Where there is hatred, let us sow love. Where there is injury, pardon. Where there's darkness, light."

When we arrived back at the beach house, we heard on the evening news that the billionaire Malcolm Forbes had died. The news report recounted the lavish parties, collections of fine art, and motorcycle rides with Elizabeth Taylor. "Talk about a full life, huh?" I said.

Mychal didn't say a thing, but his silence spoke volumes.

A few weeks later, the gay writer and activist, Michaelangelo Signorile, would break the news of Forbes's secret gay life on the cover of *Outweek* magazine, bringing the topic of "outing" into the mainstream.

There was no such outing, however, following Mychal's death a decade later at the World Trade Center, for there was nothing to out.

He proved that someone openly gay could lead a full, healthy, and rewarding life in the Catholic Church. Not a prisoner of the past, Mychal was, indeed, a pioneer of the future.

My own calling, however, was short-lived. I found it increasingly difficult to belong to a church that was becoming more and more exclusive, a church that had even begun to deny gay men from entering the priesthood. The Church was asking me to hide my light under a bushel basket—but I was God's perfect creation, remember?

The poster for "The Saint of 9/11," the documentary about Father Judge's life and death, depicts Mychal in his Franciscan robes walking alone along a beach. Staring at that image, I remember our own walk along the beach that day, and I take comfort imaging myself in the arms of this gentle man who loved me unconditionally and who died so I might have life to the full.

There's a movement brewing to have Father Mychal Judge consecrated as a saint, the first openly gay saint in the Catholic Church. I'm not sure what he'd think of that, but if he asked for my two cents worth, I'd say, "Who better than you?"

Mea Culpa, Mea Maxima Culpa

Helen Boyd

Even now I have the urge to walk into a confessional and plead guilty to being human, and thus vulnerable. Vulnerable to bouts of jealousy, desires of the flesh, mortal and venal and whatever other kinds of sins I might have forgotten. It was that "sin of pride" that always caught in my throat because I knew it was mine. Even as a child I didn't go to my chores like the Little Flower St. Teresa, oh no: I fought my mother with the devil's tongue, advocating only on my own behalf that my day was ill-used in emptying wastebaskets and folding clothes. No doubt my mother muttered, "God save her" a few too many times during my elaborate verbal defenses as I've always, and inexplicably, felt that all's well between me and my God. I own being human and all the innate frailties of that condition, but I'm not letting Him off the hook, either: my logic is that if He is so omnipotent, He could have kept me from feeling seduced by the smell of lipstick and the tickle of a dangling earring on my neck, and He could have given me a head that wouldn't have called Him out on this shell game of sinfulness. What kind of game is it if when you lose you lose, but when you win you lose too? What kind of nut, after all, would force a child to start out in this world with a soul blackened already with sin?

That's why I wanted to help out, relieve people of their guilt in being who He made them. "Bless you, my child. May you walk in the way of the Lord,"—and by that I would have only ever meant the way of inconsistency and peevishness. Just like Our Lord.

Long before I knew about the pleasure of waking up next to an exfoliated man whose eyes are smudged with yesterday's eyeliner, I had much bigger plans for myself. At nine, I wanted to be a priest, a real one. I felt my mother's need for a priest in the family keenly, and so set out to be the holy one: draped in a cassock and smelling faintly of cabernet and incense, I would sit behind lattice and call grown men "child" as I asked to hear their sins. That was what I wanted—not so much the cabernet, as that would come later, and I'm allergic to incense, but that power to send people on their way, to grant them relief from their human concerns, their indeterminate lusts, and need for revenge, and all their endless, endless coveting.

They didn't even know I thought all that when they kept me from the priesthood, of course. They only knew I had a vagina, and apparently that was enough. My heartbreak upon finding out I would be barred from fulfilling my mother's hope was only ameliorated a little when my mother tried to explain the difference between the Church in heaven and its perfection, and the Church on earth and its imperfection. Call me a Protestant, but I was pretty sure the "good old boys" in robes had gotten this one wrong: I set out to be a priest in my own way. My mom got her priest at long last—oh did she. The sinners come to me and tell me their sins.

I want to wear panties, he says.

I get hot and bothered when I tie my husband up, she explains.

The first time a man bent me over I sure as hell did feel like a woman, he admits, nearly gleefully.

The first time I strapped it on, she says, eyes sparkling . . . .

But you get the idea. These are no willing sinners; they would have rather been "normal" they tell me, instead of trans, instead of kinky, instead of fem dommes. Wouldn't we all rather have desires Dr. Phil would approve of? Monogamous, vanilla desires, the kind that live next door to chastity, would be much easier for most of us, and cheaper too: no toys / no lube / no porn. But that's not what we were given. It's not what we have. What we have instead are complicated lusts, psychosexual yearnings, needs to be spanked or regendered or held down (against our will, but with our permission).

My mother isn't happy about having a daughter who is an *author cum priest* and it's certainly not what she expected, nor what I intended. I didn't plan for my family ever to know about this, and they didn't when my husband was still a closeted transvestite who only wore *inside clothes*. I never intended to drag anyone else into this, but then Betty never intended to drag me into this, either. But I did drag them into it, we did: *mea culpa, mea maxima culpa*. I say it the way my mother did, fist to my heart to emphasize the *mea*. It's my fault, only mine.

On the great scorecard of weighed intent and oblivious pride, I may turn out okay. My objectives must count for something: I renamed myself to write about being married to someone trans, so that I could chronicle our kinks and queerness in a way that let my pious parents pretend they weren't related to us. My intent probably doesn't count for much since there's the road to hell and all, paved by the likes of me, and because, as Father Brennan pointed out during his homily when I was fourteen and lusting after the pretty boy who looked like Sid Vicious a few pews further up, *Whosoever shall look on a woman to lust after her hath already committed adultery with her in his heart.*

I'm guessing there's no exception for Anglo-Asian boys in leather jackets.

But still, my poor mother didn't sign up for this even if she's also guilty, in her own way. They were always the type of parents who put A papers on the fridge and wouldn't resist the urge to tell their friends that their sixth child, their youngest, the one who might, in another time, have been sent to a nunnery, had published a book. "We knew she'd write a book," they might have explained, "when she sent her Sunday School teacher scrambling for a dictionary." But they didn't know. I didn't even know I'd write a book about being married to someone trans until I did, and I was as surprised by writing it as I was surprised to be married to a man who would become a woman.

But oh, mea maxima culpa!—I even liked it! Surely wanting to see long, lean legs in thigh-high black stockings in the air is a sin, no matter that those nylon-clad legs are your husband's. Surely there's a special circle in hell for perverts like me, the married-by-loophole perverts, the gender perverts, the doubters, the priests of perverts. (I took a test once that told me I'd end up in the second circle with Catherine the Great; I'm looking forward to asking her if the horse story was apocryphal.)

I can at least fulfill the role the good Church Fathers have denied me. I listen to sinners and not least of it, I try to help them find ways to be the perverts they are with peace in their hearts and some kind of moral center. They used to saint the ladies who worked with lepers, I figure, so helping the people called perverts by the world feel forgiven is the least I can do. I still want that priesthood, but they still won't give it to me because of my vagina, and now too because I've been christened queer, so I spend a lot of my time talking about vaginas and criticizing the Church, and especially this Pope Maledict, for treating people with vaginas in ways that are not in keeping with a Church that is, after all, referred to as Mother Church and whose walls are full of paintings of madonnas and whores and female saints with their breasts on plates. Women are more than a majority within the Catholic Church: they are its heart. Women shouldn't be treated as *less than* by the Church whether those women are Catholic or not.

When I told my own Catholic parents about Betty and her transness and our intention to stay together despite our same sex-ness they reminded me of what it was I had learned from the Church, *their* Church, the Church of Al Smith and Dorothy Day and Oscar Romero. We told them that Betty dressed like a woman sometimes, and would possibly become one, or live as one, and my father—my seventy-nine year old Catholic father—said. "Don't ever let anyone treat you like a second class citizen." My mother nodded in agreement.

And that was all he said.

And that was all he needed to say.

And that's what I tell the perverts who come to me to confess their sins because that's the only Catholicism I'd ever bother practicing. Sometimes the Church on Earth just gets it wrong. So to be clear: sometimes girls are supposed to grow up to be priests, and gay men, and lesbians, and trans people shouldn't be treated like second class citizens.

Welcome to Church.

NUNS

Don't Sing: Growing Up Lesbian in Catholic School

Maria V. Ciletti

I knew I was different from most of the kids at St. Mary's Elementary School when my teacher, Sister Mary Lena asked me not to sing. Sister Mary Lena taught first grade and was the first African-American nun I had ever met. Her cocoa skin glowed in contrast to her blocky, white habit bandeau, coif and guimpe, and her perfect, white teeth. She was as energetic as any six-year-old and had a voice that could put Diana Ross to shame. From the first day I saw her I thought she was amazing and beautiful, and I would have done anything to please her.

Our first grade class (1966-1967) was scheduled to be the opening act of the upcoming Christmas pageant. Every Tuesday and Friday afternoon, all thirty-two of my Parochial school uniform-clad classmates and I would trudge down the green-tiled corridor to the gymnasium to practice for the big event.

Excitement filled the disinfectant-tinged air of the gym as we approached the stage. At six years old, you think you're pretty hot stuff just being in one of these events. Sister Mary Lena would line us up on tiered rafters, the same ones the older kids in seventh and eighth grade choir used during their big shot performances. One by one we filed on to the wooden rafters: petite little girls in the front and tall awkward kids in the back.

Being taller than all the girls and most of the boys in my class, I was pushed way back into the far left hand corner of the stage. After we were all positioned, Sister took her place behind the conductor's podium. She pushed back the long, billowing sleeves of her black tunic, picked up her little wooden baton, and tapped it on top of the podium. Once she had everyone's attention, she'd raise her little stick and commence orchestrating our little group.

Granted a troupe of first graders singing on stage may not sound like the Mormon Tabernacle Choir, but after several attempts at "The Little Drummer Boy," Sister tossed her baton onto the podium in frustration and approached our group.

"There seems to be a problem—somewhere over here, on the left."

Sister waved her black-robed arm in my direction. "You, back there—Mina."

"Yes, Sister," I stammered, my voice cracking.

"Mina, sing 'A new born king to see, pah-rumpa-pum-pum.'"

I did as she requested, but instead of the voice of a six-year-old angel, something closer to the croak of a forty-year-old woman who smoked a pack of cigarettes a day erupted from my young vocal cords.

The entire class burst into laughter and Sister Mary Lena cringed as if she had heard nails on a chalkboard. "Okay, that's enough class," Sister scolded. "Thank you, Mina," Sister said with a forced smile. "Class, let's take a five-minute washroom break."

As my classmates clomped down the choir rafters and out into the hall in two single file lines, Sister pulled me aside. "Mina, come here a minute please."

"Yes, Sister?" I answered, my face still hot from embarrassment and my knees trembling as I stood before the beautiful nun.

Sister Mary Lena kneeled down so our faces were just inches apart. "Mina, when we begin practice again, this time don't sing, just move your lips, like this." Sister then moved her lips, but no sound came out.

"But Sister, if I just move my lips, I'm not really singing," I protested.

"Of course you are, my dear," she answered, patronizingly patting my shoulder. "Jesus knows you're singing and that's what's important now, isn't it?"

Sister said it and I bought it. But I was crushed too. Talk about feelings of inadequacy. I got my first taste of the many rejections I would later endure from women in my life that I thought the sun rose and set on.

Second grade was no different. My teacher, Sister Mary Agnes Rose, was the polar opposite of Sister Mary Lena. Sister Mary Agnes was eighty-years old if she was a day. Two to three times a week Sister Mary Agnes would become confused and mistake the janitor's closet for her classroom and would have to be escorted back to her room on the second floor by Julio, our janitor.

As every Catholic knows, in second grade children receive the Sacrament of First Holy Communion. We all endured endless hours of rigorous religious instruction: When to sit, when to stand, and when to genuflect. We learned when to make a full sign of the cross, and when to make the baby sign of the cross on your forehead using only your thumb nail before bringing the thumb to your lips to kiss the nail (just before the reading of the gospel). We were terrorized with the consequences of mortal sins and given the remedy of the Act of Contrition to atone for our venial sins, but to this day I am still confused about how many venial sins equal a mortal.

Two weeks before we received the sacrament of First Communion, we had our First Confession. This, to me, was the scariest part of it all. As a class we were led in a single file line down the dark aisle of our church, which smelled of incense and mold. We were ushered into the hard, mahogany pews by shushing nuns and instructed to kneel and prepare ourselves to face God (as represented by the priest who sat in the other side of the confessional). Between confessor and priest there hung a spooky white curtain through which we were encouraged to bare the darkness of our eight-year-old souls. When it was my turn in the confessional, I could only come up with four sins: I lied three times to my parents and was mean to my little brother. Those transgressions earned me a penance of three Hail Marys and one Our Father. Apparently being mean to your little brother carried a lot more weight than lying. I whispered my penance into my folded hands on bended knee, as instructed, and then rejoined my classmates at the back of the church, unable to deny the feeling that a burden had been lifted from my heart.

Finally, the special holy day arrived. While the other girls in my class were excited about the frilly, white, miniature wedding dresses and veils they would be wearing, I secretly envied the boys who got to wear sleek, navy blue suits and white dress shirts instead of the itchy, white crinoline dress my mother bought for me at Hill's Department Store.

The day went off without a hitch. My parents, grandparents, and aunts and uncles beamed with pride as I walked down the aisle, hands clasped in prayer, to receive the holy host for the first time. After the mass they all came to our house for cavatelli, coffee and cake, and I got a silver and black Timex watch from my parents as a First Holy Communion gift.

Sister Mary Agnes Rose not only gave us instruction on the sacraments, she taught penmanship as well and was my first teacher of cursive writing. She may have been frail and forgetful at times, but when it came to teaching she was as sharp as any other teacher. I had been experiencing some difficulty with reading that year—later diagnosed as reading dyslexia—and this condition not only interfered with my reading comprehension, but it also affected my ability to write letters like "J" and "Q." No matter how hard I tried, I would write the letters backwards. During our penmanship classes, Sister Mary Agnes would walk around the room carrying a wooden ruler stuffed under the front flap of her nun habit, observing us as we worked on our writing assignments. When she came to a student who wasn't doing as she instructed, she would smack the ruler on top of the desk, making a sound that would scare the bejesus out of everyone in the room. If the student continued to make errors, she would demand that the student lay their hands flat on top of the desk, and then she whacked their hands with her wooden weapon.

I never understood the logic of this since some kids, including myself, got whacked so often, I figured our hands would be crippled by the third grade, and we would have to resort to another means of communication. To this day anytime I write the word "January" or "Quota," I break out in a cold sweat for fear that Sister Mary Agnes Rose, long since dead, is looking down from heaven, ruler poised for one last whack.

By the time I reached junior high, I knew in my heart that I carried a dark secret inside of me. At this stage of adolescence, the only thing the girls in my class talked about now were boys. They endlessly chattered about which boy was "tuff," who was "going" with whom, or how so-and-so was so lucky because she got kissed by Jimmy Modrelli underneath the bleachers. But while these girls daydreamed about boys, I daydreamed about them.

At this level of my Catholic education, homosexuality was added to the list of mortal sins and it terrified me. Not much was said on the subject, except that homosexuals, with their tortured souls, lurked in the shadows preying on innocent Catholic boys and girls, trying to convert them to their sick, perverted ways.

I didn't want to be a pervert; I didn't want to be the twisted, sick person that our religion teacher warned us about, but I knew in my heart if I didn't do something, that is who and what I would become. I tried with all my might not to think those thoughts, but they haunted me when I lay awake at night. And no matter how far I pushed them away, nothing could quell the tingling in my stomach the next day when I'd see Capri Pagano do a split jump during cheerleading practice, or when the girls in my class rolled up their uniform skirts practically to their hoo hoo's, trying to entice our male classmates.

I found it particularly difficult to concentrate on parallelograms and trapezoids in math class when Jennifer Tucci sat in front of me. Her lustrous chestnut hair cascaded onto my math book while the scent of her Love's Baby Soft perfume permeated the air. Jenny was also a cheerleader, and therefore way out of my league. Even though she sat in front of me in many of my classes, we never spoke much, except for one time in the girl's washroom when she asked me if I had an extra tampon, and I almost fainted.

Junior high was torture enough, but then throw in the mandatory shower after gym class requirement and it was enough to send any closeted baby dyke over the edge. After gym class we were all required to strip off our diocese's approved one-piece gym uniforms and take a five-minute shower under the watchful eye of our gym teacher, Sister Mary Francis. Each girl had to walk by Sister Mary Francis on her way out of the shower room so Sister could see that her skin was wet—evidence that she actually took a shower and didn't just let the water run.

I was mortified. No one, not even my parents, had ever seen my awkwardly disproportioned adolescent body naked—and now I had to parade nude in front of a nun every Wednesday afternoon? How can being gay be a sin and this be okay?

Finally I made it through junior high and into high school. Sadly, my first year in Catholic high school would turn out to be my last year of parochial school. Not because they found out that I was a lesbian and tried to excommunicate me from the Catholic Church, but because my father, in pure Tony Soprano-like fashion, tried to pay off my Spanish teacher in order for me to get a passing grade. What can I say? Dad did what he thought was best. Unfortunately, it was unethical and ineffective, accomplishing exactly what he'd tried so desperately to avoid, and I was asked to leave at the end of the school year.

Actually, leaving that school was fine with me. I never fit in with those kids anyway with their high-class tastes and high moral standards. I figured maybe the kids at public school were more liberal, since we were always taught in Catholic School that the kids in public school had no morals and were already destined to burn in hell.

My first day in public school was definitely an eye-opener. After spending most of the morning in orientation, my first class was gym class.

I jostled though the crowded halls trying to find the locker room, which was on the other side of the campus. By the time I got there, I discovered that most of the class was already dressed and out of the locker room. I quickly changed and headed out into the enormous gym. Girls of all shapes and sizes warmed up doing stretches and calisthenics, readying themselves for what I considered the usual hour of hell and humiliation.

As I heard the shrill screech of a whistle, I turned toward the sound. In the center of the gym stood our gym teacher, Miss Thompson. My heart skipped a beat. Miss Thompson was tall, with lean defined muscles in her arms and calves. Her short cropped dark hair was feathered back in perfect layers, and I immediately suspected we had a lot in common. Suddenly, I didn't dread gym class any more. Actually, I couldn't wait for Wednesdays to roll around so I could see her again in her white gym shorts and Steve Prefontaine T-shirt.

Miss Thompson clearly sensed that we shared a common bond, but she always kept a professional distance. I never had to walk in front of her nude fresh from the shower—although the thought crossed my mind. She was one of my favorite teachers and we became good friends, but it wasn't until well after graduation that she actually "came out" to me and introduced me to Sandy, her life partner of thirty-two years.

During high school, I didn't totally abandon my Catholic faith. I continued to attend Sunday mass with my Dad, right up until he passed away suddenly three months before my graduation. After which I never felt more abandoned in my life. How could a God that I was taught so loved us take my father away so soon? I carried that chip on my shoulder for a long time.

It would be fifteen years before I set foot in a church again. It was during the annual St. Mary's festival when, at my mother's insistence, my partner of ten years and I signed up to volunteer. We were assigned to make cheese puffs and fried dough twists in a dilapidated classroom of the old elementary school where I had attended kindergarten through third grade. Being in that building again brought back a lot of memories. Rose and I sat down at one of the miniature flour-covered kindergarten tables and rolled bread dough into cheese puffs and twists in a room full of women who had been doing this for the past fifty years. The camaraderie of the women and the acceptance of us joining them was a great thing.

Sitting at the same table as us was Father Mathew, a priest I remembered from sixth grade who was now the parish Pastor.

"Mina, it's been a long time since I've seen you. How have you been?" Father asked.

"Fine, Father," I replied. "This is my . . . uh . . . friend, Rose," I said, regretting the introduction as it escaped my lips. I felt like I had betrayed Rose.

Father Mathew smiled at Rose and Rose smiled back.

"So Mina, what's kept you from the church for so long? Did you move out of the area after graduation?" Father asked as he rolled a ball of dough into a long thin snake to make one of the dough twists.

"No, Father, I didn't move. I guess my life has changed," I said, my heart pounding with anxiety as the ghost of Sister Mary Agnes Rose and her ruler loomed overhead.

"I see," Father said. "So how has your life changed so much that it's kept you from the church?"

I looked over at Rose. She looked down at her ball of dough and continued mashing it into a flat pancake, her signal to me that I was on my own with this one.

I leaned in close to Father Mathew. "The church teaches that my lifestyle is a sin, Father," I said, keeping my voice low.

Father leaned back and pushed his wire-rimmed glasses back up his nose. "Oh, I see," he said quietly.

"So you can understand why I haven't been a regular at Sunday mass," I added.

"You know, Mina, it doesn't have to be that way," Father answered, glancing over at Rose and then back at me.

"How so Father?" I asked.

"In your case, Jesus loves the sinner, but hates the sin," he answered, wiping his flour- and oil-covered hands on a greasy piece of paper towel.

"What's that supposed to mean?" I asked, curious that maybe the doctrine had changed while I'd been away.

"That it's okay that you have those feelings, but just don't act on them," Father simply stated. "The church doesn't condemn folks for having homosexual tendencies; the church just doesn't want them to practice them."

"So it's okay to be gay, just don't do anything that is gay?" I asked, trying hard to keep the sarcasm out of my voice.

Rose stood up. "I'm going to see if there's more dough," she said.

Father Mathew nodded solemnly. "It's very simple really. It all goes back to the celibacy requirement. Catholics are supposed to remain celibate until marriage. Then sex should only be used for procreation," he said.

"Father, in this day and age, do you actually believe that? That Catholics remain celibate until marriage, then once they're married they only have sex to have a baby?"

"I can only hope," he said.

"And gay people shouldn't be having sex at all?"

He nodded. "It's all right there in the Bible."

"So marriage is sort of like a permission slip to have sex?" I asked.

He nodded. "The Catholic faith is firmly against gays marrying. If you look in the Bible, that's where you will find the evidence that homosexual acts are a sin," Father said. "There is never any point in the Bible where it's okay for gay people to marry and that's what God wants. If you'd like, Mina, we can make an appointment to discuss this further in my office," Father said, reaching into his shirt pocket to produce his business card.

I reluctantly took the card. "Thanks, I'll think about it," I said, knowing full well that I wouldn't. I finished rolling out my last cheese puff and excused myself from the table. I found Rose in the little girl's bathroom washing up at a tiny bathroom sink that only came up to her knees.

"Sorry I abandoned you like that," she said. "I just couldn't sit there and listen to him anymore."

"That's okay. I probably should have left when you did. I would have made just as much progress. I don't know why this bothers me so much. What do I care what he thinks?"

Rose patted my shoulder and handed me a paper towel to dry my hands. "It's how you were raised. It was ingrained in you to care about what they thought."

"Yeah, who really knows what God wants? The rules keep changing. I remember when it used to be a sin to eat meat on Friday. Now it's only a sin if you eat meat on Fridays during lent. So what about the people who ate meat on Friday before the rule changed? Are they burning in hell because they ate a sausage sandwich at a football game on a Friday night?" I asked.

"It's silly," Rose concurred.

"But you know what really bothers me? It's their high and mighty attitude. They pass judgment on us without even knowing us. 'Hate the sin, but love the sinner'. Give me a break," I said as we walked down the musty hallway of the school and out into the bright sunlight.

"Look, we love each other and we have a good life together. Isn't that what's important?" Rose asked as we made our way through the crowd of people waiting for cheese puffs, sausage sandwiches, and cavatelli.

I nodded. "You're right." And as I looked at Rose then, I smiled, realizing that I'd learned to sing despite them. It had taken this long journey all the way back to where I'd first been silenced to finally understand that no matter how badly someone thinks you sing, there will always be someone else out there who thinks your voice is music to their ears.

Hive

Beth Kiplinski

I thought the Church was like a bee's nest when I was a kid. Complete with sentries, who greeted you at the door. Usually men in suits, an occasional priest. And what was the honey? Money. Solace. Expiation. Unload your sins like pollen. Do the bee dance of penitence.

Queen bee Mary. Mother Church. Jesus was a dead hornet. The mass droned on until we all swarmed out.

Nuns like sow bugs in their flannel habits. I imagined the honeycombs where they must live. But they always noticed when I tried to follow; stared me back the way I came.

They were not like other girls.

They weren't brides. They were soldiers of Christ like they told us at Confirmation.

In castles. Behind moats. The elaborate architecture of the Catholic churches of Chicago. Spired. Gothic. Like those African Termite towers I saw on TV.

Warrior ants.

My cousin Ben got drafted to Vietnam. He got killed too. They said he went to heaven. I know for a fact there is no way he went to heaven. He'd done things he'd never confessed. To my sister and me. And why would hell or purgatory take him? *Just because the Army did?* I don't think so. I would think even the devil had higher standards. I guess all souls have some redeeming trait, but Ben would seem better served by reincarnation. He'd flunked. Make him do it all again. But leave us out of it.

I want to forgive him more than anything in the world. But all I get to is a sort of erasure.

So, I am only able to vow to forgive him. Vow and wait. I can't manage it yet. I do try. One day I will forgive him, that is my vow. I do it for me, not for him.

The sting of hate. The sting of guilt. The sting of lies. The sting of being scolded. Bees can go either way—sweet honey or pain—and so it was with the Church. We were trained to sting ourselves.

I loved and hated those nuns. I didn't want to hate them. I vowed not to. I wanted them all to love me. Many of them did. But just as many of them were stern and strict and sadistic. I wanted to live in a big, happy hive. I didn't like how dark the nuns' habits were. Why couldn't they wear yellow? Yellow and black like bees? Or at least black velvet, with a big yellow sash, or maybe a yellow tied-off rope like the Franciscan brothers wore. Then they'd be like bumblebees.

My mother never let us ride the L Train. It was dangerous, she said. This made it fascinating. I'd watch it from the window of the car, rushing around, speeding up and slowing down, letting people in and out. A moving church. A mobile hive. I used to think everyone on it was dead, on their way to heaven or hell. I looked for Grandma, Aunt Susan, even Ben. I saw all of them several times, from a great distance. I never waved. It wasn't proper to wave at the dead, or to let them know you were looking. Death was a little shameful. Everyone had more or less failed.

I loved the confessional.

Not the part where the priest opens the little screen, but right before, and right after. When you could hear him talking to the person on the other side. I was safe, if only for a brief moment. And the priest didn't really scare me because I never confessed anything that bad. I kept to the greatest hits, rotely rattled off "disobedience to mother," "fighting with my sister," "saying a cuss word," "not doing my chores."

I wondered how different it would be if nuns could do confession. They'd do away with the door. The nice ones anyway. You'd be able to hug them, sit in their lap. They'd brush your hair when you cried. You'd tell them everything. There'd be no safety before or after though. They made me feel raw like meat. You could stick your finger right into it and it would sink all the way down if you pressed hard enough.

Sex was just another cruel thing that boys did.

I didn't call what me and Madeleine did sex. We both wanted to be nuns. We didn't care about sex. We wanted to live together and sleep together in the abbey. And what kind of service would we do? We both agreed a hospital would be best. We wouldn't be afraid there. People were in a compromised position.

Of course, it was a boy who called us dykes. We were in the ninth grade at St. Brigid's and we did everything together. We were best friends.

We didn't know what a dyke was and had to ask Sister Clare. She fumed. Then she called our mothers, and all the classes that Madeleine and me shared we got moved out of. One or the other of us. I thought of that Biblical saying a lot then: "What God has joined let no man tear asunder."

And Sister Clare was one of the nice ones.

They learn to sting themselves. They don't wear yellow. They never will. You must carry your cross, suffer Christ's wounds.

Bees can go either way, and so it was with the Church. I drifted away. Because what was the honey? What was the honey?

A Nun Story

Susan Leonardi

I spent much of my childhood and adolescence in love with nuns. In love with the Ideal Nun, holy, glorious in her flowing habit, and glowing with the love of God and His creation (including me, of course). But also in love with particular nuns, who might be a tad less perfect but were, on that very account, approachably human. Sister Mary Perpetua, the third grade teacher at Holy Trinity, for example, was stern and demanding enough to induce fear and trembling but indulgent enough to let me read in the cloakroom (on the pretext of being in charge of the shelf-long library) when I finished practicing my penmanship or dividing 657, 666 by 252.

By the time I was a high school sophomore and thoroughly enamored of my history teacher, I took for granted my intense feelings for these otherworldly women. Sister Mary Virginia, though, inspired—appropriately enough at hormone-ridden fourteen—something new. While she wasn't nearly so stern as Perpetua, my heart beat wildly whenever I caught a glimpse of her in the distance or, even better, a glimpse of the dark hair sprouting out from under her headdress, a glimpse of her thin ankles—encased in thick, black stockings—when she crossed her legs. Coming to school early and leaving late—a longstanding habit—became less about escaping the boredom of home, with its increasing number of demanding babies, and more about the chance to exchange a word with my beloved.

Sister Mary Virginia let me carry her books from the high school to the convent, conveniently located across the street. She kept me after class and concernedly lectured me on the advisability of broadening my social horizon beyond the clique of three that Mary, Deanna, and I (the class nerds) had become. She talked to me about history—did I realize that Roosevelt *knew* the attack on Pearl Harbor was about to occur and did nothing to stop it?—in ways that challenged my naïve patriotism and kick started my critical faculties. Tall (or at least a few inches taller than my 5"2') and elegant, she had a little gesture, a sort of regal sweep of her slender right hand, that I tried to adopt. I practiced speaking in her measured tones. I had it bad.

And then, junior year, came Sister Mary St. Daria, new to the high school, quite young, and—rumor had it—equipped with a graduate degree in chemistry from some prestigious but ever unnamed place. Most of my classmates were distressed that memorization of the periodic table, which had gotten previous chemistry students through, was not going to suffice for passing Daria's class. She was passionate about her subject; she wanted us to *understand* how and why the smallest change of molecular structure could engender such dramatic difference. She wanted us to *love* chemistry.

And so I did. I spent hours at night reading ahead in the textbook, going over my notes, sketching molecules, and dreaming of Daria's small, pale face with the pink-rimmed, blue eyes (behind granny glasses) that widened and brightened as soon as she started to teach. I knew even then that the line between loving chemistry and loving Daria (how daring it seemed to call her that, even in my head) was a thin one. Thinking of myself as a potential scientist was novel and not always comfortable, but if Daria thought I could do it—and she seemed to—well, it sounded more exciting and ambitious than being an English teacher.

Of course, as a nun (my intended vocation since the days of Perpetua—how else could I escape the ordinariness and tediousness of marriage and full-time motherhood?), I might not have the choice. I would, as Perpetua did, as Virginia did, as Daria did, take a vow of obedience and therefore study what my superiors thought I should study, teach where they thought I should teach, live where they told me to live. (That I secretly envisioned *myself* as the Sister Superior and therefore able to make those decisions, is of only minor relevance to the narrative.)

The reality of this vow of obedience hit me hard when Sister Mary Virginia was suddenly transferred to a boarding school in the Midwest. She wrote me a couple of sweet letters, assuring me that I would flourish if only I could be with her in this new and magical place. Why didn't I suggest it at home? Fat chance. I could barely convince my parents to let me go to my parish high school rather than send me to the tuition-free public equivalent.

But that didn't prevent me from imagining myself on a plane to Iowa—or was it Illinois? Like the kids in the English novels I devoured, I'd live in a dormitory, but this one would be cheerful and lively, my companions a hundred eager-to-learn girls. I'd be waking and eating (I conveniently repressed recollections of the watery porridge and meager, greasy dinners I'd read about) and sleeping near that lovely and intelligent nun. I'd absorb from her and her colleagues (none of them mean and petty like Sister Gabriel or Dickens's headmasters) more knowledge than I ever could at this dumb school that didn't even offer physics, trig, or Greek, subjects I longed to learn, subjects that the neighboring boys' school took for granted but were considered too advanced for us girls, destined as we were to raise—and only to raise—the next generation of devout Catholics.

But Daria was making a difference. She was offering us something advanced, something mysterious, something profound, something challenging. And in spite of the fact that she was less beautiful and elegant than Virginia, she slid easily into place in my teenage heart. As Steven Stills would later sing, "If you can't be with the one you love, love the one you're with." Besides, Daria had her own, un-Virginia-like charms. She seemed so vulnerable, so shy, so grateful that I stayed after class to ask questions, so touchingly unwilling to let me carry her books, as though I were almost an equal rather than a mere eager child.

Forty years later, I put Sister Mary St. Daria into a novel. A novel about nuns.

I tried to become a nun myself when I was eighteen—over the vehement and violent objections of my parents—but it didn't work out very well. I found the convent stifling, my classes sophomoric, the constant asking-of-permission infantilizing, and the lack of privacy—especially the reading of our mail—infuriating. Worst of all, there was almost no contact between us postulants and the real nuns, "the professed." I had less access to the objects of my desire (neither the Mistress of Postulants nor my subject teachers could possibly be placed in this category) than I had in high school. The nunnery liked me about as much as I liked it. Mother Superior, my own mother claims, called her one day and asked her to take me home because I was trying to take over the convent.

I was bitter for a while. For one thing, I wanted my departure to be *my* choice, not theirs. For another, they didn't let me say good-bye to

Cheryl, Zoe, and Peggy, my fellow conspirators. No, the Mistress of Postulants stuffed me quietly into my mother's car when everyone else was at breakfast. No chance for drama or tearful farewells. Nor could I write to the friends I left behind. Nor would I ever be allowed to visit—or return. I brooded a bit over the indignity and the injustice of it all, but college beckoned, and there I studied philosophy and there I met a young man, and well, the conventional narrative would have me say, "and I never looked back."

But I did look back. I went over the terrain of those conventual months again and again, not because I regretted leaving but because I knew there was, in my relationship to nuns—the only academically-oriented, semi-independent women in my young life—something sustaining, something inspiring, something *necessary.*

Every time I tried to analyze their hold on me, I reran in my head the queer and inconclusive ending to the Daria story. Before school let out for Christmas vacation junior year, Daria had asked me to stay after class. When the room finally emptied, she pulled a thick and slightly battered paperback from her book bag and handed it to me reverently. "I think you're ready for this," she said. She brushed my arm with her small thin fingers and slipped out the door before I had a chance to thank her properly or even to register the prosaic title of the precious volume in my hand: *Introduction to Organic Chemistry.*

I was flattered beyond words. I was ecstatic. I was more in love than ever. I spent my holidays reading and trying to absorb the difficult material. I barely even missed Daria, so close to her did I feel turning the faded pages of her book; so eagerly did I await the week after New Year's when I could flaunt for her my newly acquired organic chemistry vocabulary; when I would ask her, humbly, if I could borrow the book a little longer.

Chemistry class was first period. I hurried to my usual spot in the front row of tables refusing to be sidetracked by the excited admiration of Barb's fuzzy, pink sweater and the going-steady ring around Suzy's finger. My heart was beating fast. I'd hoped Daria would be a minute early, just so I could ask, casually, if she had a good vacation. Or should I say "a Holy Christmas?" Or "A Happy New Year?" I needn't have weighed the phrases: she wasn't early. The bell rang and Daria had still not arrived. We took our seats, but in the absence of the teacher, the post-Christmas conversation buzz continued. And continued and continued. No Daria.

Finally, about fifteen minutes after the hour, tall Mary Eugenia—Sister Memorize-the-Periodic-Table—strolled in. She unrolled the huge Periodic Table of the Elements that hung above the blackboard at the front of the classroom. "I'll be your chemistry teacher for the rest of the year," she said. "Sister Mary St. Daria has gone to teach at the college level, which is where she really belongs."

No kidding. The relief in the room was audible. Sister Mary Eugenia was a known quantity and she seldom flunked anyone. How hard could it be to remember that Fe was iron and Mg was magnesium—or was it manganese? I, on the other hand, didn't even try to stop the tears that rolled down my cheeks for the next half hour. The periodic table was superficial, I sniffed, and Sister Mary St. Daria was gone. She hadn't even said good-bye. Later when I locked myself into my room at home, I realized that of course she *had* said good-bye, had even given me a farewell present. She meant for me to keep the book.

And I did.

When I finally acknowledged my love for Daria (and for Virginia and Perpetua before her) as more than the simple and quite common erotic charge between good teacher and eager student, I was married and the mother of four. I started sleeping with women and writing about nuns at about the same time.

My partner of twenty-three years was never a nun, but she did have a temporary fixation on Rosalind Russell as the mother superior in *The Trouble With Angels*. She waits with gratifying impatience for each week's installment of the nun saga.

My nuns live in a monastery in the foothills of the Sierra Nevada. They're a contemplative rather than an active order. They don't wear habits. They dance and sing. They talk and plot. They take pleasure in Sister Kathleen's homemade scones and Sister Bernadette's pasta. They don't get transferred. When one of them decides she has had enough of monastic life, the leave-taking is ceremonial. Leavers are encouraged to return, whether to visit or to stay. Sometimes the nuns fall in love with one another. Sometimes they sleep together. Always they work at what it means to live in a community.

I love these women. I spend happy hours with them. I may be sitting at Peet's, tea in one hand, pen in the other, but I'm really walking the Manzanita-dotted hills of Julian Pines Abbey in the company of Sister Anne or Sister Ming (hardly anyone calls them Sister, of course) or, best of all, Beatrice-the-Abbess (by this time, in the third volume of the series, the ex-abbess).

It has been thirty years since my last confession. I'm not a believer in God anymore. I don't go to Mass, except for the imaginary one at Julian Pines, celebrated by Sister Karen, their priest. They're queer women, these nuns, even the heterosexual ones, and I fit right in. Sometimes I get mail from similarly besotted women: "I wish I could live there," they write. Lucky me. I can.

Sometime during my pregnant years, I lost *Introduction to Organic Chemistry,* and I long ago lost Sister Mary St. Daria. The sisters of her order (who now welcome visits from their ex-es) have lost her, too, they've replied in response to my inquiries. As I had long suspected, her "transfer" to college teaching was a cover for her leaving the convent altogether and returning to be pedestrian Polly Parker or Betsy McBride. I hope she's alive and well. I hope she's happy. I hope she spent most of her life teaching chemistry to adoring students at a wonderful women's college. I hope she married a great guy if that's what she wanted, but my fantasy is that she has loved some good women and has an especially fabulous one with whom to grow old. I'd like to send her my nun books. She probably wouldn't mind—do you think?—that I used her "real" name.

Maybe she left it behind for me.

My Heart, Also Sacred

Nora Nugent

My parents, may they rest in peace, coveted a Catholic school education for each of their numerous offspring. No sacrifice could be deemed too arduous if it contributed to achievement of this goal. In the pre-JFK days of the late 1950s, fellow Catholics would conspire to assist. That's how my sisters and I ended up on sunrise journeys in the back of a milk truck, rattling along with the icy, pasteurized bottles.

La Jolla, California, then as now, is a bejeweled township for the elite with Mary, Star of the Sea as its parish and Stella Maris Academy to instruct its future generations. We were Navy brats temporarily housed in corrugated tin Quonset huts on the dusty flatlands of Miramar Air Base, miles away. But during after-Mass conversations in the military chapel's sanctuary, someone who knew someone who knew that pivotal someone else hatched a plan and I shivered amidst rigid wire crates packed with dairy products each morning for my initial two years of grade school.

Happy cows of Ralston Farms peered from fenders on the boxy International van that deposited us curbside on the first day of school. I tugged at the tartan pleats of my unseasonable wool skirt and ventured into my academic future.

Across a polished concrete pavement, my first grade teacher breezed toward me. Black garb habitual to nuns enrobed her lithe body, long skirts swaying like a gently pealing bell with each purposeful step. Her starched, white headdress was strikingly unusual; rather than merely framing her face in tight martial folds, the fabric creased fan-like around her head suggesting, abstractly, unfiltered cigarettes wired together into the holiest of tiaras. She extended an open palm toward me, and only then, when her soft lips parted in a beatific smile, did I notice a front tooth fashioned from gold. The morning sun glinted off this metallic dental surface, mesmerizing me and completing my enchantment.

I knew the feeling in the very moment of its occurrence, though many years passed before I knew to name it love. As she welcomed me to first grade, Sister Maria Domingo paved my entrance into an intriguing and new emotional land. She was a nun in the Order of the Sacred Heart of Jesus, but it was my heart, also sacred, she laid claim to. A young Latina with a creamy, bronze complexion, her eyes enveloped and enticed me, encouraging my nervousness in a manner this type of woman still does today. I raised my young head to meet the broad welcome of her smile. In an instant, I felt valued by a person I admired, embraced by her caring concern. No, I didn't know the word for it—nor that in this case it would be considered a social aberration—but I basked in the warm radiance of love.

I clutched her proffered hand and its promise and followed her lead into the classroom. I'd have done anything for Sister Maria Domingo, phonics and arithmetic included.

Smart kids sat in the back of the class, deemed as requiring less attention, and before long I merited a desk in the very last row. We were accorded certain special privileges—most importantly, an extended choice of reading matter—and were expected to perform additional responsibilities. When Pope Pius the Twelfth lay dying of an illness that famously involved uninterrupted hiccups, a turquoise transistor radio leaned against its plastic stand atop a shellacked plywood credenza and we were directed to monitor its static hum, listening for the death report so the class could begin our prayers without delay. I hoped to be the one to hear the news, but I didn't wish to bring sorrow to Sister Maria Domingo. Fate spared me my conundrum when the pope passed from this world outside of school hours.

I mastered lessons easily, but first grade seemed fraught with hidden fears descending upon me with frightening regularity, jarring the school day's routine. Air raid sirens screamed from the intercom's rusty screen circle or, sometimes, earthquake warnings bellowed their staccato interruptions. Students practiced preparedness by squatting beneath desks where gravel remnants embedded in the waxed linoleum pierced the tender flesh on my palms and above my sagging knee socks to impart a distorted stigmata.

Routine fire drills required us to queue up on the asphalt playground beyond aluminum tetherball poles. Once, remembering my navy cardigan still draped inside across my chair, I raced back into the classroom pushing against the orderly tide of my escaping classmates. I didn't know if this disaster was or wasn't real, but my parents had impressed upon me the cost of replacing a school uniform sweater. Sister Maria Domingo was never so disappointed in me. *Didn't I realize the price of a garment was incomparable to the price of any one of God's precious souls?* Though my parents would publicly voice their agreement with her stated principle, I knew I'd chosen the wiser course. But the shaking head and stern tone of Sister Maria Domingo blanketed me with loneliness and I ached to recreate her unabashed initial approval.

The school year wore on. With each new achievement, though, my beloved teacher appeared less enthused by my accomplishments. Her praise became more pat, unauthentic, merely rote. I didn't represent a hard enough nut to crack, I guess. The specialness she'd first conveyed she'd seen in me seemed to have diminished in her view over time and I didn't possess the wiles or confidence to win back her affection. Though I yearned for what we'd so briefly shared, I could only swallow my loss and pretend not to care.

Eventually our time together reached its end when I advanced into second grade. From my vantage across the playground, waiting in line for my turn at tetherball, I noticed other cheery little girls beam when Sister Maria Domingo aimed her tilted-head smile their way, when her delicate hand rested lightly across the span of their small shoulders as she bowed from her waist toward them, the pendulum of her silver crucifix swinging like a dowsing wand.

Mornings in my family's household were a flurry of regimented activity. The sharp toot of the milk truck horn interrupted a silent predawn, so evenings were the time when bologna sandwiches were shoved into wax paper bags and fresh underwear was laid on the dresser top, designated for the morrow. Breakfasts were simple and hurried.

With few liberties afforded us, my sisters and I reveled in selecting our own particular cereal. Milk made me gag, so my criteria centered upon choosing a product that would soak the milk efficiently, each bowl a race I hoped would end in a tie between grain and liquid. I settled on Spoon-Sized Shredded Wheat for my morning sustenance. The miniature biscuits seemed designed to achieve the perfect milk-to-cereal ratio.

My sisters and I read the back of our cereal cartons while we plowed spoons into our mouths with symphonic rhythm. Nabisco Company touted a promotion to draw attention to their miniature product: tiny plastic figures designed to rest on the end of an eater's spoon handle. When I received a dime for each A on my report card, I taped twenty cents to a torn cardboard box top, then checked the mail every afternoon for a month until my plastic purple Martian arrived. Reverently, I slid the Martian over the shaft of my spoon, its little arms hugging the silver flatware. I discovered a new friend, a friend who belonged only to me.

It wasn't enough to share breakfast with my new friend, I carried this Martian in my pocket with me everywhere. During the day, I felt comforted by the presence of my companion, a confidante to whom I could whisper my secrets. Reaching clandestinely into the folds of my skirt and clutching the figurine in my fingers gave me a sense of belonging that I'd never experienced before. As an adult, I'm still not a joiner, but as a child I recognized the camaraderie I viewed around me and understood it only by its absence in my own life. But with my Martian, I finally knew this sought-after sense of connectedness with a best friend of my very own.

Catholics, of course, are required to attend Mass on Sundays and Holy Days of Obligation. But above and beyond that, ecumenical "deals" are available, and the most astute church members make savvy use of them. Nine First Fridays is perhaps the very best of these bargains, second only to the scapular deal.

The scapular deal is the *sine qua non* of Catholic liturgical promise. Simply stated: *If you're wearing a scapular when you die, you will go to heaven.* No questions asked. Just *go to heaven.* A scapular is two postage stamp-sized portraits of Jesus and/or Mary, one in front, the other in back, tied together by apparent shoelaces and worn around the neck. The downside is the physical annoyance. Made of fabric, a scapular slides around, comes out of the neckline, and cheaper ones can bleed when wet. But this deal is fantastic and it's puzzling why there aren't more takers.

Nine First Fridays is the other deal that's almost as good, though it requires some effort to accomplish. But once you do, you're set. My sisters and I completed several series. The structure of this arrangement? Well, *anyone who attends Mass and receives Holy Commu-*

nion on the first Friday of nine sequential months is guaranteed to see a priest at the moment of their death. Guaranteed!

But read between the lines on this one: a person may *see* a priest—say pushing coins into a parking meter across the street or tapping a melon in the produce section of Whole Foods—but if that person is not attuned to Eternal Life they may not sense the imminent closure of Finite Life and might not realize they're missing their final opportunity to request administration of the Last Rites.

Despite the caveat, this deal seemed to me to be a good one, so my sisters and I routinely—some might say, religiously—attended Mass on the first Friday of each month. Other immediate benefits included a waiver of the start of the school day—if Mass went late, our tardiness was excused. Additionally, since fasting is required to prepare a body to receive The Body of Christ, we were sent to school with cinnamon toast for breakfast which we were then permitted to eat afterwards in class. I loved cinnamon toast.

One First Friday morning I balanced on a padded kneeler in a narrow oak pew of Mary, Star of the Sea Church, my fabric book bag bulging beside me with carefully wrapped cinnamon toast. Arms akimbo, a child-sized plaster Jesus rose from a bank of twinkling votive candles beckoning me to come unto Him. A priest's dolorous Latin dirge resounded from behind the white marble altar, center stage. My mind wandered to my Martian friend hidden within my skirt pocket. Its lure was strong and potent but I remembered, "*Thou shalt have no false gods before thee.*" And what would this Martian friend be if not a false god?

Latin droning continued, the morning congregation chiming an occasional response. I exhaled a deeply weary sigh. I wanted to be a part of this Eucharistic event. I wanted to be religious, but in truth I was washed in boredom, not the Blood of the Lamb. This scenario didn't ring true for me. I experienced no connection.

A long-handled wicker basket stretched between the pews, interrupting my thoughts, raking in coins, bills, and sealed donation envelopes. With the suddenness of a child's clarity I wondered if this club I knelt in existed primarily for money. I could be a member, we could all be members, but membership required payment. Did religion have nothing to do with beliefs and everything to do with finances? Did the adults around me get that? Had they decided this was okay?

I peeked over my prayer book at the parishioners resolute in their piety. Beside me knelt a woman cloaked in steely concentration, an ivory lace mantilla resting on coifed, silver hair. She robotically intoned the Latin responses, turning gilt-edged missal pages, ducking her chin with each whispered name of Jesus. Hand in pocket, I squeezed my Martian into my fist. *No false gods before thee!*

When cued, I headed up the parquet center aisle to the front of the church to receive the Holy Sacrament of Communion. The priest lifted what looked like a Necco wafer candy from his chalice and placed it on my outstretched tongue while an altar boy positioned a golden saucer at my chin to protect against an unlikely spill. Head bowed, I minced my steps back to my pew.

Even before the host dissolved in my mouth, my hand reached into my pocket again for my plastic friend. *Thou shalt have no false gods!* But the allure was so, so strong. I weighed the two sides of my inner debate: this Catholic club, so empty to me; or, the immediacy of my cherished bond with the Martian toy.

In my eight-year-old head I conducted a quick cost/benefit analysis. In doing so, I factored in the Nine First Fridays promise: I held a guarantee I'd see a priest before my death. If I fell away from the Church and its teachings now, I'd still have one final chance at the moment of my death. A hedged bet.

We sat, we stood, we kneeled as the ceremony continued. Only minutes to go before the end of Mass, but I couldn't wait. I pressed my Martian friend between my thumb and forefinger, this friend who I knew would never abandon me. I lifted my friend into daylight and surreptitiously wedged its tiny form into the spine of my Saint Joseph Daily Missal.

How are you today? I breathed into my purple Martian's countenance. And with that inquiry, I spiraled through the ether in a glorious free fall away from the church of Catholics and into a life of my own making.

Vague Recollections

Doreen Perrine

What could be salvaged from the blackness of those forlorn years? A small, wooden figure of a half-naked, dying man hung in every room of that unhappy household. Would he ever resurrect? Once, her drunken father hollered she had ruined his life. Eight at the time, Jane cried out to the crucifix clinging to the slick wood paneling of her bedroom wall, *"Jesus, help me!"*

Vague recollections, sufficiently blocked, of too much hitting, scratching, screaming and, years later, too much therapy, marked the litany of abuse underlying the prevailing notion: her childhood had been martyred to a deaf icon. She internalized a personal mantra to turn eighteen and just get out. The additional outcome of joining a Bible cult had never crossed Jane's innocent mind until she turned eighteen and ran off to Philadelphia to live with "the chosen few." She merely exchanged the hostile God of one dysfunctional family for that of another.

Long before eighteen Jane had her not-so-innocent descent into delinquency. Smoking and shoplifting at ten had actually become a saving grace from the stodgy good-girlisms of so many requisite expectations being heaped upon her.

Someone, who wouldn't come forward, had placed a thumbtack on the fifth grade nun's seat. It wasn't Jane. The miserable creature, perhaps the reincarnation of a Roman emperor in her thwarted power trip, enjoined the principal in a thumbs-up/thumbs-down ritual for each child in the class. The entire class was ordered to stand beside their desks in frozen silence to await the sister's divine judgment. When Jane's turn came, the nun hesitated. Jane was nondescript, not good, not bad, just there, just surviving the seemingly endless purgatory of her depressing childhood. Her parents had bought a weekend home that year and, left in her older siblings' charge, Jane's brother had begun to molest her. Jane no longer wanted to live.

Still, when the nun's thumb went down to condemn her, Jane cried. Her world had split. The "good girls" no longer permitted her to hang on the periphery of their friendship club. Despite being lumped in with the "bad kids" like a discarded toy, miraculously, Jane's life was about to become easier. She no longer needed to bear the impossible cross of acting good and feeling bad. The nun had confirmed that she was just bad.

Genuflect, sit, kneel, stand, make the sign of the cross, and repeat the homily, we are one apostolic faith, had all merged into an antiquated lie as the cynicism of Jane's raging teenage-hood set in. Often stoned during mass, she gazed numbly up at the sparkling colors of the stained glass windows and relegated the meaningless recitation to dull ritual. The only appeal force-fed religion now held for her was a visual embellishment. Colorful windows could only lead out.

What was wrong? She had new friends that her reputation for deviance and her scathing sense of humor had won her. Like her, they felt the bitterness she expressed in biting, subversive remarks. The postpubescent age of abstract reasoning had evolved into a bold cynicism and, even though she was attending an all-girl Catholic high school, nuns no longer held the same almighty sway. Nevertheless, Jane tapped obediently on the keyboard, "The quick, red fox jumped over the . . ." to the tune of shouting, *"Let me out!"* The nun who taught typing had locked some poor girl in the closet. If only fifteen-year-olds could metamorphose into quick, red foxes.

The incest ended when, at twelve, she'd broken down in a tearful confession after which her father had beaten her brother with his fists. Though the matter was never discussed, she was indelibly scarred by the guilt of the unforgivable *ratting out* of the prisoners in the next cell—what she'd come to view her siblings. Hearing his bleating cries rise through the slats of the floor vent, Jane punched out the glass of her bedroom window. She wanted so badly to escape.

Yet, even Jane had culled some notion of tolerance from somewhere. Two girls, much too chummy for the other girls' taste, had become the subject of harsh ridicule. Having never heard the unthinkable word, *lesbian,* in that narrow world until her early twenties, Jane had thought the pair were simply close friends. Naively, she believed her brother's forcing himself on her at a young age was at the heart of her extreme lack of attraction to boys. Jane was *damaged goods* and, rather than embrace the *heretical* alternative, had assumed that, like Jesus forever bleeding on his cross, she was destined for eternal suffering. The taboo term, faggot, had subsequently meshed with her foggy grasp of suburban slang like slut or scumbag. Never uttered at school or home, hush-hush language fell spiraling into the blank chasms of a hell-bound void like medieval ships careening off the edge of the flattened earth. Still, as bitter as she supposed she had a right to be, Jane refused to condone the cruelty of her delinquent friends; it just wasn't cool to harass those terrified girls. "It's their business," was all she said.

Two short years later, had she become a flesh-and-blood doll, dressing up as something she could never hope to become—a gender it had been made excruciatingly clear was more entitled, more godlike than her own? It was the same pivotal year she'd mustered the spunk to tell her father, "If you hit me, you're going to have to kill me because I'm going to fight you to the death!" To Jane's amazement, he simply laughed, walked away and never laid a hand on her again. Puberty had changed something integral. No longer an invisible child lost in an imaginative world of pretend possibility, she'd learned to identify abuse for what it was.

Still, she longed for her mother's approval—or at least an understanding—of her boyish, dress-up fantasies. "Is something wrong with me?" she ventured sheepishly. Her back to Jane, her mother gazed blank-faced into the arching mirror flanking her bedroom wall as though it would produce the required response.

Unable to decipher her mother's tacit reaction, at fourteen, she confessed her mysterious pleasure for dressing in boy's clothing. Along with kissing the girl next door, this was one step beyond earlier endeavors of cutting a doll's hair so that she'd been transformed into a hippie guy—it was the sixties, after all. Later, finding her dolls left naked by her brother behind the neatly folded towels of the linen closet, Jane could never bring herself to play with them again.

Nothing up to that point having earned the unattainable approval she yearned for, Jane knew better than to count on her own mother's limited understanding. This was the same mother who'd scratched Jane's arms so badly she'd had to wear long-sleeved shirts in summer to cover the bloody redness; the same mother who'd repeatedly thrown Jane out of the house so that she'd once stared like a teenage

Oliver Twist into the lit windows of other people's homes on Christmas Eve. It was snowing; she'd begged her mother to take her back. Why should this moment of potential revelation for her self-identity differ?

That was her mother's own helplessness reflected in Jane's question that had kept her from responding. It took years for Jane to understand: Her mother's stultified world had been as oppressive as her own. Yet there was something redemptive in her maternal lineage—her feisty aunt and adoring Irish grandmother who'd taught her to say, "yes, yes," but do what you want anyway.

At the beginning of senior year a crossroads in her future flashed before her eyes. In math class, as the nun dictated a command for total silence, the student in the desk behind Jane muttered something and the nun mistook her for Jane. The nun slapped Jane's face. The crossroads opened as Jane debated whether or not to throw her textbook at the nun. *"Don't ever touch me again!"* Jane growled as she flung the book against the blackboard and the trembling nun jumped back in her orthopedic shoes.

Years lapsed into the forgetfulness of estrangement during which Jane had put herself through college and lived apart from and barely spoke to her unsupportive family. In her late twenties, her mother begged her to take her back into her life. Denouncing Christianity altogether in her desire to nurture hope for a better future, Jane had cut the cord with her agonizing past. Still, when her aging mother asked her forgiveness, she'd offered it.

But Jane had learned forgiveness elsewhere—from her grandmother's kindhearted example, from her Jewish art teacher's encouragement of her creativity, and from the magical connection to painting which had sustained her like a loyal, lifelong friend; not from the roles she'd been compelled to don like her stiff, plaid school uniform or from being ousted from the class play by Sister Claire because she'd once dared to speak out of turn.

Years later, she dreamt she saw herself standing on the flat, black tar of the same bland schoolyard. The nun's tall, penguin-like figure towered over the fence as Jane flipped up her middle finger as she walked away from the school. Delinquency, for what it had been worth, had forged the strength to confront the demons of what she'd been taught was strictly taboo—in her subconscious and her real life.

Then, alone and celibate for nearly four years in her thirties, her mother wanted to know why she was no longer dating. Although Jane had believed she loved the last man she'd been with, Jane had ended things when the relationship had become too sexual. Even the intense loneliness of those hermitic years was preferable to the pretense of self-inflicted heterosexuality. When she'd lost her virginity, she'd gaped in puzzlement at her boyfriend at the time and flatly asked, "Was that it?" Had she, like her mother's persecuted example had taught her, been playing the oppressed martyr for too long?

"What would you say if I told you I was gay?" Jane asked in a tone of childlike rebellion.

Her mother clutched at her chest in an exaggerated gesture of the melodrama she'd long grown accustomed to. "Do you want to give me a heart attack?"

Oddly enough, her mother later became incensed at a neighbor's criticizing a woman in the apartment down the hall who was a lesbian. "That quiet girl never bothers anyone!" Despite being pumped up on morphine to stave off the extreme pain of her cancer-wracked body, her mother's anger was genuinely piqued.

Not until after her mother's death and Jane's coming out a year after, had Jane's sister mentioned their mother's questioning of her sexuality. "So long as she's happy," her mother had, apparently, declared. The richest inheritance she could've possibly left was this previously unimaginable acceptance for who her daughter was meant to be.

Still, Jane was dumbstruck when her father, from whom she now maintained a healthy distance, handed her the silver medal her mother had worn for most of her adult life. A small, girlish image of Mary was etched on its circular center frame in looping filigree and, on its *verso,* her mother's first name had been inscribed in fine, cursive writing. She returned it to the bed of square cotton in the tiny gold box in which her father had handed it to her.

This question of whether to wear what seemed to embody her mother's largely unreflected, guilt-ridden life, plagued Jane for nearly a month. Why wasn't she buried with it? What could Jane possibly do with this symbol of what had always been, for her, the horribly, oppressive belief system of her turbulent past; an abusive past to which the Church had not only turned a blind eye but, as Jane saw it, had sanctified?

She'd been pegged by malicious nuns for a neglected child her parents had been too screwed up to speak out for. It no longer mattered. Just as when her first grade nun had hit her for some minute, childish sin and Jane retaliated with a sturdy kick from the sole of her saddle shoe, she had learned to speak out for herself—albeit in far less physical means.

Jane is Buddhist now. She believes in compassion, respects all beliefs, and abhors violence. She has marched on numerous occasions against war, written a play to give voice to victims living with the aftermath of hate crimes, and was harassed out of a teaching job for reporting child abuse. She has rediscovered the gift of her matriarchal heritage and come to embrace certain, seemingly unrelated icons, not for worship, but to cultivate what she views as the divine within. She possesses statues of Kwan Yin, bodhisattva of love and compassion, and the Virgin of Guadalupe whom she sees as the transformation of Mayan Earth Goddess into Madonna as something she can live with.

Jane wears her mother's medal at all times. Not in deference to a religion she could never personally comply with, but as a connection to her mother's maternal spirit. For Jane, it has become a symbol of the growth they had eventually evolved toward. Even the enlightened moments of her mother's dying process when they daily pronounced, "I love you," was a hallmark of renewed life for them both.

Soon after her death, Jane dreamt her mother was folding her socks, lovingly like mothers of children she'd always been envious of when she arrived at school wearing two different socks, her hair unkempt, falling asleep at her desk—her parents had been drinking and screaming through the night and she and her siblings had had to step gingerly over broken glass to get their own breakfast—again. Now, Jane felt her mother had returned to do for her what she hadn't been able to do then.

For this, the resurrection of her mother's nurturing presence in Jane's dream life, she wears the medal like a talisman. For her, this image of Madonna simply stands for the woman who stood faithfully beneath the cross of her tortured, dying son, the tender Mother of us all—Catholic or not.

Good Habits to Hang Onto

An Interview with Sister Soami of the Sisters of Perpetual Indulgence

Sr. Soami (pronounced: so-am-i), formerly known as Sr. Missionary Position, was one of the four founding mothers of this venerable order in the queer community of San Francisco in 1979. On the occasion of the Order's tenth anniversary he altered his name to Sr. Missionary P. DeLight, in honor of the first Sr. Missionary Delight/John Glorioso who had just died of AIDS in Baltimore. In 2002 he honored another deceased brother and AIDS activist, David Baker/Beautiful Dove with the adoption of his new name, Sr. Iamosama DeLite, the Sodomite of the Most Holy and Beautiful Dove, Rumi Sufi Heart Now, or for short, just Sr. Soami.

So who are the Sisters, Sr. Soami?

With a profound bow to Sr. Phylllis Stein the Frangrant and Sr. Kitty Catalyst, dedicated archivists of the Mother House, I will adapt our "sistory" as revealed in the many sisterly Web sites around the world, by saying that we are an Order of Twenty-first Century Queer Nuns dedicated to the promulgation of omniversal joy and the expiation of stigmatic guilt. We combine social activism with glamour drag for public edification and personal enlightenment. We produce public parties; we lampoon political and clerical party lines; and, we celebrate queer diversity and community.

As Sr. Sarong Soright is wont to say, we work to raise money for AIDS charities, fight for queer rights and visibility, and promote HIV education and safe sex, crystal meth harm reduction, and transgender awareness, never taking ourselves so seriously that we forget to have fun. The Sisters regularly visit local hospices, bringing joy to the people there. We also have some very intense one-on-one sessions with the people we meet while out. Ours is a "ministry of presence." The Sisters frequently act as educators, lecturing to classrooms of students and informing the cute boy at the bar about the risks of unsafe sex. And if you've ever been to one of our bingo games or any other event that is hosted by the Sisters, you have seen us in our role as MC and hostess. We employ the sanctifying grace of camp humor as a survival strategy and for social and spiritual transformation. We support playing and praying in public. Being a Sister requires a lot of different skills and an investment of time, energy, and money. And of course, there are the vows!

Which are?

PROMULGATION OF OMNIVERSAL JOY to bring laughter, humor, and a lightness of being to all situations. The Order tries to exorcise the gloom of conformity while performing the role of devoted Sister and sacred clown. Formerly we aspired to Universal Joy. However, with scientific reports of global warming and a collapsing galaxy, we are preparing the faithful for some major cosmically conscious leaps and transformations into the Multiverse, which we hope and pray is out there.

EXPIATION OF STIGMATIC GUILT to end the centuries of oppression that have been laid upon the hearts of so many. Absolution is achieved through ending shame relating to gender roles and sexual behavior.

HABITUAL MANIFESTATION to reveal our vocation, and perform public ministry while wearing the habit.

PERPETUAL INDULGENCE is both a name and a way of life. The Order claims a perpetual indulgence from self-punishment, guilt, and despair.

By eradicating guilt and promoting multiiversal joy, we aim to end prejudice and intolerance toward those who "dare to be different." By manifesting in habit, the Sisters and Brothers challenge gender stereotypes and the oppression of organized religious orthodoxy, which still refuses to accept queers (or, indeed, anyone living an "unacceptable" lifestyle) as being equal members of society with a right to their sexuality.

In the early years of the Order, Reverend Mother and Sr. Loganberry Frost, trained by Maharishi himself, instructed us all in the ways of Transcendental Meditation. In honor of those early teachings, our vows include a pledge to support one another in our individual and collective enlightenment. Yes, we are a part of a cosmic scheme and are plotting your very salvation.

You just mentioned Sisters and Brothers. Are there Brothers of Perpetual Indulgence as well?

Some of our houses worldwide do have women assuming the roles of fathers and brothers. Guards, bishops, and cardinals have also emerged. Lesbian luminary Cardinal Titti promenades in Sydney, and Pope Dementia the Last still pontificates in San Francisco.

But, when your filmic icons for priests are Spencer Tracy, Bing Crosby, and Anthony Quinn and for nuns are Audrey Hepburn, Julie Andrews, Shirley MacLaine, Sally Field, and Whoopie Goldberg, who do you think would inspire you? I do admit that Monty Clift's parish priest in Hitchcock's *I Confess* gives me pause with his tortured vulnerability.

In actuality, in the intervening quarter century since our inception, we have become more inclusive with les/bi women, transpersons, and even a heterosexual male, Sr. HedraSexual, taking the veil.

So why be Sisters? What is it about the image and role of a nun that speaks to you?

The habit of the Roman Catholic nuns had lost its relevance for the noncloistered orders during the 1960s through the 1980s. But we self-respecting drag queens could not allow such fabulous attire to moulder in convent attics and closets. Truly, our intent has never been to trash the Roman sisters, but rather to honor and emulate their unstinting devotion and work within our communities and on behalf of our faithful lay folk.

So which Catholic values would you say the Sisters exemplify, or which do they particularly excel at?

All the corporeal and spiritual works of mercy, of course. Then there are the seven deadly sins we have been known to flirt with as well. And our Rosaries of Perpetual Indulgence spring from our most

Catholic roots planted in the divinely feminine. Our rewrite of the Hail Mary goes like this:

Ave Prayer
Hail, O Divine Mother,
Source of Wisdom and Delight.
Blessed are You among the Deities
and Blessed are all of Us
Your Loving Companions
Holy Maiden, Wise Womyn, Crone,
Protect Us from the Earth Defilers
Now in this Hour of Our Need. (Nema/Amen)

Are the Sisters a postmodern Reformation of sorts, to rival that of Martin Luther's efforts half a millennia ago?

Yes, and our *Play Fair* safe sex pamphlet was our Wittenburg testament to a morally bankrupt church still unable to develop an honest and enlightened theology of sexuality after two millennia of dastardly diddling amid serial crimes of gross hypocrisy and venality.

Sisters Homo Fellatio, Loganberry Frost, Loretta (Sensible Shoes) Timothy, and Theresa Stigmata (*Photo credit:* Sr. Homo Fellatio and Sr. Missionary Position)

Can you comment on nuns as contemplatives versus social activists vis-a-vis the Sisters?

Our perpetually indulgent sisters are definitely not of the cloistered variety but very much of the theologically liberated, social activist cloth. In addition to our many good works already mentioned, we have a long tradition of participating with the peace movements in our various countries. In early 2007, at a major Peace Rally and March in Washington DC, I was honored to carry our red banner with the white stenciled message we have been delivering since the early 1980s: WE REMEMBER . . . US NUNS . . . KILLED . . . WITH US GUNS . . . IN EL SALVADOR . . . STOP THE WAR. To the assorted alternative media that recorded me, I delivered our Rosary of Five Sorrowful Realities of Terrorism Sponsored by the United States of America:

1) The Mass Murder of Indigenous Peoples throughout the Americas, Sixteenth Century to the Present.
2) The U.S. Nuclear Bombing of the Civilian Populations of Hiroshima & Nagasaki, 1945.
3) The U. S. Directed War in Viet Nam, 1956 to 1975.
4) The U.S. Supported Israeli Directed Massacre of Hundreds of Palestinians at Sabra & Shatila Refugee Camps, 1982
5) The U.S. War on Iraq, 2003 to the Present.

Sisters Theresa Stigmata, Loretta Timothy, Mary Media, Rosanna Hosanna Fella Bella, Succuba, Searching for Men, Vicious Power Hungry Bitch, and Loganberry Frost (*Photo credit: Sr. Homo Fellatio and Sr. Missionary Position)*

We recite as many as five Ave Prayers after each Reality.

On these occasions we invariably meet many Roman Catholic Sisters, mostly in modern attire, but some in their orders' traditional robes. I have always felt their sororal solidarity and appreciation for our parallel path on the road to peace and justice.

So who was the first Sister, and where did the idea for such a profoundly queer order come from?

In mid-1970s Iowa City, the later-to-be Sr. Vicious Power Hungry Bitch (VPHB) had formed a drag troupe called the Sugar Plum Faeries. They did one set of numbers in nun's habits that had come from a convent attic in Cedar Rapids, ostensibly for a production of *The Sound of Music* (ahem!) and were never returned but went to San Francisco when VPHB moved there in 1976.

I joined him there at the end of 1978, immediately after Harvey Milk and Mayor Moscone were murdered. Within my first two months, I met my first, self-identified fag nun, Sr. Assunta Femia, of independent orders and living in the Haight. Inspired by him and the robes hanging in VPHB's closet in our flat near Mission Dolores, on Holy Saturday 1979, I donned a nun's habit for the first time.

Some fifteen years before I had studied to be a priest with the Capuchin Franciscan friars until I was rejected when I confessed my repressed gay feelings. But that day, in the city of St. Francis, I reclaimed my earlier calling to the religious life, and along with Sr. Vicious Power Hungry Bitch and Sr. Roz Erection, I sashayed out into the streets in full, traditional habit to challenge the world. We were met with shock and amazement, but captured everyone's interest as we made our way all the way to the nude beach at Land's End to frolic with the pagan babies there assembled. At each location we were embraced and honored. "Good Afternoon, Sisters." "Happy Easter, Sisters." "Bless me for I have sinned, Sister." It was a glorious afternoon.

It sounds seminal. So tell me more about the beginnings of your historic order.

Our next appearance was at a softball game where our pompom routine all but stole the show, and by the time the Castro Street Fair had rolled around, we were ready to recruit more members. In the fall of 1979, Sister Hysterectoria and Reverend Mother went to the first Spiritual Gathering of Radical Faeries at a desert ashram in Arizona called by Harry Hay and Mitch Walker and encountered even more men with the calling.

In the next several months I, along with the other three "founding mothers" of SPI (Sr. Vicious Power Hungry Bitch, Reverend Mother Abbess—now deceased—and Sr. Hysterectoria (aka, Agnes deGarron) recruited ten others—mostly Radical Faeries—to form our order of gay male nuns. By January 1980 we named ourselves The Sisters of Perpetual Indulgence. Sister Hysterectoria, utilizing his nonprofit dance company, commissioned the SF Neighborhood Arts program to make our habits. He was inspired in his design by the style of Flemish fourteenth century noblewomen/nuns. Sister Succuba, a calligrapher, created the name banner under which we Sisters made our first public appearance.

And where and for what was that first glorious appearance?

It was at a march and rally in San Francisco against nuclear power on the first anniversary of Three Mile Island. Some organizers had told us not to come as *we were politically incorrect; we were drag queens; we were not germane to the issues at hand.* (As if anyone on the planet could not be!). But like I said, Sr. Succuba had calligraphied our gothic SPI banner, and Neighborhood Arts had sewn our first fourteen habits, while at the convent we'd been making black

Sister Clara Cumpassionata, Novice Sister Right, and Sister Soami (*Photo credit:* Willi Cole)

and white pompoms for days, and the rally in Golden Gate Park would be just two blocks from the two convents that housed ten of us. So we gracefully showed up at the Civic Center, jumping in between the giant Mutant Sponges from the Farralon Islands and Haight hippies pushing a coffin marked Capitalism. En route we alternated cheerful pompom routines with a "Rosary in Time of Nuclear Peril." It was a meditation on the Five Sorrowful Nuclear Realities: the U.S. Bombing of Hiroshima; the U.S. Bombing of Nagasaki; Karen Silkwood Killed in Oklahoma; The Chernobyl Disaster in Russia (added later); Three Mile Island in Harrisburg. The Ave Prayer in between decades implored the Great Mother to protect us from the earth defilers. On that first outing we established the range of our ministry, from silly satire to thoughtful spirituality. We were soon front page news, chasing hate-mongering Christians out of the Castro and Polk Street neighborhoods.

And what about your charity work? When did that begin?

Our first charity work was a collaboration with the Metropolitan Community Church for gay Cuban refugees. It was a church hall bingo followed by a salsa dance party directed by Sr. Unity Harmony. So many people turned out for the event that a second seating had to be thrown together to accommodate all of the bingo players. We called the games in English, Spanish, and Sign Language. As the gaming ended, the tables were collapsed and the disco ball began to spin. When the lights dimmed in the MCC gym around 3 a.m., we had collected $1500 for the cause.

When did you first take on the Roman Catholic Church itself?

Two days later! We protested at Jesuit-run USF at their 125th anniversary party, where they tried to deny the existence of their lesbian and gay campus groups. Years later the sisters were thrown off that same campus for distributing condoms.

How did the Sisters first get involved in AIDS activism and fundraising?

In 1982, when the city's health scene had hit crisis levels: STD's were spreading at an alarming rate and the "gay cancer"—it wasn't even called AIDS yet—was contaminating everyone with fear and prejudice. Registered nurses Sister Florence Nightmare and Sister Roz Erection joined with a team of Sisters and medical professionals to create Play Fair!, the first safer sex pamphlet to use plain sex-positive language, practical advice, and humor. It was paid for in part by a South of Market sex party benefit at the old Cauldron, along with proceeds from the sale of holy relics: little vials of ashes from the burned down Barracks Bath House.

Our annual Dog Show in the Castro became the first AIDS fundraiser, and that same year, pushing the political envelope, Sister Boom Boom ran under the "Nun of the Above" ticket in the race for Supervisor of San Francisco. Amidst all of the brouhaha about whether or not s/he should be allowed to run, s/he campaigned hard, spoke eloquently, and won over 23,000 votes. Frightfully close to winning.

Is it true that the Sisters were the ones who organized the first AIDS Candlelight Vigil?

Yes. That was in 1983. One of the many speakers to that weeping and angry crowd was Sister Florence Nightmare, RN (aka Bobbi Campbell), our first AIDS poster boy. He was not only a health care professional, but an advocate for PWAs and was himself HIV positive. His "gay cancer journal" series in the San Francisco Sentinel of a year earlier combined observations of a man living with Kaposi's sarcoma with the practical insights of a medical professional. He and his lover appeared on the August 8th cover of *Newsweek*. The article, about gays and AIDS, was the first time that the topics were handled in a fairly unbiased manner, bringing the entire nation face to face with AIDS.

Were the Sisters recognized by the gay community for all their service work?

Oh yes. For our efforts the previous year, the Sisters were honored with five Cable Car award nominations including outstanding theme event, outstanding athletic event, and outrageous parade float. I believe we won three of those awards.

And what about the Pope's visit in 1987? How did the Sisters respond to that?

The Sisters "schismed" when the Pope visited San Francisco in 1987. While most of the Order sided with much of the lesbian and gay community in wishing the city to disinvite such an international homophobe, Sisters Chanel and Sadie the Rabbi Lady constituted themselves as "The Official San Francisco Papal Welcoming Committee." Sister Vicious and Blanche deRoot called me back from the missions in Tennessee to prepare the liturgy for a Mass Against Papal Bigotry which we held in Union Square along with the Canonization of St. Harvey Milk. That and a few other actions and antics are said to have landed us the prestigious honor of being placed on the Papal List of Heretics. Personally I have my doubts we are on such a list, but not because we are not deserving.

What happened next?

For our tenth anniversary in 1989, the Sisters threw a huge gala event, Sistericus, with the Seattle Sisters joining in the celebration, helping to raise much-needed funds for Project Open Hand and AIDS Emergency Fund. Later that year, and for the next four years, we partnered with the City of San Francisco, Community United against Violence, and the Gay Men's Chorus to make Halloween in the Castro a safer event. Since then, donations collected at these mega street parties have been doled out as community grants for worthy causes. The Sisters' Pink Saturday nighttime street party in the Castro during June's LBGTI Pride continues this funding tradition.

Then in 1991, Sister Roma! introduced her STOP the Violence Campaign in reaction to the rise of violence in the streets, especially hate crimes. A window placard system was devised to mark safe homes to run to in the instance of an attack or the threat of an attack. The Order distributed window signs and whistles in various neighborhoods and districts of the city as well as on college campuses.

The Sisters also mobilized against Rev. Coal and his gospel of hate at the Capitol Christian Center in Sacramento. Demonstrators chanted outside of the Easter Morning services, finally drawing security and parishioners from the inner sanctum. The Sisters also put on events benefiting the Women and Cancer Walk and raised the first legal $1000 for SF Proposition 215 legalizing medical marijuana. Sister Phyllis Stein the Fragrant rode in the California AIDS Ride from San Francisco to Los Angeles, raising thousands of dollars in the process. Sisters have served medicinal brownie and tequila communion at Burning Man, as well as hoisting a queer youth prom, numerous art auctions and fashion shows, and lots of fundraisers, including one to support Princess Di's many charities after her tragic death. We've marched with Californians for Same-Sex Marriage and performed an exorcism of radio-show hostess "Dr." Laura to free her of her hate-filled speech against gays and lesbians.

And with the guidance of Srs. Merry Peter, May Joy, Bella DaBall, Sharin Dippity and Mary Timothy, our *Joy Darshans* enlivened the Castro neighborhood this past year to again route the fundamentalists plaguing our streets like locusts.

Your work is never finished it seems. God knows San Franciscans are blest, but tell me about the Sisters in other locales.

We now have houses around the globe. In 1980 Sr. Gazza Gumdrops did his novitiate with us, and in 1981 he and Mother Inferior Across the Abbyss established the Order of Perpetual Indulgence in Australia. The Sisters there colonized New Zealand, Thailand, and England. Toronto, Seattle, LA, and Germany spontaneously combusted with our blessings—or was it parthenogenesis? No, they definitely were not virgin births! Sr. X (RIP) of SF was the godmother of the Parisian Sisters. I believe England begat Scotland and we are not sure who infiltrated Uruguay and Colombia. In the last two years, Srs. Edith My Flesh and Helen Wheels at the Mother House have assisted in the formation of new houses in Portland, San Diego, Palm Springs, and Las Vegas, and the Russian River SPI has established a mission in Eureka. The Missionary OPI, under the Reverend Mother Generalship of Sr. Clara CumPassionata, operates from Des Moines and Kansas City through Tennessee and on to Philadelphia and Rhode Island. More than a hundred of our 500 sisters worldwide attended our June 2006 Conclave in Los Angeles to celebrate the Order's tenth anniversary there. And even as you go to press, we joyfully report a new house has formed in Arizona.

Sounds like vocations are on the increase. But is the whole nun thing so well understood that non-Catholics know exactly how to be a Sister, or do the Catholic-raised Sisters find themselves instructing?

Sisterhood and brotherhood do transcend the Roman model. All communities of support and faith embrace these attributes. That being said, I do confess to observing in my own motherhood the little tyrannies of a Catholic rearing with a zeal for rules and instructions in orderly ways. Fortunately, the pagan babies and radical faeries with whom I live inculcate solid anarchic values to balance out this human equation.

In some ways we queer sisters are little living holy cards, tableaux of beatific possibilities and prayers in action. St. Augustine said, "singing is praying twice." We say, "singing and sashaying in transgender dress is praying thrice." I don't know if this puts us on the fast track to heaven, but these little heresies have certainly enriched our earthly sojourn. We will continue to serve notice to those parts of Catholicism mired in a degenerate and legalistic priestly caste, to please redeem itself, repent of past grievous errors and reclaim those sadly silenced but not forgotten impulses to renewal which the saintly Pope John XXIII delivered to us almost fifty years ago.

Speaking of saintly, have any of the sisters been beatified?

Our dearly departed sisters we call *Nuns of the Above*. Many are memorialized on our four panel Names Project AIDS Quilt: Sisters Florence Nightmare, Marie EverReady, Unity-Harmony, Sleaze duJour, Rosanna Hosanna Fella Bella, Salvation Armee, Loretta (SensibleShoes) Timothy, Lucious Lashes, Marquesa DeSade, Sushi Psychedelia, Reverend Mother, and our Saints Ramon Vidale, Brownie Mary, Jimmy, Bobby, Walter, Mel, Morgan, Robert and so many more—yes, we have our role models and our spirit guides.

How does one become a Sister?

As Sr. Right proclaims, it takes a special type of person to become a Sister of Perpetual Indulgence. It is not for the prude, the blue-nosed, or the faint of heart. Sisters are called to be sacred clowns in their communities. Above all, sisters are activists who are continually working toward the betterment of the world around them. And, contrary to the idea that being a Sister is just about the glory, there is a great deal of unglamorous work that needs doing. So, in order to maintain the level of integrity for which the sisters have become known, we do screen all prospective candidates. Through a period of postulancy and a novitiate we test a Sister's call to service. Each individual, with the help of his or her house, determines whether the sisterhood is right for that prospective member. Please visit the SPI/OPI websites if you would like more information on becoming a nun. Go to http://www.thesisters.org

At the risk of sounding 1970s folk mass corny, whatever the love of God is, you make me feel it, Sister—through the power of your work, the goodness and relevance of your message, and your sincerely loving queer spirit.

Ah, those 1970s folk feasts. . . I was teaching high school in Freeville, NY, then, struggling to come out and attending Mass at Cornell U with the Berrigan Brothers and feisty, lavender-clad lesbians circulating whole wheat loaves to the congregants, with jugs of Almaden Rose. . . Jesus never tasted better!

May I have your blessing?

We are all blessed, dear editors, by the thoughtful, good works we do together. Sincerest congratulations on your efforts herein. Your rewards are in the here and now.

SAINTS

Ritual, Wonder, and Miracles

Vince Sgambati

I recently attended a local Catholic Charities Awards Dinner. Two friends of mine, Michael DiSalvo and Nick Orth, who founded a Catholic Worker house, *The Friends of Dorothy,* were honored for their care of people who suffer terminal AIDS-related illnesses. For years, they have opened their home and their hearts. Their gentle voices and touches have comforted many at the moment of death. I was thrilled that these two gay men were finally recognized for their remarkable work, but couldn't help thinking as well that in a neighboring state another Catholic Charities had ceased their adoption services in response to the law insisting that they allow gay people to adopt. Having grown up queer and Catholic, I'm accustomed to such conflicting ideology.

Mike and Nick's home is warm and inviting, and the walls, cubbies, shelves, and tabletops are adorned with Catholic icons—a kind of *Catholic-gone-queer* motif. The excessive décor is outdone only by the excessive attention both men give to their live-in guests. I've attended mass at their home a number of times, and I've often wondered if the folks present—a circle of social justice activists and social outcasts—mirror Christ's early followers more closely than the current leadership of the American Catholic Church which is increasingly reflecting the ultra-right televangelists.

About twenty years ago, I attended a particularly contentious City Council meeting. There were more than the usual number of conservative evangelical Christians present and a handful of conservative Catholics attempting to shove queers back into their closets and seal the doors shut. After hearing one too many times that homosexuals are essentially the reason for all that ails America, I had to respond: *Some folks here seem to think they know exactly what Jesus would think of us. It's odd because we don't really know a whole lot about*

Jesus, but it appears that he was an unmarried man who spent most of his time with twelve other men and a few strong, independent women. He sounds a heck of a lot like the queer folks I hang out with.

In retrospect, I was retaliating with my own queer version of "shock and awe," but my words were heartfelt, nonetheless. And though Mike and Nick are amazing men, they are not so very different from many dear friends and acquaintances I've had over the years who have committed themselves to speaking truth to power. My own activism has taken many forms. Though I've never self-identified as a Catholic Worker, when I attend mass at Mike and Nick's home and take in the candles glowing in front of the numerous icons, listen to the words spoken, share the consecrated bread and wine, and smell the aroma of the meal to be enjoyed after mass, I'm reminded that much of what I do has its roots in my own Italian Catholic upbringing which was filled with ritual, wonder, and miracles.

At age four, after recovering from a respiratory infection, I had continued to run a low-grade temperature, and our family physician was concerned that I might be developing rheumatic fever. My grandmother gave my mother a picture of Padre Pio and instructed her to place it under my pillow. At the time, 1954, Padre Pio was a Capuchin Priest living in Foggia, Italy, and famed for suffering from the stigmata and possessing the gift of bilocation, the ability to appear in multiple places simultaneously. Millions, mostly Italians or Italian Americans, were devoted to him and believed him to be a living saint.

My mother dutifully placed Padre Pio's picture under my pillow. The next day, in our living room, she smelled flowers. Overwhelmed by the fragrance, she walked into the front hallway and called upstairs to inquire if my aunt had sprayed air freshener to which my aunt responded that she had not. My fever broke that afternoon. When my grandmother visited later that evening, she told my mother that upon Padre Pio's intercession the faithful petitioner smells flowers.

Such were my childhood stories. The Catholicism that I grew up with was the Catholicism of immigrants and first-generation Italian Americans. Years before, they had been the marginal Catholics, an embarrassment to the more reserved and rational American Catholic Church. I remember crossing the Third Avenue Bridge, from Harlem to the Bronx, in a blizzard in my father's old Buick, weighted down with my aunts and grandmother sitting in the back seat, each one of them tipping the scales at a minimum of 225 lbs., with two of my young cousins straddling the women's laps. In the front seat were my father, driving the car, my mother, and me. I snuggled into my mother's muskrat fur coat like a fledgling rodent seeking warmth. Out came the Rosaries. My mother, aunts, and grandmother prayed us across the bridge. God the Father, and to a lesser degree Jesus, may have been distant dieties, but there were many intermediaries to call on. Mary was their favorite, and the clicking of Rosary beads was a familiar lullaby.

I knew non-Italian Catholics, but their forms of worship, like their familial expressions, were more staid. Their devotion wasn't reflected in reproductions of The Last Supper over the dining room buffet, or vigil candles burning in front of statues with heavenly gazes. Their worship was less impressive and didn't pour into the streets. They didn't have feasts and processions where men carried the *giglio* bearing large statues of patron saints.

For Italians, being Catholic was high drama. Religion didn't stop at the church door. In fact, except for baptisms, weddings, and funerals, religion had little to do with the church. My father rarely attended mass, but once when he came home from the hospital after discussing my mother's diagnosis with her doctor and told my maternal grandmother and me that my mother had cancer, his rage was directed against Jesus. He threw his hat at the crucifix that hung above our kitchen door and cursed Jesus, saying that they should crucify him again for making my mother sick. Years earlier, when his father's second wife had died, an orderly had to restrain my grandfather from throwing a statue of Saint Jude out of a window in the hospital. And there was also the story of my maternal great-grandmother who vowed to dedicate an annual mass to Saint Felix, the patron saint from her hometown, Cimitile, if he would see fit to cure her pneumonia, so she would live to raise her children in this strange, new country, America. To this day, the descendents of immigrants from Cimitile, Italy, attend St. Felix's annual mass at Our Lady of Mount Carmel Church in Harlem.

For many immigrant and first-generation Italian-American Catholics their feelings toward Jesus, his mother, and the saints were as volatile and compelling as their feelings toward benevolent, but domineering parents. My great-aunt would place her religious statues head first into snow banks when her petitions were not answered, then within a few hours rescue them from the cold and beg their forgiveness like a repentant child with tears staining her cheeks. And once my maternal grandfather, suffering from gallbladder problems, promised his pocket watch with diamond insets to the Madonna if she would spare him surgery. His prayers were answered and his pocket watch hung from a gold chain around the slender neck of the chestnut-haired and full-figured statue of the Madonna perched above the main altar at Our lady of Mount Carmel Church.

La famiglia were my primary teachers, and lessons were taught around kitchen or dining room tables where multicourse meals nourished larger than life stories of family, politics, and religion. But soon the church and parochial school became the literal center of my world, halfway between my house and my father's Italian-American grocery store.

After school, Dominic Di Cico, Elieen McKenna, and I would run across 104th Street from Saint Mary Gate of Heaven Elementary School, to our cathedral-like church, enter the doors (which required all three of us to budge) and kneel at a marble altar railing in front of a larger-than-life crucifix hanging above the main altar. We'd squint without blinking at the tormented figure of Jesus. Of course squinting without blinking tends to distort vision, but as three highly imaginative kids who felt a kinship toward the Children of Fatima, we weren't about to concern ourselves with such rationalizing.

I'd ask, "Did you see Jesus move yet?"

"No, did you?" Dominic would answer.

"How about his eyes? Did they open?" Eileen would ask.

Finally one of us would squint just right. Jesus' head would turn, or his eyes would open, or he'd smile. "There He goes! He moved!" Followed by the three of us screaming, and then running from the church.

Many of our priests and nuns had performed missionary work and their stories fed the overactive imaginations of their young students. One elderly nun who'd occasionally fall asleep at her desk repeated a story about a young woman who sacrificed her infant in devil worship. After stabbing her newborn on a sacrificial altar, the young mother floated above the heads of her fellow devil worshipers. I'd suffered nightmares every time she repeated that story, but I still longed to hear it again. I also devoured the stories of saints. They were my heroes, more courageous than Hercules, or Sinbad, or Gulliver.

My growing obsession with Catholicism played out in many childhood games. Necco wafers were hosts and bathrobes were vestments. A favorite toy was a plastic music box altar. A silhouette moved back and forth within the altar to the tune of "Ave Maria." The hologram glued to the silhouette would alternate between images of the Sacred Heart and the Madonna. Soon the music box broke from too much use. For my twelfth birthday, I asked my parents for an Extreme Unction crucifix. I would slide out the crucifix exposing the secret compartments where holy water and candles were hidden. My friends quickly tired of me performing last rights on them, but they enjoyed it when I'd choreograph elaborate funerals for deceased pet fish.

It was inevitable that I would go through a period of wanting to become a priest. An understatement—I wanted to be a martyr. My family balked at the idea of my entering the priesthood. Anything that drew me away from family was a threat. Especially the church with its demands of leaving one's human family behind. Regardless, during late elementary and early high school years, I attended annual weekend retreats with neighborhood buddies. I was the youngest in the group. When my father would pick me up at the end of a retreat, there would always be one or two men who would tell my father how devout and committed his son was. My father would smile and engage in polite small talk with my admirers, but I knew what he was thinking. He had little use for priests and would frequently comment about the empty bottles of liquor he noticed in garbage cans as he walked past the rectory on his way to work while the priests were still sleeping off their hangovers. My fleeting crushes on girls—the school janitor's daughter, the lead dancer in a friend's tap recital and, of course, Debbie Reynolds and Sandra Dee—gave my parents hope. *He won't become a priest; he has an eye for the ladies.* Well at least they were half-correct. I didn't become a priest.

Within this milieu of a pre-Vatican ll Catholic education built upon a foundation of Italian Catholicism, attraction to my own sex began to surpass my little crushes on girls and a concern for justice began to surpass my need to fit in. I sang in the church choir and remember a time that we performed at a home for people with mental retardation. As we followed Sister Mary Elizabeth up some stairs, single file of course, several of the young men living at the home descended the stairs. One tall, thin man with long fingers that he repeatedly shook next to his ears appeared quite anxious. He made deep grunting sounds. Several of the boys around me glanced at each other and chuckled. Though I was curious and a bit surprised by the young man's behavior, I was more distressed by my schoolmates' response. *Weren't we Catholics, and shouldn't we emulate Jesus' compassion?* During this same time, I began to find the boy sitting next to me in class more appealing than the janitor's daughter, and Richard Chamberlain left Debbie Reynolds in his dust.

An outsider's assumption might be that Italian Catholicism with its rigid mores, especially around sex, and especially in the early 1960s, would have felt overwhelmingly oppressive to a queer youth. But behind dogma was story, and it was the story that sustained me and made the flickering candles, and smell of incense, and portraits or statues with benevolent expressions that much more precious. The stories I learned were of love and compassion and mercy, and even though they rarely matched church practice, I still believed in them.

Being a child of first-generation Italian Catholics, I learned to be leery of religious leaders. When my mother was a young girl growing up in Italian Harlem, Italians were not welcome in her German/Irish parish's main church; they attended mass in the church basement, since Italian newcomers and their expressions of worship were considered an embarrassment. No doubt issues of race and a perception of Italians not being *white enough* also came into play. My mother told me that one day when the church basement was filled, she and her sister and aunt attended mass in the main church, subjecting themselves to glares and smug expressions. It wasn't until most of the German and Irish congregants had left and a new Italian pastor replaced the prior pastor that Italians were welcome in the main church.

I knew that priests were fallible. After all, they had not been immune to ethnic bigotry. I'd question why non-Catholics couldn't go to heaven, or why the souls of unbaptized babies would linger in limbo, or why we could only see movies with a certain rating. Suppose an actor I liked was in a movie that the church did not deem appropriate for children? Talk about the church interfering with my queer sensibilities.

I don't mean to suggest that I was free of Catholic minutia. I remember spitting out a perfectly good Nathan's hot dog in the middle of a subway station because I suddenly realized it was Friday; and I wore a scapular around my neck until it was two limp, faded patches hanging from knotted pieces of thread, because dying while wearing a scapular was a sure ticket into heaven. I even wore it while taking a bath, just in case—God forbid—I should fall asleep and drown, or slip getting out of the tub and bang my head against the tile. But on more important matters, like movie ratings or whom I was permitted to have a crush on, I was a bit more critical.

Ironically, my Catholicism was the only light that existed in my hastily constructed closet, which was horribly dark and lonely and separated me from my family and friends. I found solace in the stories of Jesus, the Apostles, and the saints. And I found company in the images that reflected these stories. Catholic paraphernalia, especially that which reflected centuries of a uniquely Italian-Catholic imagination, and which years later would fill Mike and Nick's—my Catholic Worker friends—home, was as reassuring to me as fig trees wrapped in burlap for winter, Italian folk songs, and sauce simmering on Sunday mornings. My closest friends became the sainted ghosts immortalized in paint or plaster or marble. And the more I heard or read about them and their lives and the people they cared for and loved—the *least of these*—the more I understood that there have always been outcasts relegated to the margins of societies. This was a closeted, lonely boy's burgeoning understanding of the dynamics of power and privilege, but it would be a few years before I applied these understandings to the "isms" of today's cultures. And it would take many more years before I'd connect such understandings to my own oppression and the oppression of my queer brothers and sisters.

As a young adult, it became more and more difficult for me to be a practicing Catholic. I guess I was too busy being a practicing homosexual, and the church had become more and more vocal about the incompatibility of the two. Ultimately, it was the Catholic Church's silence in response to the early years of AIDS that severed any lingering connection I may have felt to the Church. I remember marching in a Gay Pride Parade past Saint Patrick's Cathedral, and the march stopped for a moment of silence to commemorate those who had been lost to this exploding pandemic. I had already buried a number of friends, and I stared at the barricades stretching across the front steps and literally, if not metaphorically, separating thousands of queers from the cathedral and Catholicism. I thought of the hours I had spent inside, kneeling among the flickering candles in front of the images of understanding friends. At that moment, Saint Patrick's was simply stone, housing more stone. How the Catholic Church could turn its back on so much suffering was beyond my comprehension.

I still held Catholic stories sacred and they continued to inspire my activism including the work I did around HIV and AIDS. In 1987, I volunteered in the buddy program through what was then called the AIDS Task Force. My buddy was a one-year-old boy with HIV. His foster mother told me that she had asked to have him baptized in a local Catholic Church, but that the priest had refused. She felt it was because of the child's illness. Two years later, another priest in the same church agreed to perform the baptism. But for me, it was too little too late.

Over the years, I maintained minimal involvement in what might be considered Catholic forms of worship through my Catholic Worker friends and occasional visits to a priory in Vermont, but it wasn't until I became a parent that I felt compelled to revisit my giving up on the Catholic Church. After my partner, Jack, and I adopted our daughter, we obsessed over what to do regarding religion. Friends recommended Our Lady of Perpetual Grace, a small, Roman Catholic Church with a multiracial congregation. This latter attribute was very important to us: Jack and I being European American and our daughter, Mona, African American. One of our friends who recommended this church was the head of the Black Catholic Chancery at the time. She and another friend, a married priest, had baptized Mona several years earlier on Winter Solstice in a Congregational Church (a landmark stop on the Underground Railroad).

We decided to give Perpetual Grace a try. Mona was three years old at the time. We knew a number of people who attended the church, most of them African Americans. Our family began attending Solace about seven years ago, Jack and I with ample trepidation: *We don't care what you think of us, but be nice to our daughter.* But the three of us have been and continue to be treated with kindness and respect by the clergy and laity of the church.

Most recently, in the wake of Hurricane Katrina, Our Lady of Perpetual Grace has brought us unexpected comfort. It turned out that a number of the African-American parishioners were from the storm's hardest hit areas or had family living there. Our daughter, Mona, was born in the Gulf region. So a Catholic Church and Catholicism have become an integral part of our family life. It's a small, uniquely diverse and supportive community. Mona is growing under the watchful eye and within the loving embrace of doting elders. Last year, she became an altar server, which makes mass more tolerable for her since she gets to share top billing. I've watched our daughter move through familiar rituals: first communion, altar service, and Christmas Eve performances. Of course, the broader issues of Roman Catholic dogma and politics are a continuous challenge for our family. Fortunately, Father Jim, a patient man and a cordial listener, accepts my occasional tirade, and often shares my concerns. He is not a political progressive by any means, nor is he a right-wing ideologue; he's just a good man who's trying to do a difficult job with integrity and compassion.

My truce with Catholicism is tenuous at best. Jack and I wanted to give Mona a spiritual starting place in a relatively familiar, supportive, and multiracial religious community. But, we are critical observers. Even our physical presence as a queer family bears witness against official Church bigotry.

Mona is a very different child than I was, traveling a very different path. When Mona first met Father Jim, she asked him why little kids couldn't receive communion. I was reminded of my own persistent childhood questioning. But unlike Mona, as a child I never thought to question the central tenet of Catholicism. Last year, during Father Jim's Easter Homily, Mona leaned toward me, "Is he saying that Jesus' body rose from the dead?" She sat back and thought for a while. Finally she said, "Okay, maybe a soul can go up to heaven, but once a body is dead, it's dead." My analytic daughter's thinking is much more rational and earthbound than was her father's mystical thinking. But then she's not a queer, Italian Catholic boy growing up in the 1950s and 1960s.

I've moved beyond the beliefs of that boy, but not completely. For about two years we had attended Unitarian Universalist services in conjunction with attending mass at Our Lady of Perpetual Grace. Too much cultural disconnect. I'll never be soft-spoken enough or mild-tempered enough—nor be able to completely relinquish my superstitions—to be a diehard Unitarian Universalist. I mean, what's religion without a little guilt, repression, and hocus-pocus?

My ninety-five-year-old mother moved in with us five years ago. In her bedroom, I scan the plaster and plastic replicas of Saint Jude, Padre Pio, the Madonna, and a host of other saints, or watch her lips move while she whispers novenas, or hear the click of her Rosary beads. The Catholic icons in my mother's room, Our Lady of Perpetual Grace Church, and Michael and Nick's Catholic Worker house are familiar. They appeal to the queer, Italian-Catholic boy within. They're more than marble or plaster or wood; they represent stories of overcoming rejection, humiliation, and scorn—stories of compassion, resilience, and mercy. One Catholic Charities organization turns its back on queer adoption; another celebrates two queer men for their amazing capacity to love. I'm still learning from the bittersweet stories of Catholicism.

Queer Thoughts on Catholic Bodies

Anthony Easton

ONE:

In paintings of the crucifixion, often the wound on the side of Christ's belly looks like a womb. I imagine all the souls that were given birth via that womb, and how the people crowding the cross's base may have caught those souls. The apostolic succession, Christ to Peter, Peter to the Popes, has a populist mirror here. All began there for the people of God. I am of the body of Christ. I am in the people of God. When the Holy Spirit came down like a dove, I was there, and when Christ died, that wound leaking water like amniotic fluid, I was there. Being part of a corpus means that all of Christ is in me as well as all of his children. Like all nature, it is cyclical. The moon waxes and wanes; the tides rise and recede; people are born and die, and Christ is in the middle of that circle. She gives birth to the placenta of new life, her breasts suckling, nurturing, and loving us.

TWO:

Christ lived, he lived in the time of the gospels, and he lives today. I do not understand what it means for him to live historically, no matter how much I read or absorb—there were struggles and contexts that are just too gone for current Christians to understand. He was too large for us to speak for him. It is difficult for me to say: I am doing this because God told me to. But because God was before time began, and because he will be there when time ends, I also know that the message of God is continually emerging. I will die in a few decades. I cannot know what will happen in the fullness of time. But it is my duty to follow him, and his son, to the best of my ability, for the length of my stay.

THREE:

I believe that I am broken. I am a sinner. What I do with my sexual gifts, can be as destructive as what I do with my love. Seeing Christ on the cross is being in the middle of the ocean, in a capsized boat—and being pulled from the storm waters.

FOUR:

The body that I eat is the body that consumes me. Christ on the cross, after being whipped, and scourged, after he was stripped, and dragged to The place of Skulls, after his side was opened, and the temple curtain was torn, after thirty-three years of drama (the scandal of his birth, the flight into Egypt, the stories in Thomas of him making clay birds live and then killing them, the showing up of the rabbis at twelve, and the decades of mysteries, before the final drama unfolded). The story ends with a corpse—and memory.

FIVE:

We slip into the great unknown, and our bodies become artifacts. Full stop into something larger and stranger, or as worm food, it doesn't matter. On our deathbed, we do not know what will happen. The sea is mother to us all in her tides, in her life-bearing qualities, in the salt water like a global amniotic sac, in that all life came from it. When we die, we are born back into that sea, like a sailor without a map, past the temporal lives, alone—no crew but a single captain.

SIX:

As I am writing this, I am looking at a postcard that I bought when I was in London, of Andres Serrano's *Piss Christ*. All this talk of flesh and bodies, that's what the boys in the bars and the boys in the church have in common. What a piss queen has in common with a Piss Christ: the body of Christ immersed in human waste, in human filth, in the basest of humanity, makes it holy again.

SEVEN:

As Christians, we are aware that language will be forever inadequate to explain our relationship with the divine, but we are forever contained by language. In the Gospel of John, this contradiction is the first thing that he tells us: "In the beginning was the Word, and the Word was with God, and the Word was God." (John 1:1, KJV) Desperately we still use the phrases, the terms, the explicit speaking out, that gives us pause, or hope, or comfort, or meat (sometimes, milk). I went from the Latter-Day Saints to the Mother Church, because I believe in bodies, because the language we use to describe bodies comforts me. This is ironic, because the LDS Church believes that God has a body of "flesh and bones"—but being told that and experiencing the mysteries of the Eucharist are different things. I believe, most days, in the body and blood of Christ in the Eucharist. I never believed in the flesh of the Mormon God.

EIGHT:

Patron saints come when you need them, and for me the doubting Thomas is the patron saint for men who desire male flesh or even divine flesh. When it is written in the Gospels about his impertinent questions, and desire for closeness, he functions as all saints do, asking questions. Specifically, he wonders what the literal flesh of Christ means for us.

Caravaggio's rough trade painting of Thomas punctures who I am, as a man, as a Catholic, as a queer. Thomas slides his whole hand into this wound, this gaping, black-red sore. To believe in it all: God made flesh, flesh on the cross, and flesh rising again, means having to touch that flesh. Other questions flow from that touching, like water flowing from His sides: How do men touch each other's flesh with love—is this something that Christendom is good at? Is demanding holes in hands and holes in sides, love? Or, is a willingness to be prodded and poked, love? Who is showing the love that we are supposed to emulate? Thomas who prods, or Christ who allows Himself to be prodded? Not being able to answer these questions means that in some basic ways, my relationship to the body of the Lord, and to the bodies of men, remains mysterious.

Sometimes, I pray through Thomas, hoping to talk to him, when his curiosity, his doubt, his faith, and his ambiguity threaten to drown me. Such as when the wine and bread mingle in my mouth, the flesh of it all, I hope then I have Thomas's desire for something tangible.

NINE:

I remember as a kid having very earnest theological discussions about the end days, with Alistair, a fellow believer in populist American apocalypticism (Jehovah's Witness versus LDS), and in the literalism of children, I was convinced that the floor of heaven would be crowded, and there would be a giant screen, and all of the sins that you committed, all the darkness, the evil, the secrets, the humiliations, and the viciousness would be broadcast. God would judge it, but everyone would see it.

In the reptile brain that doesn't repair itself from childhood drama, sometimes I worry that those conversations with Alistair will prove true. That the second coming will happen in my lifetime and that my sins (my queerness, my bitterness, my casual cruelty, my despair, my refusing to marry) will condemn me. Admitting a desire for children, and a husband, is a way for me to say that maybe if I'm good enough, I will be saved with the rest of the good boys and girls.

TEN:

Growing up, the Holy Ghost was described over and over again as the still, small voice or as warmness, and I was always convinced that I was too much of a sinner, so dark and evil that God had abandoned me. I was never a happy kid. I remember the first time I walked into a Catholic church to attend mass, and I felt awe, the still, small voice, the warm feeling, the sense of order and construction, and all of those things left out of my childhood.

My first orgasm with a boy, when I was fourteen, was at an Anglican all-boys boarding school. We did things with mouths and cocks and hands, on a hillock, a mile or two from that school . . . his flesh was warm, and he was tender. Nothing still and small, but a raw kind of ecstasy. It happened years before that Catholic mass, but the two are in the same shelf of my interior library. He was an altar server, and the rigor of that blooming into something mysterious was sacred to me. The feeling at my first mass was like that orgasm. I think the Holy Spirit is like our sexuality: warm and free—it descended on the Pentecost, and people went crazy with joy. It came to Theresa and she rolled with it toward sainthood—it comes to me.

ELEVEN:

I listen to *Gay Messiah* by Rufus Wainwright when I'm writing this—and I'm thinking about how Rufus handles all of these questions, about being saved, and wanting to be loved, and prayer, and everything else I have been writing about in a roundabout way. Rufus believes that there is a messiah for us, who understands tube socks, 1970s porn, Studio 54, and Liz Taylor—he sings a line that is supposed to be intentionally shocking, about being baptized in cum.

So far, I have been a relatively orthodox Catholic, talking about the death and wounds of our Lord and savior. I wonder what happens when I talk about Christ as a celebration. I am devoted to the body of Christ, that handsome Jewish man who loves us all. To his hair, his neck, his belly, and his feet—to his penis, and to his back. The real, historical Christ wasn't as handsome as the man who is depicted now, but he must have had charisma. What happens when we think about the line *Jesus Loves Me* a bit further?

Baptized by the divine savior's cum, he bleeds and weeps for us, but his semen is left undiscussed. Augustine taught us that it was the root of all evil, the seed from which grows the tree of the knowledge of good and evil. But we wouldn't have life without that rebellion. I want to be loved by all of Christ. I want to see his penis.

TWELVE:

I go to mass sometimes at the chapel of the local university. The people are fairly conservative, and sometimes it's strained. But at 10 p.m., when everyone is huddled in together for the last mass of the day, on the floor, I forget this. Boys around me, young, with hard bodies, and young faces, open to the love of God, the waves of hormones leaking out around us. Sometimes I get a hard-on during these events.

I used to think that the hard-on was because I love cowboys, and that first-year students, lonely and fresh from home, were close enough. There is some of that here, no use in denying the obvious. But the Holy Spirit might be using me as a vessel, filling every inch of me, expanding, rising through my body. My erection is a physical response to the glory of God.

I wonder if they both work together—if my love and openness for Christ, and the people of Christ, and my desire to fuck them are from the same place. But then I remember that when I get to know people a bit better, figure out who they are as people, my love for them increases and my sexual desire decreases. The gift of Eros extends past the solipsism of my own body.

THIRTEEN:

I take the wafer, between my teeth, once a month now. It used to be three times a week. I wonder what it means, that bread made flesh—that's the key to all this talk of bodies, isn't it? I take Wellbutrin daily, for the same reasons I used to take the Eucharist. Because I thought it did something, because I thought it made me healthier. And just as Wellbutrin makes me a little more on edge, communion has caused me to be a bit more anxious.

I struggle with the feelings in my heart when the man in the front slips it between my teeth. The wafer is thin and it sticks, it's hard to swallow. I try to guess exactly when the body of Christ emerges into the host. I want to believe the word made flesh, where language is not an abstraction of a thing, but the thing itself—so the words that a priest utters are not symbolic but alchemical: tin into gold, bread into flesh, communion into church.

FOURTEEN:

I have left questions furled with this essay. Beginning with what happens with Christ's body interacting with mine: the moral and aesthetic effects of touching one's penis, or falling in love with handsome young men in long robes; the texture of the various rosaries you owned, and how it felt to let them slip through palms and fingers; the sorting out of which casual sex is proper to talk about in reconciliation; signing up for the Church because of the pretty things on the walls, the writing on the body of Sebastian; how talking about celibacy is a turn-on, how remaining a virgin is a turn-on; how blockages make you go around something; on being a male bride of Christ; on the disappointment in not wanting to fuck any of the monks in the monastery you went to hoping to find God; how you didn't wank once that week. I tried here, to negotiate a path around these questions, disappointments, revelations, and blockages, because being Catholic has taught me how to move my body. It still does.

Series of One

Lisa M. Kelley

My family lived in the foothills of the Adirondack Mountains in the shadow of the little Catholic Church in town. Walking to mass and the masses themselves are among my earliest memories. I was a good Catholic girl and I knew God was watching. I was told regularly that He was watching. I walked quietly to church knowing that any diversion from me on Sunday was bad. Once, when I was four, when we got home and my Sunday dress, tights, and shoes were safely away, I asked my mother something that had been puzzling me. "Who is Leda Snott?" My mother didn't know and wanted to know where I heard that name anyway. "In church. We all say her name every time, '. . . and Leda Snott into temptation . . .'" I trailed off and learned what I had been hearing and saying in unison all that time, was wrong. I was wrong. It was a first for me. I was four, the first child, the first grandchild, and unaccustomed to being wrong. I didn't like it. I tried harder, determined it would not happen again.

Questions, I learned as a child, are not always a good thing. This was especially true of the questions about God and the things I learned in church. Good Catholic girls weren't supposed to ask. And saying things could be sinful. When I said, "Heaven sounds boring to me," I was sent to the corner to think about it. A later comment, "If people in heaven can see people on earth, I don't think they are always happy. Aren't they sad when they see something bad happen?" received similar reactions. My Grandma tried to help me understand. She assured me God could see everything, even my thoughts. And my thoughts, like the ones I had been having recently, could be sinful. I became guarded and I performed. God could see everything I did and after the seeing came the punishment. If I colored and one of the precious, to me, crayons broke, this signified a bigger deal than simply a fractured piece of colored wax. It was a big deal because something as simple as a snapped crayon was God's punishment. My grandmother would tell me, "God is punishing you because . . ." There was always something to be pointed out as the cause of the punishments. God was always punishing me. He broke my crayons, lost things, and hurt me by making me fall. I learned in no uncertain terms that anything bad that happened to me, no matter how large or small, was my own fault. Anything bad was God's punishment of me.

I decided at a young age that I did not like God. He was mean to me. I did not tell anyone my feelings because I was aware that my dislike of God was a sin. I became good at guarding my thoughts. The belief that everything bad that happens to me is my own fault follows me always. Church gave me the fear of God and the hope of Jesus. I knew him and his kindness. I could not imagine he would hurt me. When my mother told me of Jesus and his love for children and the way he would let the children speak, I saw there was never any punishment from Jesus and I knew I loved him better than God.

My childhood had God, and Santa Claus, hovering just out of sight and seeing and knowing everything. They became somehow synonymous for me. God and Santa, I knew, were always watching and judging my worth. I lived with the belief that someone could always see. When I was in kindergarten, my mother left and I was told she was somewhere getting a baby. I was told I would, when my mother came back, have a baby brother or a baby sister. When my mother came back, she did not have a baby with her and she was sad and I did not understand. Then one day there were so many people at our house and not one person wanted to play with me. I was used to people thinking I was cute and wanting to play. No one wanted to play with me despite my best efforts, but my hopes for fun resurfaced when I saw the most beautiful baby doll on the desk in a box. I wanted to hold her. People wouldn't let me and I threw a fit, stomping and crying. Nobody cared and I was taken away. I didn't understand. Soon after things were explained to me in various ways and one of my nightly prayers became scary to me, "if I die before I wake . . . ." It could happen, I now knew.

Soon Death and a baby sister I could not hold hovered near like God and Santa. There were other stories shared with me at this point. I grew with these. The stories carried specific messages for me and the details ebbed and flowed depending on the telling. My mother almost died when I was born, and I almost died, and the baby sister came home in a box, and I was bad because I wanted to hold her, and now she was watching me too. I hurt her feelings sometimes, I was told. Death became a concept that was not foreign to me. It could happen anytime to anyone. It was embedded in the stories I heard.

At that point in my life, God and Santa and the baby were watching everything I did. When I learned that my baby sister was named Angela, I thought that this must have been why she died and came home in the box. I knew the angels were with God, so I thought all it would have taken to save her would have been for my mother to just give her a different name. As it was, my grandmother told me my sister was watching me, and Grandma let me know when I hurt the baby's feelings about something. I felt I was a constant disappointment to those watching. I heard that Angela died because she was too good for this world and God loved her so much He wanted her with Him. I got the message that I was a disappointment and not good and God didn't love me as much as He loved Angela. I was not wanted.

I felt I was never good enough and one day at twelve, with nothing to lose anyway, I reported that I decided to not go to church school anymore. The weekly dismissals from the classroom separated me and disrupted my invisibility. I had become good at not being noticed otherwise. It was a long practiced skill born of dodging God, Santa, and a dead sister. My mother did not push the issue. I still went to church with Grandpa and took comfort and delight in the weekly premass ritual. I was not there for God; I was there for stained glass window images and quiet and time with Grandpa. I was a girl so this was all I had. My brother, who had come later, could hunt and fish with him, but I, a girl, could only go to church for time with him. I never asked why Grandma didn't go, but I did notice at twelve that Grandma wasn't so quick in pointing out the ways God was punishing me. Instead she turned her attention to teaching me what it feels like when someone walks on your grave and which leaves, when pulled, can tell how many lies I have told, and what will happen if I ever open an umbrella inside again. Everything still pointed to me being bad.

I wanted to write, but I stopped writing almost as soon as I started because the images got scary and because anyone could see them. When I wrote there was evidence of me. I became more visible on paper. It was safer not to.

Soon after I ended church school, I had a boyfriend. This was a very good thing, I knew. I started thinking that maybe I could be good. Everyone seemed happy with me and talked with me more and asked me about Kendal and told me about his family and bought me new clothes for no reason. But I again became a disappointment when I broke up with Kendal because he wanted to kiss me. On the lips. He was the prettiest boy in the class but I did not want to kiss him.

School was an escape but it was not fun for me until I played basketball with Coach C, who had the most beautiful eyes I had ever seen. Once during practice, I sprained my ankle and she helped me from the gym. I was on crutches for a while, but the thing I remember most about being on the team . . . all of those games, all of those sweaty practices, and the communal locker room after . . . is leaning on Coach and her arm around my waist as she helped me from the gym. I did not write about this. Soon after, I learned I could not be an altar boy. Church itself began to lose meaning for me, and, try as I might, I could not hear me in the mass. I moved on. Stained glass stopped being reason enough to go, so I didn't. But I still crossed myself sometimes. Still I do.

Despite the negative components of day to day, I did perfect not being noticed and I started to write for me. I made peace with the sins I was committing by being me and I found places to hide my writing.

The first time I saw the person who would later become my best friend, my love, my lover, my partner, was Freshman Orientation at the university that would be my escape for the next four years. This is not a glimpse across the crowded room story. She was sitting two seats up and one row over from me and I was thinking as I looked, "Boy or girl?" There were no discernable clues. The shoes were Reebok, the CB jacket blue and green, Levis, the hair feathered and in the in-between long and short classification. Very eighties. I later learned that her name was Patrice. Sophomore year we were roommates and life took on new meaning. It seemed that there might finally be room for me.

Still writing for me, I took a creative writing workshop. I was also taking a Psychology class where I learned of Freud. I started writing about sex.

I wrote about sex and women and love for women and obsession with women. There is the London story with the woman who leaps unceremoniously into the path of an oncoming train. There is Virginia (it is embarrassing to think of her now) who loves Tony. I am Tony. There is the unnamed woman who actually "masturbates with a thought not her own." In all of these, I am the guy, the narrator, the one who follows, observes, obsesses, and has sex with the women. One after the next. As a narrator, I am easy and nonselective.

One day, a professor suggested I write something from the female perspective. I did not appreciate the suggestion but I wrote a story from the perspective of a woman who walks into the ocean. She just keeps going. There is no sex. The professor read the story and asked me to be one of the editors for the university literary magazine. I accepted. The walk to the English building on campus took me past the chapel. I didn't go in, but I slowed regularly to appreciate the stained glass windows. I was on the outside now.

I still wrote from the male perspective, but I had more material.

Someone told me I acted like I had a crush on one of the young women in the sorority I had joined. I denied this with convincing vehemence and immediately staged a crush on Paul. He was in one of my writing classes. We arranged times to meet and critique each other's work. He joked that we were destined to write the Great American Novel together. We went to one of the sorority formals together. He was tall and handsome and I wondered what he was doing with me. We did have a good time. We did not kiss. I convinced Patrice to join the sorority.

Eventually I graduated. I tried to become the person I thought I was supposed to be. I did not write once again. The summer after graduation was the summer of weddings. I was bridesmaid or maid of honor, depending on my friendship ranking, in three Catholic weddings that summer. I was in Patrice's wedding and immediately after, I embarked on a summer of self-destruction. I drank too much and smoked too much and did things I did not want to do with people (men) I did not want. I didn't know what else to do. College was over. My options had ended.

I got a job.

I dreamed of dying. Repeatedly. I dreamed of lying on the floor of my bedroom while two women slept in my bed. During the day I taught. I lived alone. I thought all of this was what I was supposed to do. James, the science teacher, began stopping by my room more and more often. He asked me out. He actually said, "I think we'd be good together." I told him no and I called Patrice. "I think I am not entirely straight," were my exact words. She was not surprised.

She was 300 miles away. I was a high school teacher someplace in rural New York State. I cried. I listened to music. I drove on back roads late at night. I hoped to not be able to find my way back, but I always did. When I found the Catholic Church in town and attended a mass, I toyed with confession. "How many Hail Marys would this one take?" I wondered. Even with Jesus, I decided it was safer to be silent.

Late one night Patrice called to tell me she would be divorcing and moving to California. Four months later, I followed. We were roommates once again, and both trying to find something as we averted our eyes.

I wrote a story about two women who run away to join a circus. They just leave everything behind and the narrator becomes a solo act on the high wire. She has a unique perspective. My narrators are never guys anymore. It amazes me that I used to do this, a subconscious bowing to rigid expectations. I thought that to write about a woman the way I did, I needed to be a man. I am shocked at everything I did not see.

In California the waves touched the shore in a rhythmic embrace and I heard the silences Patrice pointed out. California echoes in my mind with images. As I would light a cigarette and smoke, it was my defiance I blew out into the salty air. I crossed myself. It was automatic and there was no longer the inner intonation of *fathersonholyghost.* There was only the familiar motion.

In California, I found a Catholic church and during the sunlight of a weekday that was not a day of holy obligation, I walked inside. I was in the light of stained glass windows, eyeing the confessional, and knowing that I had left this behind. Still I genuflected and crossed myself before I stepped outside and continued around the city lake that is Lake Merritt. Later that day a woman, not Patrice, handed me a beer and told me about a time she was homeless. Later she would speak her poetry to me. I carry these images with me.

Once Patrice and I could be honest with ourselves, we could be honest with our feelings for each other. We touched each other in new ways and we grew to trust what we have together. When the time was right, we declared ourselves married on a day that threatened rain, and then gave a rainbow. I took comfort in this as we proclaimed, "By the power we give ourselves," and declared ourselves married. I don't need to look further than me, us, what we have.

We return to the coast of our births for too many reasons to say. There are good things in this, but I look back daily. California brought us to ourselves and to each other.

I am more present in the places left behind than I am in this little town where winter comes. I am in the moments of the past because there is nothing to keep me here. There is only Patrice. The warmth of her body. The comfort of her embrace. But I had these there, too. I cannot make peace with the approaching winter. I cannot let the ocean go. I cannot remove myself from these moments that have more dimension than anything I have seen here. This little town is flat and winter is approaching.

I am not here.

Right now I am in her arms once again watching the sun set across the waters of the bay.

I know what I want. I keep looking.

One Sunday we go, at my request, to Catholic mass at a church near our home. I want to find something; I expect to find something there. But it is clear that my love and my marriage are not recognized as I am marginalized repeatedly by the mass. There is nothing for me and my dissatisfaction with all that is not here is palpable. We do not return to the church. I try, instead, to find something in reading about spirituality. I discover Hans Urs von Balthasar. I look to him and his Catholic Theology for answers he cannot give. But the symphonic nature of truth ebbs and flows like the Monterey tide I left behind. I pull Stephen Mitchell's translation of *Tao te Ching* from my desk drawer and read from time to time. My shelves at home are a resting place for various spiritual reckonings. I find pieces of the things I would like to believe interwoven.

I am surprised when one day Patrice and I watch steam rising from the freezing surface of Lake Champlain. She comes home from work and she says she has something to show me. She drives me to a secluded spot by the water. It is beautiful, like the lake is exhaling, steam rising into the sharp air and meeting the intense blue of the cold, cold sky. I am learning to see the beauty in winter. I am here and I am learning to let go.

That is not all. Here in the expanse of country, with only trees and clouds waiting placidly on the horizon, I have time to consider myself. I am coming to know who I am in a new and unforeseen way. I am my own worst enemy. This takes on new meaning but, I still believe the things that happen must, after all, be my fault. I still think about all I have left behind: pieces of me. I am, I say, on a spiritual quest. This takes shifting forms.

I am a writer and I am a dyke with Catholic roots on *a spiritual journey.* I am learning to see the beauty and the power in this; it was here all along. I talk with Patrice. She is patient. Together we have strength and power and love and more than I could ever have imagined. Even in the rural immensity of winter.

I cross myself.

I am here.

WORK REFERENCED

Monk, Richard C., Kenneth T. Lawrence, Walter Hofheinz, Robert C. Monk. *Exploring Religious Meaning*. 5th Edition. Prentice Hall: 1998.

Holy Scenes

Emma Day Jones

Scene. Baptism. A church lit blindingly white. There are two women wearing white robes present. One of the women sits on the edge of the baptismal font and pours water onto the other who is kneeling in the font, facing her. There are cries of ecstasy.

When this scene first enters my mind I am disgusted with myself for thinking of something so sacrilegious. Not only sex in a church, but queer sex. (It doesn't occur to me that because the church is dedicated to the expression of love it only makes sense that the love I find myself longing to express be situated there.) I try to erase the image but it's been drawn in permanent ink. I draw lines through it but the black marks somehow fail to overcome its bright whiteness. I long to rip it to shreds but given that it lacks physical substance this is not possible. And so, the scene sits impressed upon the front of my brain. Still, I claim victory because at least I do not write it down. As long as I do not write it down then everything will be okay. It will be as if it never even happened. Until this moment it never even happened.

In this moment I tremble as I write this, fearing whatever other "sin" and/or truth will be revealed here to me for the first time. For every time I write I feel as though I am confessing, confessing thoughts not yet actions but sins all the same. The pen is my voice, the paper the priest, and there is no partition between us on my desk, which acts as a confessional. Just two bodies face to face, trapped in a small, wooden box until one of us concedes. Either my pen just comes out (no pun intended) and lists my offences or the paper gives up on trying to force them out of me. My pen is usually the first to surrender and even when it isn't the words and the sin exist all the same. They sit in the pit of my stomach causing such discomfort that even if I wanted to confess, so that I might reclaim the privilege of communion, nothing would truly be gained by it. The joy of eating and drinking of Christ would be short lived because anything consumed would come right back up.

Scene. Communion. The church lit blindingly white. A woman lies on the altar. A second woman enters, a white towel draped over one of her shoulders and a glass bowl filled with water in her hands. She sets the bowl down on the altar and proceeds to wash her hands. She wipes them dry with the towel and then begins to make love to the woman on the altar.

The eroticism of this scene proves to be more overwhelming to me than that of the first. What's implied if communion is actually to be taking place, if both body and blood are present, makes me sick. Nevertheless, I'm drawn to the idea represented, that eating and drinking (so to speak) of the female body can be a form of praise. What's even more striking to me about the scene is that the body has been given up not for one but to one. As a result, the only thing one has to confess to partake in this communion is love, not sin. But then I remember it's a kind of love that's viewed as a sin.

As such I continue to tremble as I write this and prepare to launch into an Act of Contrition as soon as I am done because that's what you do. You sin, you confess, you offer penance and then you move on. No questions asked of you. No questions asked by you. But I can't move on. I'm stuck. Stuck on the questions I want to ask of the Church and those I must eventually ask of myself. Who says this is a sin and why? If God made women and God made love, why would He not want women to love other women? Why did this image appear to me? What does it mean? And most importantly, am I a lesbian? But I am not here to question, I am here to confess. This is the problem with confession, and why I normally avoid it. For me it's always complicated everything while allowing for the resolution of nothing.

When I am done writing this I want to be able to say that what these women are doing is or isn't sin and that I see them because I am or am not a lesbian. I want to say that I see women not as objects by which the Church is desecrated, but as beings by which Catholicism becomes tangible. (If these scenes do nothing else they show that desiring women is helping make religion more tangible to me than it ever was. And this is happening despite the fact that I have yet to experience women, well, tangibly . . . I have yet to make love to a woman.) I want to be able to say of this image when I see it that it seems perfectly natural. (And perfectly brilliant.) I want it to make sense to me that altars have become beds, the host nipples, and the chalice, that most holy of holies—the vagina. I want to say all of these things, but I can't say what I am afraid of. I can't say what I'm not supposed to believe, not in confession.

What I'm supposed to believe is that the scene is filth, barely a step above pornography, that there is nothing beautiful or sacred about two women having sex on an altar. There is nothing beautiful about it at all. There is just me, my subconscious really, and it's trying to make the religion I was raised in and the desire I find myself being devastated by fit with one another. There is just me longing for my longing to be deemed holy. The guilt I fail to feel at wanting this silences my pen.

Scene. Anointing of the Sick. A bedroom. There are two women present, one lies on the bed, the other is dipping her fingers into a vial of oil that sits on the nightstand. She then proceeds to trace the shape of a triangle over various parts of the other woman's body. First her mouth, next each of her breasts, then her navel, and finally her vagina.

Appropriately, when this image wakes me I find that I have been sweating with a fever. The moisture on my body is repulsive and I ache in so much pain that I make a bargain with God. If He puts an end to this temporary physical illness I'll do the same to my sexual one. I'll stop writing these scenes down. I'll stop writing them, but then I won't stop seeing them. I could go on with them forever, or at least until I've run out of sacraments. And then the scenes I see and the sins I commit involuntarily would simply be replaced by those I create and knowingly partake in. I would continue to sin, seek it out in fact, despite myself because I can't do anything else. The scenes exist within me whether I write them down or not and they aren't going to vanish anytime soon.

Scene. Crucifixion. A bedroom. A woman lies in the bed. Another stands next to it, blood pouring from her body. The woman in bed wakes, turns to her lover and on seeing the blood asks her what's happened. The bleeding woman does not respond. The woman in bed asks again. "You," answers her lover, "You."

This scene does not appear in my mind as any of the others, but is provided as a prompt in a writing class. The instructor has decided most everything about it; who the characters to inhabit it will be has been left up to me. I choose for them to be women. There are no questions here. What's happened and happening is quite clear. I am the woman in the bed. In my desperation to show my lover just how much I love/want/desire her I've cut her insides so badly with my nails that she won't stop bleeding. She bleeds for my sins, for how much I love/want/desire her; like Christ, she will die for them.

O my God, I am sorry for my sins. In choosing to sin, and failing to do good, I have sinned against You and Your Church. I firmly intend, with the help of Your Son, to make up for my sins, and to love as I should. I firmly intend, with the help of Your Son, to make up for my sins, and to love as I should. To love as I should. To love as I should.

Dance or Die

Jim Leija

Bryan,

Do you remember the private, all-boys Catholic high school we went to? It had that ridiculous motto: "Builders of Boys. Makers of Men." I went back to that school for the first time in years. I passed the statue of the Virgin Mary. Her fingers were broken, and had been glued back on. It happened a long time ago. Her fingers were broken, almost like a warning. She's one of the only women in the place, so she couldn't get too involved. The broken fingers made sure of that. She could only watch, silently, as they built men out of boys. As they built the perfect khaki-colored world. As they nourished despair. She has no power in this world of men, and her fingers could easily be broken again. So she stood with her arms out, as if to say, "I am at your mercy."

I thought of you, Bryan.

We met when I was a junior. You were younger than me, a sophomore, and I remember you were *the* "queer kid," over-the-top, effeminate. And, somehow, people would always say "Do you think Bryan is gay?" And I would think, "Is it possible that he's not?" You were kind of an open secret, and none of this was ever directly addressed by anyone in the school; maybe if we ignored it, we wouldn't have to deal with it as real.

I always thought of you as a kind of imperious, Napoleonic figure. You were notoriously difficult, defensive, a little snooty, generally unpleasant. You were a fabulous liar. We'd make fun of you because you would make such outrageous claims, like the time you told us that you wrote romance novels under the pen name "Tami Hoag." You claimed that you would write the novels and that your aunt would publish them in her name. We asked you to prove it. Of course, you couldn't. You claimed you had an older boyfriend; claimed you dressed as a woman when you were with your *other* friends. We were intent on catching you in your lies; on backing you into a corner and making you squirm. We enjoyed destroying your outrageous fantasies.

The truth is that you didn't really have any friends. You were even too gay for me and my friends. You remember Jake and Mike. They are still two of my best friends, and the funny thing is that we all turned out to be gay. We didn't know each other were gay at the time. I was the first to come out once we all got to college, but after that, one by one, we figured out that our small, all-boys Catholic high school was a veritable Midwestern Castro.

I'm sorry that we used you to turn the attention away from ourselves. You were just more obviously gay than any of us. A red herring to throw everyone off our trail. We felt more normal, more protected, because we thought we were better than you. And we weren't as effeminate, or outspoken, or . . . I don't know what.

I know I was never very friendly toward you. I couldn't be. It would have been too dangerous; guilt by association. And that was just something I wasn't ready for. But you must have seen through us; you must have known the truth about us, probably better than we knew the truth ourselves.

You loved the school musical. I remember you singing and dancing in the chorus. You had those eternally rosy red, round cheeks, and wore those dorky glasses. And you would come to rehearsals wearing black, tight-fitting, stirrup dance pants which accentuated your protruding pot belly. But the thing we absolutely made fun of the most was the t-shirt you wore: a black T-shirt, emblazoned in silver letters with the phrase, "Dance or Die." Dance or die. Oh, that T-shirt! It was a constant source of amusement to us and, of course, to all the other proud and practicing homophobes at school. Dance or die. That's what we started to call you, Bryan, in the days and weeks following the appearance of that T-shirt. Mockingly, we would call you "Dance or Die."

I always had a lead in the school musical. It was the only thing I lived for during those three months, and I loved every moment of being on that stage. After the final Saturday evening performance, we would have a huge cast party, kind of like a school dance. And when the party was over I would think, "There's no reason to come back to school on Monday."

During the cast party that year, I heard that you dared that guy Joe Camillini into kissing you. He was a typical high school jock. You dared him to kiss you, and his friends egged him on.

It makes a lot of sense, now that I think about it. You knew what you were doing. You knew that you would hang yourself the next day. You knew that this was your last chance, your last impulsive, fearless act to get exactly what you wanted out of this guy, before you killed yourself. I don't know if he kissed you. I hope that he did. I hope that you got the chance to have that electric feeling, that feeling of the first time you kiss another man, when something so absolutely off-limits becomes suddenly yours. You deserved to have that.

You loved being onstage; you loved the musical theatre. After your suicide, someone mentioned that you had talked about the attempt beforehand. But no one took you seriously because you had lied about so many other things in the past. But, Bryan, you had said, "Now that the musical is over, I don't really have anything else to live for. Maybe I'll kill myself." Dance or die.

When we arrived at school on Monday morning, there wasn't an official announcement. All these rumors were going around, and, at first, I thought it was just a joke. And then the choir director told us it was true. And a strange silence ensued.

Jake and Mike and I, we can't remember any response from the school. No grief counselors. No "all-school meetings" on suicide prevention. And most certainly, no discussion about *why* you killed yourself, because that would require the school to admit that it was a terribly dangerous place for young, gay men. To us, it seemed like a cover-up.

I remember your funeral. Your mother was so stoic, your father a mess, sobbing violently while she remained calm. I looked at them suspiciously. I had heard that your parents had forced you into reparative therapy. Maybe that was just a rumor, I don't really know, but I didn't trust anybody at that point. I had a hard time looking at them, and not blaming them for what had happened. They must have been suffering, but I didn't care. I didn't want to be there. I wanted desperately to be anywhere else at that moment. I sang at your funeral mass with some of the other guys from school, and we processed through the church, passing your open casket—you looked so harmless, so perfectly harmless. But I never cried at your funeral. I never felt I had the right. And, sure, we comforted ourselves with the fact that this wasn't the first time you had tried, that you had had mental health problems for a long time, that you were a grand liar—*and how could we know to take you seriously this time?*

When you decided to kill yourself, you knew there were others like you, but they wouldn't confess their secret. You looked around and felt so consumed by the absolute hypocrisy of the place.

No, that's not it at all. You looked around and thought, "This place is so drab. I must do something fabulous. Spectacular. Something they've never seen before." You had to develop a plan; to imagine when it would have the most impact, be the most dramatic. You always had a flare for the dramatic.

You knew it had to be a hanging. No messy blood. No sloppy corpse. You were more than a little vain; you knew well enough to preserve the body. Even in death. A hanging. Because there you would hang, gloriously, like a bell or a beacon or a disco ball. And your hanging body, in all its glory, would say to us all, "I am too fabulous. Too fabulous for you. And you don't deserve me."

And in our shame, in our pity for you, you knew we would understand how insignificant and mundane and utterly mediocre we all were. You would show us all. And we would all have to file pass your open casket in terror and awe, because you had the power to do it, and we were all just a bunch of pussies, little faggots. *Who gets the last laugh? Who gets the last laugh? Who's the faggot now?* Those jocks would cry at your funeral. They would cry. They would sob in uncontrollable fits. You would turn those violent, butch boys into faggots. And they would sob from the pits of their nauseated stomachs. Others would tell them, "It's not your fault." But they wouldn't believe it. And they would fear punishment. Anticipate punishment. Expect to be punished. And no amount of penitence would save them.

We would feel responsible. And together we would forget you. We would stop talking about you. Erase you. You had not intended for *this* to happen. When you wrapped the rope around your neck, took your last look around the wood-paneled basement, your last thought was that you would live forever in glorious memoriam. But it was easy to forget a chubby little dead, gay boy.

Forget a dead, gay boy. Forget a dead, gay boy. Forgive a dead, gay boy. Forgive a dead, gay boy. Forgive, God would forgive us. Wasn't our fault, forgive us. Forget. Forgive. Forget. Forgive and forget. Forgive and forget. Forget, forget, forget. Forget that little faggot. That's all you were.

You thought we would remember you forever. We forgot you so quickly. That year, there was no mention of you in the yearbook. No memorial.

But, by the time I graduated a year later, your parents had established a memorial scholarship, a scholarship designated for a graduating senior who had demonstrated excellence in the performing arts. I was the first person to receive that scholarship.

If only you could have waited, just a little longer, things would have gotten better. Two years and you could have been at college, joining a club or going to bars, meeting people just like you. People just like me.

Reclaiming the Power of Incarnation: When God's Body Is Catholic & Queer (with a cunt!)

Jane M. Grovijahn

"[T]here is not a soul that can at all procure salvation, except it believe whilst it is in **the flesh,** so true is it that the **flesh is the very condition on which salvation hinges.** And since the soul is, in consequence of its salvation, chosen to the service of God, it is **the flesh** which actually **renders it capable of such service** . . . [so] that the soul likewise may be filled with God." Tertullian, *The Resurrection of the Dead* 8, AD 210.

Born lesbian, baptized Catholic, brokered in and through a body sexually abused as a child, embedded God into my flesh in an erotics of pain, pleasure, and powerful persuasion. I am constituted by all three core bodily realities. Imagine my surprise to be claimed and called by God into a church that scorns the female, rejects the lesbian, and resists the holiness of *creation-in-cunt.* Yes, *cunt,* my most visceral place of losing and loving God. When I dig deep into the depths of who I am as queer and Catholic with a cunt, I find thick, ancient, gnarled roots, each one grafted onto another, all distinct, yet forming one solid manifestation of me, all defining me *in flesh* as Catholic. And that flesh, with all its roots, I know, is my hinge, both opening and closing into salvation.

My deepest root, my truest self made in the image and likeness of God, is love for the body, creating in me a provocative Catholic core that refuses to let go of the immense importance of the body, as in the awesome power of the Incarnation, God be-coming flesh over and over again. Within this landscape of bodily delight, of flesh animated by spirit, another rooted part of me is an insistence on the power of the female all around me. I am driven by a fecundity of vision that reclaims the female body as God's first home. Finally, the last and probably thickest part of me is that girl-child herself, constituted by this ferocious fidelity to the female body in the midst of its degradation in childhood sexual abuse, surviving and still waiting for a Catholic imagination that can christen creation in *cunt*. What shall be birthed from my womb, doubly delineated by violence and exquisite dyke-desire? As a Catholic, lesbian, feminist survivor I refuse to give up on God and seek out that *Imago Dei* as God-between-my-legs. If God cannot be part of my sexuality, then the Incarnation is a lie. Believe it or not, my Catholic inheritance taught me that Salvation, if it was to be truly saving, must incorporate, quite literally, my cunt.

In this contested site, of both holiness and horror, I entered the abyss of God that is my life. Drawn to, but denied ordination, and excluded from all other signs of sacramental vocation by a church that defines holiness in relation to men, I became a theologian who refuses to forget how I learned to take God into my body. Little did I know that my call into God would start so exquisitely in the body—only to have that stolen and sullied—and pull me into a collision course that began in my little cunt, which was not yet capable of distinguishing me from the harm done to me.

I am in second grade and I have a terrible dilemma I cannot comprehend. Despite all the careful and exact preparations being made to help me receive the very body of Christ into my little self in my first holy communion, I know they are useless! How could I tell and who exactly would I tell that I have already been exposed to what could not possibly be God? I secretly suspect that *my* body has been left out of God on purpose. Why else would I know such abhorrent evil, and feel so thoroughly judged as unworthy. For this, there must be a reason, although I know not what that could be. Who am I to challenge the Almighty? My body was no place for the holy; the abuse confirmed this. What could the reception of God mean for me except a searing sense of not-good-enough? I felt in my flesh what I later came to call *not-God* and *God-gone-wrong*. My fleshly hinge of salvation slammed shut the door to God for many of my childhood years of wonder and awful knowing. It seemed I did not, could not possibly belong to God, and *obviously,* God did not belong to me.

I can still remember, with clarity that only horror retains, the burden of my childhood nightmares that were peculiarly Catholic. My nighttime escapades were not about the boogeyman or the monster beneath my bed. My nightmares took me to the macabre, to Golgotha, the place where death claimed the body of God. Literally standing at the foot of the cross, weeping uncontrollably, I stood frozen while Christ cried out to me to act, *do something* to take him off this cross! Shocked and sickened by the sight of a tortured body, I thought to myself: What could I possibly do to change any of this? Here was my chance to prove myself worthy, so Christ wouldn't have to die. Yet, I knew there was nothing I could do. I was incapable of changing anything. God would die and I was the only one who knew why.

Feeling God die was something no child should have to endure. It wasn't until many years later that I realized this dream was merely scripting what I was living in the sexual abuse. God was dying in my own body slowly, stripping me away from what was most my own in God. Unfortunately, no religious teaching I ever heard helped me deal with this. Instead it blamed me and scarred my sex and my sexuality as sin. Not surprisingly then, I recited the preparatory prayers with an exact vengeance, hoping these incantations could really exorcise the way evil seemed to place itself within my memory, my bodily sensation, my incessant need for a sacrament of penance: forgive me, Father, for I am sin. The power of God was unmistakable in all this fleshly experience, but where was the love, the tenderness of God that the catechism spoke of?

My tender and young roots quickly became knotted into a severe constellation of bodily diminishment that first took shape in terms of the sexual abuse, stealing my God-consciousness and leaving me with fear and revulsion. What kind of God erupts into a body like this? How could I know God without my body? What did I know of grace? Then I was faced with my other hidden, but constant way of looking for God, and that was in and through desire for the female. This entry into God, also brutalized by a Catholic church in its abusive insistence on *hetero-everything,* led me away from the divine delight in my own viscous, vibrant female-loving self. Yet, it is what made me come alive. Trying to stay consciously connected with what made me alive in the midst of regular and ravishing abuse just about killed me. Even so, I realized much later of course, that my desire for the female, my very being as lesbian, was my spirituality; it not only was what made me alive, connecting me to a foundational goodness that preceded the abuse, but it saved my life. Being queer was about courage and honor, being faithful to the body, my body, in the midst of intense opposition.

Now, fast forward twenty-five years ahead. It is Easter week 1996. I have come out, almost completed graduate school with a doctorate in theology, and I find myself on the cusp of resolution. Indelibly marked by a lifetime vocation of struggling with learning how to live again in my body, in recognizing *my* lesbian, sexually abused body as God's first home, I begin to taste the possibility of real communion in another dream of body and God and salvation. Transported back into a reality that seems to float all around me, I find myself kneeling in front of a crucifix, both enormous in body and menacing in importance. No words passed between us, but the communication was profound and provocative. Slowly I rise, quietly, with intense focus, and reach out to touch the broken body. I grasp onto God's body, feeling the flesh respond to my grip, first pulling it off of that damnable cross. What comes next, however, I am not prepared for. Instead of the crucified body of God falling into my waiting arms, almost like the images I had seen, Pieta style, I begin to pull apart the flesh and with ravenous certainty, I begin to eat the flesh of God. I eat everything with a strange sense of exhilaration and release.

Looking back, I can see that it was then, as a thirty-something-year-old adult, I received for the first time a real holy communion with Christ. Now, defiant and defined by my own God-seeking bodily integrity, I knew God was to be found in flesh both broken and blessed. No longer belonging to a God up on the cross but needing to find God in my own body, I ingested and maybe even integrated God. I celebrated in carnal imagery a resurrected faith despite a tradition that proclaims allegiance to a God who only comes when you are good enough.

Like the other ways in which my female flesh was negated, so too my sexual identity as lesbian was uprooted and distorted by religious abuse and cultural insistence on exclusive permissibility of female flesh only in relation to maleness. Up against obsessive and obscene definitions and distortions of my flesh, both in terms of the physical sexual abuse and the religious abuse of my spirit, of who I was, I encountered the battle for my soul. My lesbian, survivor-self, whose possibility of salvation hinged on flesh, both fucked-up and fucked-over by those who not only had moral authority within church and society, but physical power over me, lived an intensity of negation *and* reclamation. This very visceral fight for my spirit, the power and tenderness of God within me, constantly swirled in and through all the abuse of my body-self: the sexual abuse, the terrorism of the captivity of my lesbian-ness and its exquisite sexuality, even my God-consciousness itself.

My Catholic sensibilities, especially when living in a body deemed sinful, confirmed for me that God was a harsh judge, one for whom damnation was easy, which had nothing to do with fire, but everything to do with pain and fear. At the same time, my Catholicity also instructed me to NOT give up on God, perhaps a God I knew instinctively from within my mother's womb. A God who takes on, resides within human female flesh. I cannot explain this conundrum. I lived it constantly. The abuse was severe negation of anything remotely worthwhile within me while I still carried on a love affair with the maternal female all around me: my grandmother, rivers, new growth in spring, a night sky so black and dense it had to be full of presence, a reassurance of care in the universe. I found comfort in the way that winter made things die on the outside, yet could not, did not, remove all livingness from within them. I was like those trees who endured winter's scourge of death and loss. Those trees hinted at another version of reality and another possibility of a God-consciousness capable of restoring me to wholeness. This God-consciousness was deliciously female and fecund.

Waking with you
Is like Creation
All over again
When Life itself
Calls us by name
Seizing us
With its powerful embrace
And desire.
Mountain walls
Ocean floor
Canyons
Carved by ancient rivers
All come together
In that split second
When my body

Remembers
How exquisitely
Morning
Lays you next to me.

This is what I call my Catholic sacramental imagination, shaped and seared by my lesbian-spirit and my survivor-body-self. My livingness in both the abuse and the profundity of the female became for me an iron-clad grasp latching onto whatever could save my life at the moment, when almost everything else seemed insurmountably arrayed against me, or even the remotest possibility of what "me" could mean. This struggle for value and power, my viscous appropriation of salvation, was my initiation into a Catholic sensibility of the sacraments, the Real Presence of the divine. My imagination, driven as it was by such intense need, cherished any visible sign of God's full and immediate presence, one that did not deny the abuse but could defy its hold on me.

Perhaps what I lived during most of my young adult life was a spiritual work-out regimen of this Catholic sacramental imagination in response to my visceral need to live *somative dissonance*. Like cognitive dissonance, my flesh knew opposing or contradictory realities simultaneously. As is true of many childhood abuse survivors, my religious sensibility developed in conversation with my experience of being female, that swirled around never being quite good enough, to the more extreme experience of being rapeable, while it was also constituted by my desire for and delight in the female body. Now plant this experiential chaos in a Catholic church that is quite practiced at heightened negativity and abuse reserved especially for the female body, unforgettably theologized as "gateway of the devil," or better yet: simply "deserving death," since even the Son of God had to die.[1]

How about those saintly myths of Dymphna and Maria Goretti? What do we do with these patron saints of incest and rape victims? Of course, both die horrible deaths after we learn that it is better to die than to be "impure." Apparently our virginity was more important than our lives. How do I emulate this loss of life? As someone who could never again be "pure," I saw in ornamental myth what that

[1]This language comes from Tertullian's writing, *The Appearance of Women* and is representative of early Church theology that associates the female with sin, corruption, and sexual pollution. This legacy of Christian misogyny delineates girl-bodies specifically as damnable, which constructs a powerful facet of being rapeable.

meant and how I was supposed to become practiced in forgiving those men who just couldn't help themselves. Why would a church give these myths to young girls if not to reinforce how most of us will never measure up? Cynically, I wondered why we never learned stories of the Church Fathers learning to forgive *their* rapist.

I am a living laboratory of how human physicality is crucial in what and how we know God. My God-consciousness was wrapped around terrible threads of abuse and a deeply buried desire for women's bodies. Consequently, in an effort to coexist with this *somative dissonance*, I remained at times content to live without full access to my body-self, all the while, hungering for wholeness. This visceral battle is where God remains: thoroughly Catholic, complicated, embodied, sensual, and connected across a wide expanse of my own sexual hunger and healing.

This transgressive character of questioning and needing God from an abused body-self who hungered for the female, while what was most distinctively female within my own flesh was wrenched from me, posits a terrifying dissonance not just within me, but within our society and possibly within God itself or at least our understandings of God. My identity as Catholic is most contested by, in, and through my *cunt,* apex of desire and damnation. Yet it is the location of my most exquisite God-consciousness. Embracing my *cunt* is no easy feat in a tradition that assigns sin, actually the entire downfall of the whole of humanity, to the very first female and heralds the Virgin/Mother as emblematic femininity most worthy of salvation. Being queer and Catholic with a *cunt* is an exploration of negation in a tradition that worships the power and presence of the phallus. Being queer and Catholic with a *cunt* is also an invitation into possibility in a tradition that imagined the Christ, the chosen one of God as beginning in female flesh, divine gestation within a woman's body. My experience of the human meeting the divine continues in and through the female body, womanly flesh so exquisitely capable of connection and ecstasy. My arduous life's work as a female survivor reassembling my body-as-a-self, only to have homo-hatred and hetero-righteousness erase the possibility of integration, functions as a corrective to heretical formulations of both body and God in church and society. I have fought too hard for both God and my body, in my own refuting of heresy, to listen to the hetero-normative censoring of my self/spirit in my deepest desire that began in female flesh and seeks home in its folds.

Orthodox Easter
Easter was exquisite . . .
Seeing L dance with the gifts
Her body moving with the gifts,
Preparing the altar,
One with the gifts.
Knowing I made love to and with that body
Heard its cry of pleasure
Felt its wet release of passion
Remembering her hands wrapped
'round my body
my thighs
inside me
praising God
awaiting and hungry for
Eucharist
Celebrating the Risen body of Christ.

Growing up in a religious tradition that focused regularly on a body broken and blessed carried the unique importance of bodies. To see visual depictions of brokenness in God's body as somehow blessed, however, never actually comforted me or suggested salvation. I rejected simplistic understandings of suffering as necessary or good; it certainly was not blessed. For me, the godding power of this Catholic mystery was not in the suffering or in the obedience of Jesus on the cross but in *the body itself.* Human flesh, tortured and abused in the crucified body of Jesus became whole, capable of saving power that had cosmic implications. This metaphor clung to me in my child-like grasp of sacramental imagination. To hold onto this power of Incarnation involved my assent to the power of flesh being transformed into saving power within all of creation. What was deemed deicide—the destruction and the murder of the divine—did *not* destroy God in that flesh. Here was a Catholic imaginary that made sense. If God could hold onto the value of desecrated flesh in Jesus, could not God also hold onto its value in my own experience of bodily deicide? If this flesh could be sanctified, how much more possibility existed then in my sexual desire to find myself reflected in another female body, glistening in feminine generative power? What I began to see in and through my Catholic sacramental imagination was that the divine power of Incarnation doesn't save us from death, prevent disease, or protect us from the cost of living in flesh; it simply sanctifies—makes holy—all aspects of our bodies. Nothing is left out of the circle of sanctity even when polluted in the pathos of violation.

Odd as it may sound my Catholic heritage allowed me to pose what I now see as the power of cunt in creation.[2] Sex is meant to be redemptive. My capacity to be deeply affected by others was a given, especially in and through the abuse where I learned its intensity with utter clarity. This same capacity is also at work in my celebrations of lesbian lovemaking. My capacity to know and to give pleasure is a miracle given the early socialization I encountered, especially in terms of its foundational formation in pain.

I have learned to want
Fiercely and without compromise
Always ready to fight
So used to knowing
Shame
Between my legs . . .
Now, I listen with new receptivity
When you name
My cunt
Courageous.
Startled by the strength of that word
I long to wrap myself
Around your curves
Looking for the little windows
Where I see your soul

---

[2]The power of *cunt* in creation comes from an ancient recognition of the yoni, divine female powers of creation, a primal force of generating new life. In terms of how I understand it, I celebrate my own *cunt* as a site of powerful connection and community in precisely the place that was ravaged by acts of abuse. This capacity is salvific for me and for those I have loved. It is godly and profoundly representative of what I see celebrated in the Eucharistic celebration of flesh that is broken *and* blessed. God animates the flesh, all flesh, again and again, as capable of carrying God's own presence and power. Like Incarnation that is constantly occurring in our midst, so too Resurrection. God raises up flesh, all flesh in and through the Resurrected flesh of Jesus of Nazareth.

Playing
Hide 'n seek.
I rejoice in knowing
I no longer hide
Only seek.

The bodily knowledge I gained in my survival also gave me insight into other religious truths. For instance, knowing early on what abuse felt like, and therefore, always having reason to disassociate from my body-self, my only home, I am now able to recognize this same body-denying reality in my Catholic tradition when it pontificates about "intrinsic disorder," "moral depravity," and other homo-hating language of closets and celibacy, all disguised as God's will. This language does the same thing to my body, i.e., it functions the same way that the sexual abuse did; it suggests that my body cannot know God if constituted and expressed as queer with a *cunt*. It designates my bodily realities of flesh as evil, or to use my earlier language, *not-God* and even *God-gone-wrong*.

My learning about the holy in and through my body, both within its negation in abuse and through its affirmation in lesbian *lovemaking,* takes me far beyond contemporary discussions about sexual abuse or sexual orientation. My bodily insights insist upon the integration of sexuality as the human response to godding. In this understanding of the Incarnation, sexuality is the first and perhaps most primary, albeit forgotten, sacrament in which we see the true universal call to holiness. All of creation exists in and for God, called to embrace an ecstatic sensibility that recognizes the entire universe as part of union with God, a communion, a Cumming-into-union succinctly and sweetly in orgasmic knowing and loving of self and another. In this way, I can recognize that my Catholic sensibility has taught me to never renounce the claim of flesh as my hinge of salvation.

Worship
If I could, I would fuck
You into being.
To retell again and again
The miracle of incarnation
Where God opens her lusty
Languorous thighs

And asks me,
No, tells me:
Take this and eat.
This is my body
Blessed for you.
Always, Do this
In memory of me.

Being lesbian is a way to be faithful to the body, to embrace the integrity of self amidst constant slander. Living fully into my lesbian self is a way to honor God and demonstrate the courage of what Jesus may have known in the crucifixion, when powers of the established society, especially its religious edifice, were arrayed against who he was and how he lived. Given this, my own bodily history of damnation and reclamation refuses to negotiate access to the divine, the power of godding, with an abusive lover, even when it is the church.

In some ways, I see myself as constituted by two primal occasions of theft: the first is the robbery of my bodily sanctity through the sexual abuse and the other robbery occurs in the rape of my spirit by a church that defines my lesbian loving as evil, contrary to godding. These losses revolve around an institutional and societal inability to fully embrace our bodily life as part of the divine design and delight within creation itself, signified most emphatically in and through the Incarnation. Instead of upholding the full implications of an Incarnating God within our Catholic religious traditions, we inherit a profound negation of sexuality in exchange for an obsessive focus on proper use of genitals in procreation resulting in relinquishment of our claim to redemption in and through the body. Yet the body remains a privileged site of experiencing, knowing, and loving God. We see vestiges of this played out endlessly in daily embodied rituals of baptism, confirmation, and Eucharist. A Catholic faith has always been all about the body, our bodies and that of the body of Christ seeking union with all that lives in God.

Lay me down
To worship
At the altar of your body
Where flesh calls God home
In cries of recognition

When my hands
Meet the sea of your desire
I drink deeply
With a furious need
I long to meet
With a tongue
On fire
Speaking/sparking/burning
In hot
Pursuit of God
Completely alive
In you
Christ-in-cunt.

Perhaps my Catholic sacramental imagination taught me how to embrace or to embody God differently, and specifically as a female, lesbian, abuse survivor because God cannot become body without me. Perhaps it taught me in cauterizing ways that heresies of flesh are the most punitive kind and most in need of truthful interrogation.

Every time I encounter power and pleasure in my *cunt* when relating well to another, I experience flesh as the hinge of salvation; this is the godding power of a body broken and blessed, not damnable nor depraved.

Joy
Hands thick with passion
Playing Music with flesh
Sweet sounds of recognition
So unlike the hands that pummeled
Into an oblivion
Darker than terror.
Your hands pressing into me,
Asking me to sing upon your fingertips
Ripe with song of unspoken
And perhaps unspeakable melodies.
Sliced open, pried apart
My legs scream with searing vengeance
Because I still remember
The sound

Of a crushed cunt
Throbbing around
Narrow places
Of oblivion
Chained
Forever chained to
First memory
Of
Hands
Holding me in hate.

Both the abuse and my gift of survival as lesbian are planted deep in my God-consciousness that is Catholic to the core. I make no apologies for who I am nor do I accept any religious definition of my flesh as less than godly. I know that the space between my legs is a portal for the divine because of how it was violated and therefore vacated by what was godly. This denial in my body was truly ungodly. Although horrific in its negation, the underlying dynamic relationship I discovered between the divine and my flesh became my own resurrection into the possibility of flesh as divine habitation.

My blessing of being Catholic and Queer with a cunt has taught me that God, and therefore godding, exist only in relationship to bodily life. For me, this means posing lesbian lovemaking as part of the divine life. I can do no other. God's girl ardor needs me. So, the last poem is for God:

This night
In pursuit
Of a shooting star
I wish
Your fingers
Would
Find me
Beautiful.

ANGELS

Sacramentals

Wesley A. Russell

I wasn't Rusty, I was Wessie, sissie Wessie. Mommie was a drunk who cuddled her little Wessie, Wessie who luckily at age six weeks despite mommie's reluctance to yield her little guy now blue to Ross General Hospital to be revived and be the first successful recipient of latest surgical techniques, otherwise would be hard blue and cold for long times remembered, which influenced her drunken cuddliness.

I hear them, my dad my Mommie's hairy ape, next room, slight spank sound now and then.

I squeeze daddy's neck between my legs piggy want more squeeze say daddy piggy back, no more you can swim the eel now, no more squeeze neck good hard thing there.

Jungle Jim metal smell rubbing on nose, tight legs around shaft, urging groin to give feeling. Give me the feeling. Even stop signs downtown Mill Valley Mommie say Wessie get down, that brings danger and smell metal tight legs good feeling comes while hear come down what are you doing up there.

They talk queer sissies Powell Street San Francisco seeing guy walk funny down Blithedale from kitchenette window.

Daddy big guy prestige, bad heart, good-hearted, loved me, never criticized, dead, me thirteen. School, work, work, home, over, over, in cocoon all teen, introvert, love Catholic ritual think priest no marriage.

In bedroom my *Leaves of Grass,* Mommie say she knows why book in room, nude drawings in Leaves, where are your hands, doesn't know I get it from Jungle Jims and my bunk bed post don't need hands. Walt my new father.

I go Powell from Market to Bay to Union Square to rest tired after walking hours, feel eyes on me get red ears don't sit walk out fast but see guy's eyes meet mine then down to Market to inside store window he says parents out of town want to come home with me, yes, we ride Muni, we suck fuck all parts eat each other all night listen to B Minor Mass propped up with pillows next morning, I think he love me, go home, move out, go to Berkeley, he say naive, but together three months fuck suck cruise he bash my ignorance, make me grow, hurts, leaves me.

I go army all sex and work find myself better than most for me. Think I'm okay now. Revel in those service guys in Hawaii, Tokyo, guys grab say you no go, you stay, but I go. Fall into upstairs immaculate bunkhouse all men all nights heaven, jerked out to Korea, more of same. Better.

Home, buddy knows Cynthia and Willie and McGinnes at Black Cat and dancer on tables push together live with them on Natoma me work in financial, McGinnes stabs Willie blood on porch 532A Natoma, mamma owns, son dead, artist, personality turns into dead son, she wild, all wild, Black Cat, North Beach, Strand, Key System, Greyhound Depot, Bare Ass Beach, Chris.

No return love me mad jealous spying, crying, trying to get it not getting it. Chris laugh nice, white teeth hate him, has lovely, quiet friend fantasy, Chris out. Go to Cat, lovely, quiet friend grabs me we ride car after drop all off he tells his boyfriend you get off next we talk till dawn, no jealousy, no monogamy, argue religion he fundamentalist. Beautiful fantasy friend Richard of Chris good Chris got me him. (We together forty-eight years he die fast fifteen days sick die Dec 11 '01.)

Long years we assimilators, sibling's children our fun, Sierras, backpacking, antiwar 1960s, no hippie, no drugs, no enlightenment but each other center universe all time no doubt, no fear, no jealousy, always there, real, can't explain good fortune no way deserve.

See mud men naked hands joined front page Radical Faerie call for gathering Malibu Thanksgiving 1987 fast on Thanksgiving, whole hog radical faeries suddenly, comes some enlightenment, out to work, out to family, sister goes crazy, her children and friends oh you naive Janet not know Wes and Dick lovers all life what matter you, not know, not feel, now okay.

See guy on ground front of barn Wolf Creek, Jesus face, join him folding and stretching and sitting and roll onto Bee, sting, we go get mud, smear each other, go to circle, picture of us, write my name in notebook, picture in my copy book, compare to Whitman I know not why, I think appearance sometimes then feel soul and body being same, remember this long time, reminder over years, see him, I with my lover on Valencia or Guerrero or? selling stuff apartment sale he moving maybe going out of country no remember, hug, look in eyes.

He give me poems, one about the bee. I read it and cry, say hope he write forever, do it, they must read you those stud muffins you be their Leaves.

He Wore a Yellow Tulip

Excerpted from the novel
Now Is the Hour
Tom Spanbauer

It all makes sense when you think about it, and God knows I've thought about it. Sex is the reason why I'm out here alone on Highway 93.

Sex and my family just don't mix, like Mormons and Coca-Cola, like me and Joe Scardino, like good Catholic white folk and Indians and niggers, no way. No matter how you look at it, it's just plain weird. God on one side, and sex and Lucifer on the other. My family and the sex-shame-guilt thing.

Myself, I've always found sex with people more than a little confusing. It's a brave thing to have sex, to let someone get that close to you.

For the longest time I was afraid of my own shadow, let alone another human body with a heart. So much fear and ignorance to overcome. At fourteen I was a long way off from overcoming anything, and I'm still not so sure about the progress I've made. Back then, sex with myself was confusing enough. I knew it was wrong, I mean, my parents thought it was wrong. But honestly, it was as close to God as I'd ever felt and that was my salvation and my downfall.

My salvation and my downfall started one day after school. Mom was in her same old, red housedress in the kitchen, her back to me, her hair pin curls in a hairnet, Mom bent over some bowl like she always

---

was, stirring. This day it was oatmeal cookies, and the kitchen smelled good.

After milk and cookies, after I drove up to the feedlot and smoked one of Dad's Viceroys and listened to the top-ten countdown, I busted open the twenty-five bales of hay. I rolled the windows down and, driving back to the yard, I turned the radio up real loud and sang,

Hello, darkness, my old friend with Simon and Garfunkel and Tramp. Tramp got that look in his eyes, and his tongue went out, and he was smiling. His paw poking, poking at the air.

I carried the five-gallon bucket of water from the house and slopped the hogs and fed the chickens and gathered the eggs. It was about five o'clock. My chores were done, and the sun was still up. I was leaning up against the barn, in the sun, my bare ass against the warm red wood of the barn. I was slowly pulling on myself, feeling the deep grace of the earth and manure I was standing on coming up through me. I was just about ready, my breath was coming hard, when out of the blue, the latch on the back barn door turned, then the squeak of the hinges of the back door, then the door was open, and there she was standing right there next to me in her red housedress, her plucked eyebrows, her pin curls and hairnet, the little lines around her starting around her mouth, her almond-shaped hazel eyes looking down at me down there red and wet and poking up, my mother.

Faster than you could say "mortal sin," Mom had closed the barn door, and there I stood with my pants down around my ankles, leaning up against the barn, cock dripping one long strand of cum down onto the dry cow manure. Just me and Tramp and the trapdoor to the underworld flung open inside my heart. I couldn't move. Really, I am not exaggerating. I just fell over, didn't try to catch myself or nothing, just like a Road Runner cartoon. One moment I was in one position standing up, the next I was in the same position lying down.

The time between when Mom caught me and supper at six o'clock was an eternity. Everybody says *eternity* like it's just another word, but that day, that hour, was an eternity, something that was never going to end, and I didn't want it to end, because the end meant I had to walk in the house and stand inside my mother's almond-shaped hazel eyes. All I wanted to do was smoke and smoke and smoke, but Dad's cigarettes were in the house, on the refrigerator, plus he would miss the cigarettes if I took more than one.

Tramp, I said, Tramp, we're in big trouble.

Tramp's orange face on his black face, his tongue went to hanging out.

Tramp, I said, what am I going to do?

Tramp got that look in his eyes.

What in the hell am I going to do?

Tramp's paw went up, poking, poking the air.

I should have started hitchhiking right then. But I wasn't ready yet. It took almost three more years before I was ready for the road.

Walking to the house from the barn, my shadow on the ground around my feet was the black hole I was walking in. All I could hear was my breath. My hand on the screen door pulled the screen door open. My hand around the doorknob turned the knob. My feet stomped off on the square of grating on the floor just inside the porch.

The hallway light was off. Mom was a tall shadow standing in shadows. Her hair was fluffed out. The feeling I get in my arms that means I am helpless. I couldn't see Mom's eyes when I looked, but still I looked away from her eyes.

She said: Change into your school clothes right after supper. We're making a *special trip* to town. Monsignor Cody was kind enough to hear your confession. The man is a saint. And a busy man, Rigby John, and he is taking extra time for you. Hurry up, we have to be at the church by seven-fifteen.

At supper, when my voice said the blessing, I sounded like a Beatles album played backward. Only the scrape of forks against the hard plastic plates with the flower gardens on them. Mom's mouth got more and more and more puckered as we ate. I looked over to Sis. Sis didn't know yet. If Sis knew, she'd have had her smirk on under her bland supper expression, and there was no smirk. Dad was scowling down at his plate, just eating his spuds like the grunting, gruff old bastard he was. Tore off a piece of Wonder Bread, sopped up the gravy. But I wasn't sure if Dad was the regular grunting, gruff old bastard, or the nightmare bastard who came out only in the saddle room when he whipped my ass.

Just before we left the house, when Mom was getting her purse, Sis walked by me with her big dark Roosky eyes. No doubt about it, she had the smirk.

Going to the chapel, and we're going to get married, Sis sang.

Outside the Buick windows, the sun was pink on the cottonwoods on Philbin Road. In the fields, still patches of snow, ice-smooth and shiny, the same pink as the sun. The red speedometer was on eighty. Usually it was sixty-five, maybe seventy, but this March evening Mom's high heel had got the pedal to the floor. Speed, more of what was left unsaid. Mom stared straight ahead, her red lips, her warrior paint, a gash across her face. Stiff-armed, she drove. White knuckles. The sound of her legs, the rub of nylon to nylon. The heater, blasting warm air on defrost. In the air, her smell, from the dark blue bottle, her sister Alma's Evening in Paris.

My body was on the vinyl seat, in its Sunday jacket, its white short-sleeve shirt, its black oxford shoes, white socks, its Catholic school corduroy pants. But I was not in my body in my clothes. I was in the breath in my ears, out on the hood of the Buick, standing on the edge of eighty, my mother's almond-shaped hazel eyes staring at my slope of bare butt, my naked back and arms, hands clasped around my cock, a hood ornament going at it.

Twelve miles can be forever.

Eternity eternity eternity.

On the playground, Mom parked the Buick right next to the incinerator, where the guide wire of the light pole went into the pavement.

You know why I've brought you here, Mom said.

You have committed a mortal sin, and I've brought you here to confess, she said.

You must confess to the Monsignor your mortal sin and any other sins which you have committed. You must tell Monsignor everything, she said. Every detail to be sure your sin is forgiven.

Cold wind blew up the corners of Mom's tweed coat. The wind blew against my ears. The tree branches were no longer pink, only gray and darker than gray, black finger shadows that flipped against one another in the wind.

OK, I said.

The brass doorknob of the church was cold on the palm of my hand. I pulled on the door. Mom held her hand out flat against the wood of the door. Her fingers spread, fingernails cut to the quick, her rough, red farm hands stopped the door. Her red leaching lips.

Rigby John, my mother said. You must tell the Monsignor *everything.*

My Adam's apple stuck on the top of the zipper of my jacket. The breath inside there in my throat.

Even the dog, my mother said.

The dog? I said.

You were with the dog, my mother said.

Tramp? I said.

Rigby John, my mother said, you must confess every detail.

The feeling in my forearms that meant I was helpless. Inside the church, the deep wood smell, Catholic incense, beeswax. I put my fingers into the holy water font, made the sign of the cross. Past the choir stairs, on the left, the confessional. The little red light bulb above the middle door was on.

The Monsignor was in.

I genuflected. My corduroy pants made the corduroy bending sound. I made the sign of the cross again, knelt down in the second pew. The holy light of the stained-glass windows all over me on my hands and face. I was saturated. My mother knelt in the pew behind me. My cock a tiny burning piece of shame. My body the ugly casket for my smashed-flat roadkill soul.

The confessional door closed behind me. When I knelt down I heard the red light bulb outside my door click on. Hot inside the dark. Sweat drips going down the insides of my arms. Down to my elbows. I unzipped my jacket, unzipped the zipper all the way down, pulled the wool collar away from my neck. I quick put my hands in my jacket pockets, tried to get some air moving by flapping my hands.

My throat. The air stuck inside there. My right hand, fingertips, to my forehead, my chest, to my left shoulder, my right shoulder. Then my hands folded together, fingers pointed up to God, my elbows on the little ledge below the screened panel.

Bless me, Father, for I have sinned, I said. My last confession was four days ago. These are my sins.

The sunlight on the wood of the barn. It was warm there in that spot without the wind. The red paint was peeling off in places, and the gray raw wood was sticking through. The sky was bright blue, only one little putt of clouds up there. The cement platform at the back door of the barn was ground down to round curves of light gray cement with chunks of tiny rock. Manure all over on the platform. Dry manure becoming earth, rich earth, the shit smell of cows and milk and hay and bales of straw. The siding of the barn, little horizontal waves. My hand against the waves of red wood, raw gray poking through. Sun on the wood, the blue sky, the cloud, the dry manure—all these things were things outside me, yet by some miracle also deep within. Like the day was a movie connected to the place just under my balls.

I wanted to fuck the barn, fuck the manure-rich earth smell coming up in the patch of sun. The sun warm there, so warm against the red peeling wood, that place, so safe, protected from the wind. My hand on my Levi's button was heavy and deep too, everything deep and full and heavy, the pop pop pop pop of the rest of the five Levi's buttons. I was still sore and wet from the last time and I was still hard, hard and full and heavy. The palm of my hand just touching my belly, the hair of me down there, then cupping my balls, underneath, the dark, smelly crack. Just pulling down my shorts I almost came. Then my ass, my bare ass cool outside, exposed. Why did the wind suddenly find me there? The hairs on my ass stood up with goose flesh. Soft ass flesh against sun wood. How warm the red peeling waves. Big old horny red barn flirting with my ass.

Oh. Just the tip of my cock, underneath the fold of skin. Grab it there and pinch. The sun is bright and bright, and the little putt of cloud. The slide of my ass up and down on the wood, the so soft and all open of me down there. The first sharp roll of ejaculation, not a shoot-out this time, just a slow roll, the slow out of the end of so red piss slit one long drool down. My tongue loves so much my lips. My knees come unhinged, and for a moment, there is nothing. And nothing is full and round, everything round and round and round and full and deep and hard and soft and heavy and safe and warm and wet, in the sun, pressed against the red wood barn, under the bright blue sky, protected from the wind, just the cloud, the putt of cloud, up high up there floating away eternity eternity.

For I have sinned exceedingly.

My jacket was all the way off, on the floor, the wool as far away from me as I could get. My T-shirt and my white shirt were soaked through. My sweat smelled like my cum, the way my ass smells.

I committed the sin of self-abuse, I said.

Out of the dark, on the other side of the screen, the outline of Monsignor's hooked nose.

Tell me, my son, what are your thoughts while you touch yourself?

You could hear my sweat dripping.

Lewd thoughts, Father.

How are they lewd, my son?

Monsignor's ear pressed up against the screen.

Lewd and dark and smooth, hot, red, wet flesh, hairy, sticky. Where was there air?

They're just awful, Father. They're I don't know how to say.

Are your thoughts of men or women?

My open palm against horseflesh smooth along the withers. Cows eating raw potatoes. The slice of a shovel into wet sod. Water running thin over gravel. Sunlight on the water.

They're of everything, Father.

Everything?

Yes, Father.

Even the dog? Do you have sex with the dog?

Monsignor's hand up to his mouth, then just his index finger against his lips. On the ledge my elbows were wet. The ledge was a puddle. I was turning into a puddle.

No, Father.

But your mother said you were with the dog.

Mother said. How could she say? What words?

The dog was only watching, Father, I said. He wasn't doing anything.

Then out of the blue, I just had to say it. Blurted it out the way I always do:

Tramp is not that kind of dog, I said.

After my Act of Contrition, after I left the confessional and knelt down in the pew and said my five Our Fathers and five Hail Marys and five Glory Be's, I heard Mom get up from the pew behind me. I thought for sure we were going to be kneeling in church all night praying litanies for my soul, so I was surprised when Mom got up so quick.

Then at the Wyz Way Market, parked outside in the Buick listening to KWIK while Mom bought groceries, I realized something. Mom got out of church so fast because she didn't want to see the Monsignor, let alone talk to him.

A couple things about the ride home. A little thing and a big thing.

The little thing was that Mom bought me a candy bar, a Snickers, my favorite, without me asking for one.

The big thing was what she said when we were halfway home. Mom had just stopped at the stop sign on the corner of Philbin Road and Quinn Road. There were no cars coming from any direction in the dark night. The headlights of the Buick pressed against the dark, against the rough bark of the big cottonwoods that line the road there. A gust of Idaho wind blew so hard, the Buick lifted up off its springs. The heater was blowing warm air up the legs of my pants.

Mom kept her foot on the brake. Behind us, in my mind, I saw the brake lights glow out red in all the dark. The dash lights were amber and green and gold on my mother's face. Behind her glasses, her almond-shaped hazel eyes were still not looking at me. Evening in Paris.

Perry Como was singing "Faraway Places."

Rigby John, Mom said, there's only one solution. You and I are going to make a novena to Our Mother of Perpetual Help. Nine Tuesday nights in a row. Starting next Tuesday.

All our prayers will be answered, Mom said. All our sins forgiven. If only we pray to the Virgin.

The next day, after school, Dad's black eyes looked at the terrible place inside me that had hurt my mother.

Dad said, Your mom says you need a whipping.

Dad said, I'll be in the saddle room. You know what to do.

What to do was wait for him to get to the saddle room, unlock it, turn the light on, pull his squat three-legged stool out from under the workbench, and set it directly under the light bulb hanging down, then sit down on it.

The walk to the barn was long, the same long as whenever I was getting a whipping. My ass could already feel the welts the belt was going to raise. But the welts weren't the worst part. In a way I liked the welts because that meant the worst part was over. The worst part was the two knocks on the saddle room door. The worst part was opening the door. The worst part was behind my eyes what happened when I saw my father on his squat three-legged stool, the light bulb hanging down directly above him, the shadow of him a dark pool on the cement floor.

The pattern in the wood of the saddle room door was a swirl of universe, a red, rough swirl of wood, years and years of a tree growing. My hand was a fist. I looked over, and my hand was a fist up in the air in front of my head.

Knock knock.

Who's there?

Daddy.

Daddy who?

Daddy under the light bulb on the squat chair. Shadow Daddy. *Inner Sanctum.*

Eternity eternity eternity.

From behind the door, Dad said, Go ahead and come on in.

My palm flat up against the wood of the painted red door, I pushed.

He said, Close the door.

I closed the door.

Dad said, Now lock it.

I pulled the dead bolt into its socket, then pulled the dead bolt down.

Like always, Dad's butt cheeks went side to side on his squat chair. He put his right foot out. His foot dragged along the cement. Then his other foot dragged until both feet were square in front of him, knees perpendicular to the cement floor.

Dad said, Pull your pants down and your undershorts.

My fingers went to my first Levi's button and undid it. Then the second button. When I was on the third button, I stopped.

Something like a burp, a large lump of words, jumped right up out of my chest. My mouth was already moving before I knew what I was going to say.

Did Mom tell you what the whipping's for? I said.

Both Dad and I looked around the room to see where the strange voice had come from. He seemed smaller for a moment, only a man sitting on a squat stool. When he spoke again, he was back to proportion, which was way out of proportion. My father took up the whole saddle room.

Dad said, No. And she don't need to. Now, do as you're told.

I undid the third button, the fourth, the fifth. Hooked my thumbs onto the sides of my Levi's, slid them down. I pulled my jockey shorts down.

Air all around where I usually didn't feel air.

The look in Dad's Roosky Gypsy eyes when he saw me naked down there. Dad jumped up so quick like a cattle prod jumped him up. His eyes, then his whole face, turned away, taking the rest of his body with him.

What in the hell!? Dad said.

I looked down, and there I was, my cock poking straight out.

Get me half-naked, and it'll happen every time.

My teeth in my mouth grinding.

Pull your damn pants up! Dad said. Cover yourself, for chrissakes! And get the hell out of here!

The next nine weeks happen like one long bad dream. Tuesday nights, on one side of me out the Buick's window, the twelve miles into town flew by at eighty miles an hour. On the other side, my mother was in one of her Joan Crawford church hats, the ripple going up and down her jaw. Things could not have been worse.

But then there's the universe. This time what the universe conspired was Sister Barbara Ann's altar boy contest and Monsignor Cody's baseball game.

The contest was to see which altar boy could get the most points by the end of the school year. Five points for showing up on time. Five points for not making a mistake. Minus ten points for not showing up. Plus ten points for substituting.

The baseball game came out of nowhere. Sunday morning from the pulpit, Monsignor Cody just up and says there's nothing like a good baseball game to get the religious spirit flowing and let's beat Saint Anthony's.

Mom's novena, Sister Barbara Ann's contest, Monsignor Cody's baseball game. They all came together and fucked me up in a very particular way.

Tuesday night was the night of Our Mother of Perpetual Help devotions.

Tuesday night was the night for baseball practice.

Tuesday night no boys showed up to serve Our Mother of Perpetual Help devotions. Except for me, which means I had to substitute for the three altar boys who were at baseball practice.

Which means I would win the altar boy contest. But winning the altar boy contest wasn't winning. I never was like anybody else, and during those nine weeks of the novena, I was never more not like anybody else than ever. Of course, then with what happened later on,

Scardino and "Casey at the Bat" and all, I was in serious deep shit.

And, if I didn't know what was coming, Scardino would remind me. Every Wednesday morning, after Sister Barbara Ann announced the score, Scardino flipped me the bird and moved his mouth real slow to say: *You fucking queer, you are a fucking dead man.*

One long bad dream.

Plus, what did you win? The winner of the altar boy contest got to be the winner, plus got a black glass-beaded rosary blessed by the Pope in the Vatican.

Tuesday, Irving Field, just three blocks away from Saint Joe's, boys ran the bases, hit high pop flies, hit home runs, pitched, catched, boys ran around the baseball diamond having fun together, playing ball at baseball practice. Not me. In the candlelight of Saint Joe's I was kneeling in the congregation, praying for altar boys to show up. They never did. Monsignor entered the altar alone, stood there, and waited. For me he waited because he knew everything about me. In less than a minute, I was on the altar in my cassock and ironed and starched surplice kneeling next to the Monsignor. Mom was up in the choir loft on the organ, watching me.

When Monsignor Cody said: *I who am the most miserable of all*—that's when I got up and got the holy water font from inside Monsignor's sacristy. As Monsignor said the blessing, he shook the holy water font so the holy water splashed out into the congregation in drops.

If a drop of holy water fell on me, I thought maybe God was touching me. But if God was touching me, why wasn't I playing baseball instead of locked up in a church with a bunch of old people.

My next job was to go into the sacristy and start the charcoal for the incense.

Don't burn the damn church down.

Outside of confession, those were the only words Monsignor ever said to me. Not hi, hello, how are you, thanks for showing up, bless you, my son. Nothing. Just: When you light the charcoal, don't burn the damn church down.

When the charcoal was lit and the edges were turning white, I put the charcoal into the open censer with the black medieval pincers, then closed the censer, then took a deep breath and carried the censer and the burning incense onto the altar.

Me doing it, and Mom watching me do it. My whole life's been like that.

The big moment of Benediction was when Monsignor turns around with the gold, spaceship-looking monstrance in his hands and points the monstrance with God in it at the congregation. Mom started playing "Tantum Ergo Sacramentum." Miss Kasiska, Miss Radcliffe, and Miss Biddle all genuflected and made the sign of the cross. I sang too, and the censer was on the second step with the smoke coming out, and my hand was ringing, ringing the gold bells, never stopping the whole time, while Monsignor lifted the golden monstrance up through the sign of the cross.

And there we were, all of us, even God, inside the slanted mirror up in the choir loft, and Mom watching.

All the while Monsignor Cody was pointing God at us, every one of us, every human being one of us was praying, praying hard to God for things we wanted to have, or for things we don't want to have, for an old way to stop, or a new way to be, to not be sick, or not be old, or for special intentions, like my special intention, I mean my mother's special intention for me.

After devotions, the charcoal still burning in the censer, I opened the sacristy door, carried the censer outside and down the side stairs. Most nights it was pitch-black. When I got to the corner of the church, as soon as I stepped away from the church, the wind was cold, but I liked the cold wind because it had been so warm on the altar ringing the bells and looking at God. The wind blew my cassock and surplice, and I felt like Heathcliff in the olden days wearing those clothes, flutters of cloth, the sound of big skirts on women in the wind. This was the only good part of the night because in the dark, cold night, for a while there was no Mom, and only the stars were watching.

I didn't know where I was in all of this, or even if there was enough of me around to be something enough to make a difference. I was just putting one foot in front of the other. Trying to be a good Catholic son. I didn't see I had any choice, and I did care about being a good son, if only to keep my mother close. The rest of it I wasn't so sure about. But how could I say no to my parents, my teachers, my priest?

There were no words, no real options. What started it all, masturbating, the thing that they were telling me I did have a choice about, I couldn't seem to make the right choice. When that feeling came up in my balls, I didn't have a chance. Truth be told, I was worried about my soul. I didn't want to hurt Jesus with my sin, and I didn't want to go to hell either. Even Hemingway said it. What was immoral was what made you feel bad after. And after jerking off, I felt like shit. But it could be an hour, and there I'd go again.

What I did have a choice about happened around the same time, and it is something I've been ashamed of ever since.

It all started one Saturday afternoon about the third week into the novena. I was out in the barn, and I looked up from where I was spreading out straw in the calf pen, and there was a kid my age standing there. The light was bright from the open barn door behind him, so he was only a silhouette. Then when I got close and I was looking at his face, his face was a face I'd seen a hundred times, but nothing registered. Then it was his pale eyes behind his crooked glasses with the white tape across the glasses in the middle.

There I was, just me with Puke Price.

I looked around. Only the chickens and the sick baby calf were looking.

Then it was weird. On a Saturday in the barn, alone without anybody else from school, Puke Price wasn't that bad.

Hey, Puke, I said. What you doing here?

Puke always wore his corduroy pants up too high on his waist. His shirt was tucked in, and right there around his waist it was a bulgy mess of shirttails, bunched-up pants, and his brown belt cinched tight.

Puke said: My name's Allen.

His shoulders went up a little, and his hands made fists.

I want you to call me by my name, he said. I don't call you names, he said. My name is Allen.

Puke's big breath of air went right up against my face and up my nose.

Fried bologna breath. The worst kind of breath. There's tuna breath, and Cheetos breath, and onion breath, and boiled broccoli breath, and each one of those breaths is bad. But the worst kind of breath is all four of them; tuna, Cheetos, onion breath, and boiled broccoli breath all in one and that's what I call fried bologna breath, and Puke had fried bologna breath real bad.

I said: Allen. Sure, I said, Allen. What are you doing here?

I liked that Allen smiled, but still I stepped back because I saw he was going to speak, and words and breath go together, and with Allen you had to be careful.

My dad's here, Allen said, shooting rock chucks. We'll be here all afternoon.

Allen was the one who suggested that we play Poison. How you play Poison is you get the most poisonous stuff and the worst awful things possible, and you pour them all together in one bucket.

The bucket was a gallon bucket of oil-base paint with about an inch of slimy red in the bottom. The weed killer was in the saddle room under the bench in a gray five-gallon bucket that said POISON on it. It was a white powder. The skinny piece of an old cedar shingle was what I used to stir the white into the red until it was pink. Next, the bucket went to the gas pump. Three seconds of gasoline into the bucket. Allen stirred the gasoline in with the pink. It smelled awful.

The creosote came from the vat where Dad was soaking railroad ties. Inside the bucket it was the color of dark blood. The rat poison from the toolshed. A white powder in a red and yellow can like Kraft Parmesan cheese. Holes in the top of the can so you can shake out the rat poison. Allen sprinkled the rat poison onto what was in the bucket. The Malathion and the DDT came from in the corner of the machine shop where the sugar beet planter was. Both the Malathion and the DDT were in quart-size brown bottles with screw-top lids. The ant spray and furniture polish were from under the kitchen sink. Allen and I held our noses, and Allen sprayed the ant spray into the bucket and I poured in the Olde English furniture polish. Bluing, Clorox, and ammonia from the closet in the washroom went in next. A scoop of phosphate from the Simplot's bag. Then drops of Mercurochrome, gentian violet, Merthiolate from the medicine cabinet. Strychnine, tiny pellets in a little blue bottle from in the saddle room, from inside the cabinet Dad kept under lock and kept the key above the saddle room door. I found that key when my dog Nikki died. Battery acid from a battery from the pile of dead batteries in the weeds next to the wood granary. Really slimy gray and white chicken poop. A dead baby chicken. A mother spider and her million babies in the web in the chicken coop window with the eisenglass. A can of Del Monte lima beans. Mush would have been good in there, or a fried-hard egg or a soft-boiled egg, but Mom was in the kitchen so we couldn't get to the mush or the eggs. A piece of Kotex with blood splotches on it from inside the big garbage burn barrel outside. Allen, not me, held the Kotex by one of the white flaps. One of my father's crusty socks.

I thought of asking Allen to puke into the whole mess, then thought better.

That's when Allen said, Let's piss in it.

Allen had a look. His upper lip curled up a little. Then, before I knew it, there he was, Allen Price's dick hanging out of the zipper under the bunched-up waist of his corduroys. His dick was really white, like the rest of him, and big. Well, not big. For Allen Price, big. I mean, you'd think he'd have a real tiny one. Then his white dick started peeing.

For a moment, I was a little amazed so I just watched the yellow pee from his dick dribble out and then up full force into what was in the bucket. I didn't know what to do. I just knew I couldn't let Puke Price get the best of me, so I undid my Levi's buttons and pulled my cock out.

My cock is a lot like me. It doesn't do what it's told right off. I have to wait. And there's no telling sometimes how long I have to wait, so I just wait.

Allen's dick quit peeing in spurts. He left it hanging out when he was done. That's when Allen's dick started getting bigger and bigger and pinker and poking out right at me.

What you doing, Price? I said.

Allen said: What you doing?

I followed Allen's pale eyes down to my own cock hanging out. It should have been no surprise, but it was a surprise. My cock was sticking straight out too. That's when Allen suggested we put another one of our body fluids into what was in the bucket, but the thought of that, the thought of jacking off with Puke Price into what was in the bucket, was just too gross, so I quick put my cock in my pants, turned around, and walked out of the barn, across the yard, and into the house. Allen zipped up right behind me. The screen door slammed.

Mom was in the kitchen, hair flying out, bent over some bowl. The kitchen smelled good.

Oatmeal cookies? I said.

Peanut butter, she said. Go wash your hands first.

After our peanut butter cookies and glasses of milk and before Allen went home with his dad, Allen and I crawled up the ladder to the granaries, then jumped down between the granaries into the secret place shaped like an hourglass.

I reached in my pocket and pulled out two Viceroys. Allen acted like it was every day that he and I smoked cigarettes. He leaned back against the corrugated-steel granary, inhaled, and didn't cough.

Out of the blue, Allen had a book in his hands. I don't know where the book came from, and I don't remember it before that moment when I was looking at it there in his hands.

It was a Nancy Drew mystery. *The Mystery of the Brass-bound Trunk.* Allen handed me the book.

Here, Rig, he said. Take a look at my book.

The book was blue-green and the regular size of a Nancy Drew mystery. It was usually in the upper right-hand corner of his desk at Saint Joseph's School. Allen always kept the book next to the ink-well, in the upper right-hand corner of his desk.

I read this one, I said. But it's the only one I've read.

I like the Bowery Boys better, I said.

Holding a cigarette for a long time in your mouth makes you cough. I was coughing. Allen took a drag on the Viceroy like he'd been smoking all his life.

Do you notice anything unusual about the book? he asked.

I turned the book around, flipped it over, patted my hand against the cover.

No, I said. It's just a Nancy Drew mystery book.

Allen pulled his legs in and sat like meditating Indians do. Then before I knew it, Allen raised his chin and was speaking right into my face. Cigarette smoke and fried bologna breath going up my nostrils.

If I told you a secret, Allen said, would you promise not to tell?

Something in his right cheek started twitching.

Sure, I said.

Promise? he said. I'll show you a secret, but you have to promise.

I sucked the smoke into my lungs, let the smoke stay inside for a while, then spit the smoke out at the same time I said: Promise.

Allen stubbed out his Viceroy onto the steel-plate floor.

Say the whole thing, Allen said.

What? I said.

Say: I promise I won't tell anyone your secret, Allen said.

A gust of wind blew up and into between the granaries. I stubbed my cigarette out, kept the filter, picked up Allen's, stubbed out his filter too.

I promise I won't tell anyone your secret, I said.

And that you won't call me Puke anymore, Allen said.

The filters went into my shirt pocket.

I won't call you Puke anymore, I said.

Promise, Allen said.

I promise I won't call you Puke anymore, I said.

Allen set the book on his crossed legs. He opened the book and turned the pages of the book, one by one, slowly, slowly.

Page forty-two, Allen said.

Allen opened the book for me to see.

The book had been hollowed out where the words had been on the pages. Only the borders of the pages where there were no words was left, and those pages were glued together. Inside in the secret carved-out hollow space of the book, there were three glass radio tubes. One short one and two long ones with skinny red parts in the filaments.

Allen's hands shook a little when he closed the book. What he said next, he said real slow.

Now remember, Rig, Allen said. You made a promise. You promised me you wouldn't tell.

There's one more thing the universe conspired on. Mom and I almost got ourselves killed by a naked man. It happened on the last of the nine Tuesdays. We were in the Buick on our way to church. It was raining. Rain like you never see in Idaho, coming down in buckets.

The swipe of the windshield wipers were back and forth, back and forth, fast as they could go, but still the wipers weren't fast enough. Soon as the wipers swiped, for a moment it was clear and you could see the road, but then, splash, it was just like we were driving underwater.

Outside my window, past the barrow pit, past the barbwire fences, the harrowed spring fields were expanses of dark brown dirt filled with shiny puddles of water. Rain splashing up on the puddles of water.

It was weird too because over there where the sun was setting it wasn't raining. Down low in the west the sky was blue, then yellow, then gold, then pink. Sun shining through all the rain coming down made each raindrop into a tiny ball of light.

There we were, Mom Klusener and Rigby John in our Buick Special speeding eighty miles an hour through a mystery shower of light and shiny rain. When we got to the cottonwoods on Philbin Road, the rain let up some, but the cottonwoods, just newly leafed out, had more of a surprise for us. The line of cottonwoods, big old grandpa trees, so big around three people with their arms out couldn't circle one, one grandpa after another after another alongside the road reaching up their big arms, lumpy, graceful, fifty feet and higher into the sky, the rain shiny-slick on the bark, the yellow-gold sunset light against the wet. Not just the trees. Everything was glowing. The yellow-gold light onto the Buick, the road in front of us, the fat drops slow falling through the air from the leaves of the cottonwoods, onto the road, onto the blue hood of the Buick, onto the windshield.

The glass of the windshield glowed, the angle of the wipers, inside the Buick even my hands were glowing yellow-gold. Mom's face, those little lines around her lips, the way she held her chin up and gritted her teeth, the light on Mom's face. Everything slowed down so slow, one long breath in and out. Mom's almond-shaped hazel eyes, one pitched south, the other east, and my eyes. My eyes looking into her eyes, that moment. Mom and I, we weren't us, and nothing was familiar. Mom and I were just there, alive and breathing in the rain and glowing light.

Just in time, Mom hit the brakes and cranked the steering wheel. Directly in front of us, the old gray '49 Ford was parked just barely off the road. All around my ears was a loud screech. My right hand held hard onto the armrest of the door. Both of Mom's arms were on the steering wheel. Her hair was flying up. We were spinning. The sun was gone, and it was gray, and outside the windows of the Buick the world was spinning. We spun around for a long time. At least while we were spinning, it was a long time. Now when I look back, I wish the spinning had lasted longer. God spins you around like that only once in a while.

The Buick stopped in the middle of the road, pointing toward town the way it was supposed to be pointing. The world was back in place, regular, the way it was supposed to be. My hand wouldn't let go of the armrest. Mom's hands were shaking so bad, she couldn't get her purse open. When she finally got it open, she pulled out her rosary. Her fingers went straight to the crucifix, then started down the beads.

But Mom wasn't praying. She was cussing a blue streak.

Her hand, her cut-to-the-quick nails, middle finger, index, and thumb, sliding the beads.

Goddamn. Son of a bitch. Asshole. Bastard.

All of them. She was saying all of the cuss words.

I was waiting for her to say *fuck* or *cunt* or *cocksucker,* but she didn't say any of those.

But she did say a word I'd never heard her say before.

To the man standing out in the harrowed field, under the cottonwoods. The driver of the'49 Ford. The man whose clothes hung out of the driver's side window. The naked man in the rain. My first time, my first naked man. The long smooth muscle of him, his hairy chest, his hairline down his belly to the dark brown-black between his legs. His brown and amber glow in the last spot of sunlight, his hands held up out in front of him, cupped. Just as I looked and before I quick looked away, that moment, a big fat drop of rain slow from a cottonwood leaf in the last light fell, the splash in his hands, crooked light.

Mom's fingers were on the bead of the first mystery of the rosary.

Goddamn Indians, Mom said. Drunken bunch of no-good bastards. A menace to society. Especially that son of a bitch George Serano.

Mom's left hand quick rolled down her window. She stuck her head out, red lipstick lips, mouth pointed up to sky.

Goddamn Indian! she screamed. Where'd you learn to drive!

I'm calling the sheriff! she screamed.

Injun George, you better get your pants on fast!

Disgusting goddamn drunk, Mom yelled.

And then she said it. The word I'd heard so many times before but never heard from her.

Queer, she said. You goddamn queer. Those Indians and their goddamn queers.

I heard this story about the Pope. When the Pope is blessing the crowd, the people up front right up close to the Pope are happy they're up close, but they're also dodging around, trying to get away from something. What they are trying to get away from is the shadow of the Pope's hand. If the shadow of the Pope's hand falls on you, it's a curse. Sooner or later, no matter what you do, your fear catches up to you.

The Wednesday morning I won the altar boy contest, and was given the black crystal rosary that was blessed by the Vatican, the shadow fell on me.

The sign of the cross and the morning prayer, Sister Barbara Ann pointed the black grease pen to the box in the ninth week that was next to my name.

Class, she said. Take a look. See who loves the Virgin the most.

The winner! Sister Barbara Ann says. Rigby John Klusener!

From out of her top drawer, Sister Barbara Ann took out a red velvet box. She held the red velvet box up so the whole class could see, then slow walked down the aisle holding up the red velvet box.

Blessed by the Vatican, Sister Barbara Ann said.

Inside the box it was white shiny cloth. The rosary was curled onto itself, a shiny, black, beaded snake, the silver crucifix on top of the folds.

Hold the rosary up for everyone to see, Sister Barbara Ann said.

I lifted the rosary up by its silver crucifix. The shadow of the black shiny beads fell onto my face, just between my eyes, down my throat, onto my shirt pocket just above my heart.

At recess, there was nowhere to go but into the boys' bathroom. All three of the stalls were full, so there was only the urinal. Allen Price stood next to me. Yellow pee coming out from between his fingers.

Scardino's miffed, Allen said. He's going to kick you in the balls again.

Fried bologna breath.

Allen's crooked eyeglasses. The piece of tape across the nose. That's when the boys' bathroom door slammed open. Allen's eyes were wide open green with gold flecks in the green. Ronald Wilson, Roger Waring, Ricky Divine, Tony Smith, Alvin Gosford, ran out of the boys' bathroom, rats from a sinking ship.

The toilet stalls on the one side of them, the sinks and the mirrors on the other side, Scardino and Breck and Muley stretched their legs out wide in one combat line across the room. Price and me were hemmed in. The boys' door behind Scardino, Breck, and Muley was our only escape.

Scardino's shoulders were back, his chin up, the grin on his face, one side of his upper lip up a little. His one tooth there that was sharp. Both his feet square beneath him.

At home in front of the mirror I'd practiced to stand like that. When I stood like that, I couldn't stand like that.

Scardino's white shirtsleeves were rolled up. His arms big biceps, smooth olive skin down his forearms, something scary how his forearms flowed down to his wrists, his big hands, knuckles big from popping. Usually some kind of ink tattoo on his arm or his wrist that Sister Barbara Ann made him wash off. His dark brown hair as long as he could get away with, wavy, combed back in a duck's ass. Brown eyes that behind something was always going on. The top button of his white shirt unbuttoned. Just down below his belt, somehow perfect how that part of him down there looked. His corduroy cuffs rolled up, white socks, black shiny wedgies.

In the mirror, the three of them lined up left to right: Scardino, Breck, Muley. Breck and Muley trying to look like Scardino. Chests out. Thumbs in their pockets. DA's. Then myself in the mirror. The cold sore I'd woke up with this morning was a big yellow pus scar across my lip. A head taller than anybody in the bathroom, skinny. My long, skinny arms and skinny legs. My neck poking up out of my shirt collar, guck, guck, silly goose. My stupid Adam's apple. My hair in a crewcut because it saved on haircuts.

Nowhere to run, nowhere to hide, just me trapped in a bathroom trapped in a body that couldn't even think of making a fist, let alone make a fist, a tall, gawky tantrum with nowhere to go, standing next to a body who was something even worse than I was. A true dork. The worst dork you could possibly get in the world. Allen Fucking Price.

Scardino stepped one step toward me. Scardino's lips said *queer,* said *syphilis lip.*

My feet were stepping backward. Somewhere behind me was the wall. Scardino threw all his weight into a John Wayne punch. I moved just enough so the punch wouldn't hit me in the face. Bam, square in the shoulder. I found the wall behind me, slid my back against the wall to the corner. The smell of mothballs from the little white beehive things you pee on, water running along the back side of the white urinal.

That was the moment, the end of the rope, cornered, the feeling in my forearms that meant I was helpless. Breathless. Shit out of luck.

A real man honors his promises no matter what, but I never have been a real man, at least not until recently. As ever, honor, when faced with Scardino and his gang, turned into a shit bird and flew out the window. I just didn't know what the hell else to do. So I said it.

I said, Leave me alone, and I'll tell you a secret.

I said, Puke's got a secret, and I'll tell you if you'll leave me alone.

Allen's crooked glasses. His belt sticking out and his pants all bunched up around the waist.

Allen whispered, Rigby, no. He whispered, Rig, you promised.

Secret? Scardino said.

That's when Allen did something that surprised us all. In that place and time, when every movement was watched, where every tiny movement had meaning, Allen broke the spell and walked over to me, stepped in front of Scardino, leaned into me in the corner. His stupid crooked glasses. Allen put his hand on my shoulder, where Scardino had hit me.

Rig, Allen said, remember? No matter what. You promised.

I slapped Allen's hand away.

It's a book, I said. On the right-hand corner of his desk. Next to the inkwell.

Scardino's little smile was all the way across his face. He laid his hand on Allen's shoulder, leaned in close to me like Allen. Scardino's thumb and index finger had Allen by the ear. But Allen didn't seem to care. His eyes stayed looking into my eyes.

What kind of book is it? Scardino said.

Allen's head was slowly headed to the floor ear-first.

I'll have to show you, I said.

A lot of commotion, then pushing back and forth, and I looked, and Allen's glasses fell on the floor. Then Scardino's shiny black wedgie stepped on Allen's glasses. Glass crushed on concrete and tile, that sound. Scardino stopped, lifted up his foot. The glasses, the parts that go over the ears, twisted, crooked, sticking up every which way.

In the classroom, the sun came in through the big east windows, big, glowing, gold sun into the room, onto the desks, onto Allen's desk, onto the blue-green hardcover Nancy Drew, *The Mystery of the Brass-bound Trunk,* in the right-hand corner, next to the inkwell.

I didn't touch Allen's book, just pointed to the book.

Scardino's big-knuckled hands picked up Allen's book, turned the book over, rubbed his thumb down the binding.

Nancy Drew, Scardino said.

It's a girl's book, Muley said.

What do we want with a girl's book? Breck said.

The secret is inside, I said.

Scardino looked around the room. Ronald Wilson, Roger Waring, Ricky Divine, Tony Smith, Alvin Gosford, were all crowded in the doorway.

The black and white clock next to the American flag said 10:55.

Five minutes before Sister Barbara Ann rang the ten bells.

Scardino kicked the boys' bathroom door open. The bathroom was empty. Allen wasn't lying on the floor anymore, no broken glass, no broken glasses frames. In the stall nearest the wall, under the locked door, in the mirror, I caught a glimpse of Allen's shoes poking out of his pants and shorts down around his ankles.

Scardino took hold of my elbow, grabbed it hard, but somehow because he had touched me, something inside me relaxed.

Back by the long urinal against the green wall and the white toilet stall on the end, the four of us stood there, Vern Breck, Michael Muley, Joe Scardino, and me, in a huddle, like I was one of them, like I was on their side.

Scardino's big knuckles, his big, smooth Italian hands, held Allen's book.

Turn to page forty-two, I said.

Scardino's fingers flipped through the pages, stopped on page forty-two. The carved-out hole inside the book.

Scardino and Breck and Muley started hooting and hollering, saying, Shit, look at that. Wow, how'd Puke do that and why is there just radio tubes in there? I'd put my rubbers in there, I'd keep pictures of naked women, I'd jerk off in there.

Sister Barbara Ann rang the ten bells. At the fifth bell, Scardino threw the book over the stalls. The book landed against the back wall, above the stall where Allen was sitting.

Radio tubes falling, more glass breaking, thin glass against concrete and porcelain. After the tenth ring of the bell, after the classroom doors closed and everyone was gone, I was alone in the bathroom leaning up against the sink, looking into the mirror at myself, and beyond, at the pile of corduroys and underwear bunched around Allen's ankles under the white stall door. Behind the white stall door, Allen was great big howls and whoops of crying. I walked up to the stall door. My hand was formed into a fist so I could knock. Then I looked at my hand as a fist, and I wondered where the hell that fist was when I needed it.

When Allen saw my shoes under the door, he quit crying. Just like when you shut the lights off or turn the water off or shut the radio off or you stop the car, Allen stopped crying.

At home that night, after the dishes were done, I went into my room. The red velvet box was under my pillow. I sat down on my bed, turned on the light on my nightstand. I adjusted the light so the light went right into the red velvet box. With my fingertips I touched each word in gold swirly letters, "The Holy Vatican."

Mom was sitting on the green couch under the standup lamp. Her hair was flying up, and her glasses were down on her nose. This time of day, she always looked tired. She was darning a pair of my socks.

I held the red velvet box out.

Her eyes, her almond-shaped hazel eyes. The look in her eyes at that moment was the look I'd forgot I'd always been waiting for.

The velvet box in my mother's rough, red farm hands.

The Holy Vatican, my mother said.

A present for you, I said.

Mom's clipped-to-the-quick fingernails.

Open it, I said.

Inside the box, the shiny white cloth. The rosary was curled onto itself, a shiny black snake, the silver crucifix on top of the folds.

The sound from out of her.

For me? my mother said.

I won it in the altar boy contest, I said. I had the most points.

Blessed in the Vatican, I said.

My mother lifted the rosary up by its silver crucifix. The shadow of the black shiny beads fell onto her face, just between her eyes, down her throat, onto her blouse pocket just above her heart.

All our prayers will be answered, she said. If only we pray to the Virgin.

As it turned out, that Wednesday after school, while I was riding home on the bus—everybody else at Saint Joseph's, even Sis, at the baseball game—at the bottom of the ninth, Saint Anthony's was three and Saint Joseph's was zero. The bases were loaded, and Scardino was at bat.

One strike, two strikes, three strikes, Scardino was O . . . U . . . T.

Scardino didn't show up for school Thursday. Or Breck or Muley.

Or Allen Price.

All day I had a day I could breathe easy. Then after school, walking to the Pocatello High School, one block from Saint Joseph's School, at the intersection, there was Scardino in a red T-shirt and Levi's and Breck and Muley in Levi's and T-shirts, standing the way they'd stood in the bathroom, spread-legged, one combat line across the sidewalk. Between me and Pocatello High School. Between me and my bus ride home.

I didn't stop to think. I was the tallest in the class with the longest legs, and I was the best runner, and I turned around and started running. My red binder in my right hand, I was pumping my red binder forward and back, forward and back, grabbing at the air. Pulling the air from in front of me to behind me. I was going in the opposite direction from where I should have been going, but I tried not to think about that. I concentrated on getting my ass out of that crack even if I had to run the whole twelve miles all the way home the wrong way.

The Memorial Building is a red brick building with columns at the entrance and big trees all around it just over the Portneuf River across the Hayes Street bridge. I was midbridge when I decided I was going to run to the Memorial Building.

All around me there were tulips. Planted in the borders along the porch with the columns and along the wide cement sidewalk into the entrance, red tulips, yellow tulips, pink tulips.

How can it be so beautiful while you are so afraid?

Scardino and Breck and Muley were right behind me, yelling at me. The doors to the Memorial Building were always locked, so I didn't think of trying to get in, so I kept running by. I jumped a row of red tulips, yellow tulips, pink tulips, like an antelope. Then jumped the other row of tulips on the other side of the sidewalk. I was beating it around the Memorial Building down the slopes of the other side. Soon as I made it around the corner, I ran smack into Breck and Muley.

We played dodge and fake for a while, and just when I saw an opening between them I could run through, something big hit me from behind. It was Scardino, and I went flying. There was quite a slope there, and Scardino hit me, and I was midair, arms and legs waving around. Seemed like I was going to take off flying altogether. I landed, and there was a buzzing around me, and things weren't in focus. Scardino and Breck and Muley were on top of me. Scardino's red T-shirt, his belly, his chest, over my mouth and nose and eyes, and there was no air. Then a fist, a shoe, something hard and square hit me in the stomach.

Right before I passed out, I almost remember wondering who would find my dead body on the green lawn with all the blooming tulips.

I finally opened my eyes, I was kneeling on the grass. I was looking at the grass and wondering if I was on a golf course. Big piles of puke on the green lawn, and I was barfing loud, and I wondered if the loud noise I was hearing was me. I don't know how long I lay on the green grass, even after I could feel the wind on my ass so I knew I had lost my pants. But I wasn't lying, I was kneeling, with my chest against my knees, my ear to the ground, my ear on the blades of green grass, sunlight and shadows on the green. My arms were out there somewhere, and my hands at the end of my arms.

I saw the shadow of it first. It's funny now that I say it. I mean, I can't help but see how ridiculous I looked.

There was a tulip stuck in my ass. A yellow tulip.

All the rest is just the end of the story. Nobody saw me, I don't think. My pants and my jockey shorts and my shoes and socks and my red binder were lying around me on the real green grass. When I was pulling my socks on, there was the hole in my sock that Mom had already darned. I phoned Mom from the Wyz Way Market. I don't remember walking to the Wyz Way Market. I just said: Mom, I missed the bus, come pick me up at the Wyz Way Market, and hung up.

In the reflection in the Wyz Way Market front window, my cold sore was bleeding, but otherwise that was me still staring back at me.

But I was different.

Different, as in changed.

Different, as in other.

My shadow a long, strange darkness coming out of my feet.

I had a nickel so I bought a Snickers. At the magazine stand, usually I stayed on the kids' side, the side of the magazine stand that was the comics.

That afternoon I stood on the other side, with the car mags and *True Confessions* and *Gent*. The other side with the freestanding book display that turned.

I was reading *Peyton Place* when Mom walked in. I didn't try to hide *Peyton Place*. I stood there on the side of the magazine stand where I wasn't supposed to be standing like everything was normal, and I looked up over the pages.

Mom wasn't wearing lipstick. She was still in her farm shoes. Her almond-shaped hazel eyes, squinted, green, one pitched south, the other east. No doubt about it. She was pissed.

Allen Price did not come back into class the next day. Or the rest of the week. And the end of the rest of that week was the end of school.

The truth is, I never saw Allen Price again. One day the following spring, Allen's father came to our farm to shoot rock chucks. I heard Allen's dad tell my dad that Allen had been sick, had spent some time in the hospital, but was doing much better at a special high school in California for kids who liked science.

California California California.

If you're a little different, if your pants don't fit and your breath is bologna breath and you like secret places inside Nancy Drew mystery books, if you're good at spelling, or you like to read Steinbeck on top of the granaries, if you're different, if you're a little bit queer, California California California must be the place you have to go.

Once Upon a Cross

Therese Szymanski

"Terri, we're short today, can you help out?" Sister Judy said to me as I walked into church with my parents for our usual 8 a.m. Sunday mass.

I glanced over at my parents, gave them "the nod," and went to get ready.

Sister Judy liked me, because I was always eager to help out, could actually lift and carry the cross, knew how to tie the difficult ropes that we servers wore around our waists as part of our robes, and the other servers followed my lead. Plus, I played the baritone in band, just like she did when she was younger.

I had a perfectly good reason for becoming an altar server—it gave me something to do during mass, so I wouldn't fall asleep. My brothers had been altar servers at our former church—so I was carrying on the family tradition.

I didn't like that my brothers had been Boy Scouts and Eagle Scouts where they got to do really cool things, while I was offered Brownies. Brownies were something you ate or cute little creatures who helped folks with their housework and lived in the forest. The Boy Scouts fostered leadership, went on adventures, and got badges for things that I would have found fun, like rope tying and forest survival, as opposed to the arts and crafts that seemed to be all the Brownies ever did.

Mom didn't really want me to do any extracurricular activities, especially any that might require her time or acknowledgment, even though she'd been a Den Mother for my brothers. But of course they were boys and she was a first-generation Polish-American Catholic, so she valued boys much more than girls. They were her princes and her girls were just supposed to help her around the house by doing the dishes, mowing the lawn, setting the table, shoveling the snow, and taking out the trash.

Altar serving let me prove that I was just as good as, if not better than, my brothers. Maybe as an altar girl, I at least could be equal to them in God's eyes, or so I thought. I always knew I could do everything the boys could do, except that I could do it better. Mom had already pounded into my head that she only wanted four kids. I was number five. I must've been provided by God when she was already in menopause, so that I could take care of her in old age. By the time I was nine, I already knew I was failing miserably at this task. Mom told me that every other day. After all, she was already fifty-four; if I couldn't take care of her now, what was she to do when she was seventy?

The Shrine of the Little Flower, our old church, where my brothers served, has been declared a national shrine, and is also widely known as the birthplace of hate radio, thanks to Father Charles Coughlin's weekly hate-oriented radio sermons from 1926 to 1941. Through his radio commentaries he reached millions of people around the world and managed to get enough donations to build the Shrine before Archbishop Edward Mooney forced him off the air.

By the way, "The Little Flower" was Saint Therese, which explains why, as a good Polish dyke, I've got a Polack surname and a French given name. Notice that it's not Teresa or Theresa, as there are several saints with similar names, and Mom and Dad determined to name me after one of the lesser-known ones so as to maximize how many people would call me by the wrong name throughout my life. My sister contends that my folks wanted to name me Therese Susan Szymanski or Therese Suzanne Szymanski, but my siblings argued that no one could say either of those and live. We won't discuss what my full name actually is.

After I finished my altar server training, when I first started altar serving, I was assigned to a three-person team with a brother and sister, Anthony and Terese. We were an unusual group since we were one of the few three-people teams, and we were all very young, like eight or nine.

I immediately developed a crush on Terese, and that made me want to excel at my job even though I was only in the third grade. Tony was in my year, and Terese was a year older, but at another school. I think, in many ways, I was the Alpha Male of our team, and that position led me to my first real crush—as in, the first real serious crush on a real person in my life.

Terese was short and had short, brown hair and brown eyes, just like Sister Judy, except Sister Judy was tall. Or at least she seemed so at the time. Even years later, when Terese and I were in band together, Terese was still short. She was first-chair trumpet.

I liked tying Terese's belt for her, and helping her out. Maybe she was a bit butch, with her short hair and maybe somewhat gruff charm, and I've grown up to be definitely butch. When we served together, I got attention from her that I normally wouldn't receive. Maybe she thought that if she flirted with me she could get me to do whatever she wanted—she was right. She thanked me when I helped her, and both she and Tony were grateful that I did the things they didn't want to do, like carry the cross, hold the book, and lead the procession.

Our cross was heavy.

I have four siblings, but at that time, only my bro' Bruce, who is six years older than me, lived at home with me and the folks. He had a cheap weight bench, and I quickly realized I could load one of his sand-filled weights at the top of the bar and carry it perpendicularly to the ground to approximate the heavy cross we had at church. I'd load it up and carry it back and forth slowly across the basement as if I was leading the processional at church. I would slide it quickly down onto the floor and out of sight the moment anyone might catch me. I didn't want anyone to see me practicing carrying the cross.

Being the rather sporty sort, I'd always been able to carry the cross at church, but I kept at this routine because I didn't want to risk ever dropping the cross. I wanted to ensure I could keep carrying it, and keep holding it as long as I needed to.

My mother, who still attends that parish, tells me they've since traded down to a much lighter cross so more servers can actually lift it. That makes me sad, because the servers no longer have to pass that measure of merit. When I served, I was proud when I'd realized many older and bigger servers couldn't carry that burden. I don't like that they've cheapened it so that anyone can make the grade I worked so hard to uphold. I was the only one of the three of us who could carry it. I did all the duties of the cross-bearer and the book-bearer, while Tony and Terese just did the candle-bearer duties.

When Pope John Paul II came onto the scene he didn't want altar girls, only altar boys. So I was told I couldn't serve anymore. The

Pope thought of altar serving as being a precursor to being a priest, but to me, it was like being told I couldn't be a Boy Scout, I couldn't drive the tri-rod, couldn't do the carpentry at the cottage—all things I *could* do and wanted to do—just because I was a girl.

What I heard was that I couldn't be a *real* Catholic because I was female. They were clearly telling me I was not worthy—not even in the eyes of God.

I didn't quite catch all the arguing that went on but the new Pope had backed down on his decisions because he'd had to face reality. I was told that due to the shortage of servers at my church, I could continue to serve, but had to step down to less-important positions like candle bearing, whenever possible.

In my new altar serving group of four, I was the youngest of a two girl/two boy team and the other girl was happy that we were relegated to candle bearing, and went on about how we were getting off easy. I hated giving up carrying the cross to the boys. I loathed being relegated to the sidelines. And I couldn't believe the other girl *liked* it, was happy about it. I stood down for one or two masses, but I resented that I wasn't allowed to do the thing I liked best, especially when I still had to tie everyone's rope belts.

I wasn't on that team for very long, but I'd serve with other groups. I'd walk into the church for mass and look over to see if whoever was serving needed my help. They usually did. But I never liked that I had to go to other groups to be validated. In my own group, I had to carry the candles. In other groups, I carried the cross because no one else could.

As time went on, I became a staple of the altar serving community at St. Martin's. Sister Judy almost always grabbed me to replace a no-show server as soon as I entered the church. I also began passing out wine and the Eucharist. If you gave out wine and there was any left in your chalice, you had to {gasp} drink it if at all possible. It was after all Jesus' blood.

I'm a Polish Catholic. At the time I was a *teenaged* Polish Catholic. It was *always* possible.

But, of course, when Sister Judy went to South America to pursue other ministerial challenges and Sister Dorothy took over, such practices—having servers stand in as Eucharistic ministers—were decided most unseemly.

So I simply pursued the next best option: I got certified as a Eucharistic minister so I could altar serve and give out wine and communion. It was all about being entertained during mass, though I did work to ensure that I ultimately served all the important masses of the year: Christmas midnight mass, Good Friday mass, Holy Thursday mass. You name it, I did it.

Years later, I still occasionally served, but mostly didn't go to mass. When I was still in high school, working full time and staying out all night on the weekends, I would pop by the church to pick up the newsletter, so that I'd have something to show my parents if they suspected I was skipping out on mass. It worked every time.

The last time I altar served I was twenty-one. Sister Dorothy caught me as I walked into church and asked me to just suit up and walk with this young team, and watch over and prompt them, because she was pretty sure they'd screw something up.

I sometimes wonder if I'm a bad Catholic for remembering things in such a bad light. Then I remember I'm a recovering Catholic.

And I still lift weights.

I still go against the restrictions of the church. I fight sexism, racism, and all other such things, because, unlike what my mother, father, and the Catholic Church taught me, I believe in equality.

I'll never be equal as far as the Catholic Church—or my mother—is concerned, and that will never be all right with me. I've given up the church, but I still responded to this call for submissions. I was a server, and taught to serve. I washed the priest's feet on Holy Thursday and I learned how to hold a position when I had to hold a cross that weighed nearly as much as I did for nearly an hour during Good Friday mass.

So if you ask me if I think I'll ever get over it, as a good Catholic I ought to respond truthfully and say, "No."

The Prisoners

Ed Wolf

I wake up in a big bed and I'm the only one in it. I know this is my grandmother's house because there are three pictures of Jesus on the wall. He's hanging on the cross in one. He's sitting in a field with a lot of children standing around him in another. One of them gets to sit in his lap. In the third, his heart is really big and it's on fire. My grandmother always carries lots of pictures of Jesus in her pocketbook when she comes to visit us in Florida. She hides them around the house so we can find them and remember to go to church when she's not there. Sometimes she leaves pictures of the Pope too.

I must have fallen asleep on the bus last night. Someone picked me up and brought me here. But I'm almost nine and too big to be carried. I wonder what it felt like, to be carried all that way?

This room is very bright with all the sunshine coming in through the windows. I know I'm awake, but it's like a dream too. I remember the long bus ride that brought us here. My mom had waited until my dad went to work before she told my sister and I that we were going to live with grandma and grandpa in New York. She sat down at the kitchen table and wrote a letter. Then she put it in an envelope and wrote our dad's name on it. She was crying and I felt really sad watching her. She left the note on the table, leaning against the rooster that had salt in it. When I was on the bus I would think about him coming home and finding that letter. I roll over in the bed and wonder if he cried when he read it.

I must have gone back to sleep. The door to the room is open and I can hear sounds coming from downstairs. When I get out of bed I see that someone has put pajamas on me. When I go into the bathroom to pee, I don't have any underwear on. I'm embarrassed because someone saw my body and the priest at St. James Church said that was a sin.

I go out the bedroom door and into a long hallway that leads to the top of the stairs. My mom grew up in this house and has told me all about it. I put my hand on the railing that she and her brothers slid down when they were little. I want to slide down it too, but I know my grandmother wouldn't like it.

This house is big. The long stairs lead down into a huge living room. There are two couches in it and four big chairs. Everything is neat and clean. It looks like no one ever sits in there.

I can hear my sister. She's asking for a piece of bread and my grandmother says, "Your hair isn't long enough for a braid." My sister says, "Bread, grandma, bread." My grandfather laughs. "She wants a piece of bread." I can hear a cupboard opening and my grandmother saying "She sounds like a little cracker."

I come into the kitchen and my grandmother asks, "Where are your robe and slippers?" I don't have any so I don't know where they are. She says to go back upstairs and get them. She says, "I'm making pancakes." I don't see my mother anywhere.

When I'm back upstairs in the bedroom, I see a pair of slippers on the floor and a robe folded on the end of the bed. I put them on and then go to the window and look out. There is a high-wire fence that runs alongside the house and then beyond that are green fields as far as I can see.

In the distance, across the fields, I can see several large, black buildings. One is really big and has high towers rising up on the corners. It looks like a castle, but my mom told us on the bus yesterday that it was really a prison and that all the prisoners lived there.

When I go back downstairs my mom is sitting at the kitchen table crying. My sister has stopped eating her bread and my grandparents are being quiet. I feel really sad seeing her cry and I go and stand by her. She takes a napkin and wipes her eyes. "Everything will be okay," she says out loud. I sit down and my grandmother puts a big plate of pancakes in front of me. I'm worried about my mom and I'm not hungry.

My mother told us that when we live with grandma, we have to eat all the food on our plate. It's a house rule. I pick up my fork and put a piece of pancake in my mouth. My sister says, "Grandma called me a little cracker," and my grandmother says, "Children should be seen and not heard."

My grandfather takes us outside. It's very cold. The sun is bright and shines in my eyes, but it doesn't make me warm. I am wearing a long coat that fits me perfectly. I don't remember ever having a coat before.

We stand in the backyard and look out over the fields. Grandpa says that everything we see is prison property. He points to the castle way off in the distance and says that's where the prisoners live. He says we'll see them sometimes, working in the fields, growing the food that they eat. He says that we shouldn't be afraid of them. They're here in this prison because they want to show that they are still good men and can be trusted. He says if someone tries to run away from here, he goes to a very bad prison and doesn't come out again.

The door to the house opens and my mother comes down the stairs. She's wearing a long coat and has a hat on. I've never seen her dressed like that. She says she's going into town because she has to get everything ready for us to go to our new school. She tells us to be good and then she walks over to the car in the driveway and gets in it. My sister starts to laugh because my mom gets in the car and then it starts to move. As the car passes by, she rolls the window down and waves to us. My sister yells, "Mommy is driving," and we can't believe it because we've never seen her do that before.

My grandfather asks us if we want apple pie for dinner and we both say, "Yes!" He says there can't be any pie without apples and we follow him to a gate in the high-wire fence that surrounds the house. He opens the gate and points to some trees in the distance. We know what to do.

We run across the field toward the trees. My mom has told us how she and her brothers used to run out to the orchard on the prison property and pick apples. Now we're doing that, just like them.

The air is cold against my face and it makes my eyes water. As we get closer, we can see that the apple trees are old and twisted. My sister starts to pick up apples off the ground but I tell her no, we have to get the ones in the trees. We can't believe you can just pick an apple off a tree and eat it without paying for it. In Florida, you only see apples at the store.

We get ten apples. I put them in my wool hat and carry them back to grandpa, waiting by the fence. He is smiling at us. He tells us he remembers our mom when she was little, bringing apples home for pie.

We hear a sound and look up. Grandma is tapping on the window and waving her hand. She wants us. We climb the steps back into the house.

Grandpa goes to the prison because he works there. I sit in the kitchen while grandma makes the apple pie. She tells me grandpa is the captain of the kitchen at the prison but that in this house, she does all the cooking. She tells me to never go through the high-wire fence unless she or grandpa are watching me. I tell her grandpa says the prisoners want to show us that they are still good men. She makes a sound while she rolls out the piecrust. She says, "Your grandfather thinks everyone is a good man."

She wipes her hands off with her apron and sits down at the kitchen table. She says that if I ever hear the sound of the siren coming from the prison, I should stop what I'm doing and get into the house immediately. If I'm already in the house, I should find her right away. If I can't find her, I should go up to my room, lock the door, and crawl under the bed. She makes me repeat all of this to her. Then she gives me the leftover piecrust dough and I make a turtle for my sister and a horse for my mom.

The whole house smells like pie when we sit down in the dining room. In Florida, we always ate in the kitchen but in my grandmother's house there is a room just for eating.

We all sit down at a big wooden table. There's a huge, white cloth on it, bigger than a sheet. All of the dishes are the same, just like my sister's tea set. They have pictures of little roses on them, and there's a special cup just for the gravy.

My mother is happy because she has found a job. She's going to be a secretary in a knife factory. My grandfather has spent the day being the captain of the kitchen. He tells us that today the men put peas into cans because the winter is coming. I tell him I would like to go and see the prison someday and my grandmother stares at me. Grandpa looks at her and then says, "We'll see."

My grandma sits down and puts her hands together. She is going to pray before we eat like she does when she visits us in Florida. She asks God to bless this house and the food on the table. Then she waits for all of us to say “Amen.”

There is roast beef, potatoes, bread, and corn on the table. There’s also something I’ve never seen before. It is long and green and looks like a little spear. My grandmother says, “It’s asparagus and it’s good for you.” She gets up and puts three of them on my plate as my mother and grandfather watch. I look at my mom who looks back at me. “Just try it,” she says.

I do.

It tastes terrible. Once, when we lived in Florida, I found a mushroom in the backyard and ate some of it. Asparagus tastes worse than that.

I eat my meat and potatoes and corn and I keep eating until there is nothing left but the three spears. I can’t eat them.

My sister has one spear on her plate. My mom and grandpa watch as grandma cuts it up into little pieces and puts one on a spoon and puts it in my sister’s mouth. My sister spits it out and starts to cry. My grandma says there will be no pie if our plates aren’t clean. My sister cries harder.

I sit with the spears in front of me. My sister has cried for such a long time that my mom has taken her upstairs. My grandfather is sitting in the living room, reading the newspaper. My grandmother is washing dishes in the kitchen. I try to eat another bite, but it tastes terrible. I sit there alone at the table.

My mother comes in and sits down next to me. She asks me to please eat the asparagus and I tell her I can’t. I don’t want to cry, so I keep looking at the plate and not at her. She gets up and goes into the kitchen and I can hear her talking to grandma. Their voices get louder and then grandma comes in, grabs my plate, and goes back into the kitchen.

My grandfather calls me into the living room and says it’s time for me to go to bed. He follows me up the stairs. Instead of going into the bedroom, he touches my shoulder and leads me into the bathroom. He puts a plug into the hole in the bathtub and turns the water on. Then he tells me to take my clothes off and get in.

I try to tell him that I don’t take baths anymore, that I take showers, but he turns around and leaves me there, closing the door behind him.

I take my clothes off and look into the mirror above the sink. I can see my face and my shoulders. I’m still brown from the Florida sun. I don't look like I belong here. It feels strange, having to eat things I don't want to, taking baths when I'm too big.

I get into the warm water and look at my long, skinny body. Then the door opens and my grandfather comes in. He is carrying a bar of soap and a small cloth. I put my hands over my body as he kneels down. I know that God thinks it's a sin for someone to look at me when I am naked, so I try to tell grandpa that I can wash myself, but his hands are already on my back. He gently rubs the warm cloth up and down. I can't remember anyone ever giving me a bath before. He washes my back and neck and arms and legs. My body looks so thin under his big hands. He pours water over my head and then washes my hair. He gets soap in my eyes, but I don't care. Then he pulls the plug out of the tub and tells me to stand. He wraps me in a big towel and tells me to dry myself off. When he leaves, I look at myself in the mirror again. I look like a little boy with wet hair.

He calls to me from my bedroom. When I go in, he's sitting on the edge of the bed. He tells me to take the towel off and put on the pajamas.

I look at the three pictures of Jesus on the wall and tell grandpa that it's a sin for someone to see my body. He tells me it's okay for him to see. I try to tell him that I don't want him to look at me, and I start crying. He thinks I'm crying because I didn't get any pie. "We'll get you a piece in the morning," he says. He watches me put the pajamas on and I try to do it so he can't see my body.

Then he kneels down next to the bed. He looks at me and then I kneel down too while he says a prayer. I can tell that he thinks I should know the prayer, but I don't. He asks God to bless all of us, especially my mom. He asks me if I want to add anyone and I say, "My dad," and then we bless him too. Then he stands up and I get in bed. He goes out, leaving the door open just a little, so some light shines in.

The house is very quiet. I know the pictures of Jesus are on the wall, but I don't look at them. I can see a little corner of the night sky out the window. I can imagine the prison out in the middle of the dark fields and the men inside going to bed, just like me.

The house is very quiet. I can smell the apple pie.

Winter is coming. We sit in the kitchen while grandma cooks things from our leftover food. "It's a sin to waste food," she says. She makes fritters with the corn we can't eat, pudding from the extra rice, pancakes from leftover potatoes. My sister says she likes the old food better than the new food and grandpa laughs. He sits at the table with us and reads his newspaper. He's always very quiet when grandma is cooking, even though he is the captain of the kitchen at the prison.

Grandma tells us that some of the prisoners are coming to hang storm windows tomorrow. When they are outside, we all have to be very careful and stay in the house. Grandpa looks at me over the top of his paper while grandma is talking. He smiles at me. It makes me feel like there is nothing to be afraid of.

Our mom works all day long at the knife factory. Christmas is coming and she tells me she's working hard to save some money. She showed me a giant meat slicer she bought for grandma. She keeps it wrapped up in a blanket in the bottom of my closet. I like knowing something that grandma doesn't.

I get up early the next morning. I'm excited because the prisoners are coming. I eat my cereal really fast and go into the backyard and look toward the black prison towers. I can see dust rising up above the dirt road that begins at the prison wall and comes across the fields, right up to the fence outside our house. Three trucks are coming, with men riding in front and back. As they get closer, I can see my grandfather in the front truck. He waves to me as they get closer and closer to our back gate.

My grandmother is tapping on the window behind me. I know she wants me to come into the house, but I pretend I can't hear her. The line of trucks stops and one of the drivers, who's dressed in a uniform like grandpa's, gets out and opens the gate. The trucks pull forward, next to the garage, and come to a stop.

I can hear the back door of the house opening. I turn and see grandma coming down the steps. She's drying her hands with her apron and looking at me like she's mad. Then she smiles at the men in the trucks and they call out to her. "Good morning Mrs. Collins," they say. One of them, a big, black man, asks her if she's been making one of her delicious apple pies and she shakes her head and says, "No, no, not today." She grabs my hand and pulls me toward the house. I can hear one of the men say, "Is that your grandson there, Cap?" as she pushes me up the steps ahead of her.

She says, "I told you to be indoors when the prisoners are here," and then leads me into the living room. She tells me to sit down on the couch. My sister is already there, on one of the chairs. We're both surprised because we're not supposed to sit in the living room. Grandma tells us not to move until the prisoners leave and then she goes back into the kitchen. My sister looks at me when she hears the word "prisoners" and gets up and sits next to me.

There are six big windows in the living room, and we can see out across the fields. Something appears outside the window and blocks our view. It's made of thick bars and it creates a shadow that moves across the rug. It's a ladder. My sister moves closer to me.

We're afraid at first because it looks like someone is trying to get in. As we sit and watch, we can see the hands of one of the prisoners come into view. Then we see his arms and then his face. He keeps climbing up until his legs are gone. Then another man appears. He's carrying a window in one hand and he slowly climbs up the ladder. He climbs until we can only see his chest and then he hands the window up to the man above him. We hear the sound of a hammer and then they both start to come down.

Ladders are now outside all the windows and it looks like they are putting a big cage around the house. The men are climbing up and hanging windows on all the bedrooms upstairs. When they're done and are coming down, they stop on the ladders and look at us through the window. One of them waves and smiles at my sister. She covers her face and hides behind my shoulder. One of the men, who is younger than the rest, looks in at me. He opens his mouth and moves his tongue in and out real slow. I laugh, but he doesn't. He stares at me until somebody yells and he looks down. Someone hands him a storm window and he starts to hang it.

I watch him as he works. He has a big, blue drawing on his arm. It's a picture of Jesus on the cross and three words, "Born to Sin." As he hangs the storm window, he keeps looking in at me. He has long hair and a beard and he looks really strong and a little bit like Jesus too. When he is finished hammering, he stands on the ladder and winks at me. I'm not sure how to wink yet, but I try. He laughs and then he puts his lips together and makes a kiss. I decide to send him a kiss back, but someone yells and he goes back down the ladder. The other men have finished too and now all the ladders are gone.

I get up and watch them put the ladders into the trucks. Some of them are laughing and talking with grandpa. I watch the man with Jesus on his arm. He sits all alone in the back of the truck as it drives away. I wonder what it would be like to be sitting next to him, going back to prison.

At dinner, my sister and I tell my mom about the prisoners. I want to ask grandpa about the man who looked like Jesus, but before I can my grandmother says, "At the table, children should be seen and not heard."

That night, when I'm in bed, car headlights from the road in front of the house move across the wall. I can see the picture of Jesus on the cross. He looks like the man who winked at me, but without a lot of clothes on. I can see that Jesus has a lot of dirt and blood on his skin. I look at the picture of Jesus in the field, and the little girl who sits in his lap, and I wonder why she gets to sit there instead of the others.

The house is quiet. I listen. Sometimes when I hear something outside, I pull the blanket over my head. Then, if I can still hear it, I imagine what it could be.

Then I can hear something right outside my window. Maybe it's a ladder. I listen for someone climbing up. I take the blanket off my face and I watch on the wall, looking for his shadow. I think I can see it.

Then his head appears in the window. I can see the long hair and the beard. I can't tell if it's Jesus or the man from the prison. I don't hear the sound of a siren, so I'm not afraid.

He silently pushes my window open and climbs into the room. He stands there until he can see in the dark. Then he comes over and sits on the edge of my bed.

He sits there very still. I'm not afraid. He whispers something and then touches my foot. I don't move. His hand slides up my leg and then rests on my stomach. He's trying to wake me but I pretend to be asleep. He moves up the bed and then lies down next to me. He puts his lips on my ear and whispers my name. "Edward," he says.

He slides his hand under the blankets. He moves it across my chest and then slowly down my body. It's hard for me to breathe. His fingers go down into my pajamas and he touches my skin. His finger pokes into my bellybutton and I shiver. I open my eyes and look at him.

I can see his long hair and his beard and his lips. I can't tell if it's Jesus or the prisoner. I know that what we are doing is a sin, but I don't care.

His fingers move down my body and he touches me where no one ever has before. I look at him while he moves his hand up and down and I put mine on top of his and together we touch my body. I'm shaking, but I'm not cold. I can see part of the drawing of Jesus on the arm that is rubbing me under the blanket. I can smell his skin, but I can't tell if there is dirt and blood on it. I want to ask him if I can sit in his lap, but our hands have been moving up and down on my body, faster and faster, until I have to close my eyes because everything inside is tingling and I'm being lifted off the bed, floating high, high, high above the house, somewhere far, far away.

I float gently down, back onto the bed. He is gone, but my hand is still on my body. It's wet there, like I peed on myself, but I don't care.

I can hear him folding the ladder up and putting it back in his truck. He doesn't make any noise as he drives away.

I lay in the dark all alone. A car drives by and lights up the picture of Jesus. His heart is really big and red. And it's on fire.

Easter Sunday, St. Francis Xavier

Stephen Greco

My grandfather's funeral took place on a cold January day in 1972. But it wasn't so cold as to require a coat, and that secretly delighted me, despite the sadness of the occasion. I was twenty-one and had come back from college for the day to my small, upstate New York hometown. Since I didn't own anything black I was wearing a suit I'd borrowed from a school friend: a black, Carnaby Street number so highly styled it could have been a costume for a Beatles movie—a long, Edwardian jacket with pinched waist, stand-up collar, and flared cuffs, plus bell-bottom pants, worn with a white turtleneck. I didn't want a coat to cover up all this drama, and sure enough, when I walked down the aisle of the hundred-year-old, white clapboard church of my childhood, St. Mary's and St. Andrew's, I could tell that people were noticing.

Is that Stephen—the one who used to be an altar boy?

Among the family members and friends in church that day were many of the people who had overseen my religious education: Father Gilbert, our beloved parish priest during the 1950s, when I was a kid; Father Fitzpatrick who had the same job during the 1960s and was not as well liked; Sister Dorothy and Sister Mary Virginia from our local order of nuns, the Daughters of Mary, who taught in our church's religious education program; and my bachelor Uncle John, who was also my godfather, and who helped run the parish as a lay volunteer. My mother had told me that I didn't necessarily need to wear black, but the funeral was too good an opportunity to borrow my friend's suit, which said everything about where I wanted to be in my life now that I had broken free of small town ties.

Mr. and Mrs. Rutledge, the parents of my high school girlfriend Mary, greeted us on the steps of the church after the service.

"Sad day," Mrs. Rutledge consoled us.

"Stop by and see us, if you have time," offered Mr. Rutledge, adding dryly, "Looking sharp, Steve"—which made me wonder if he had figured out why my relationship with his daughter had remained atypically chaste for seven years. I had told my family and was "out" at college, but I still hadn't made much of an effort to let old friends in on the news.

In the parking lot, my sister and I were getting into a limousine to go to the cemetery when we saw Father Gilbert.

"Good to see you, Stephen," he said, smiling.

"How are you, Father?" I replied. "Thanks for coming."

Though long since reassigned to a parish in another county, Father Gilbert had remained close to my family. People liked him because he was funny, smart, and warm. He was also quite handsome, with flashing black eyes and dark, wavy hair. During my childhood, Father Gilbert had been tireless in helping the nuns teach religious classes to those of us who attended public school. And because he was a friend of the family, Father Gilbert took particular interest in my sister and me, frequently calling or visiting our house on Sunday afternoons to see if we had any questions about that morning's Gospel or his sermon.

I hadn't seen Father Gilbert in years. He had to be fifty, but he still retained a youthful vitality.

"Attending mass regularly, I hope?" he asked.

"I don't know that the Church wants me, Father," I answered. I'd almost said, "people like me," but decided not to burden this old friend with an angry comment about the Church's attitude toward homosexuality.

He made a sad, amused face, as if I had made a joke in bad taste.

"Of course the Church wants you," he said. "It welcomes everyone."

"We'll see," I said.

He blessed my sister and me, then said good-bye.

I had walked away from the Church six or seven years before that, in the mid-1960s, just after entering high school. A visiting priest I encountered in the confessional one day told me that because I had admitted to masturbating I needed special counseling.

"I do not," I protested. "Besides, I don't think masturbation is really a sin."

The priest seemed stunned for a second.

"It most definitely is a sin and you need to talk to someone about it," he admonished me.

"Yeah?" I responded, jerking up from my knees. "I don't think so." I tore out of the confessional and never went back.

The breach had been coming for some time. It was fueled by new attitudes that were then sweeping through the Church, best represented in our little town by the open-hearted and open-minded Daughters of Mary—the antithesis of the black-and-white terrorist-nuns of Catholic lore. They taught my friends and me catechism, but they also lent us books on philosophy and theology. They encouraged us to ask questions about the historical Jesus and study the origins of Christian doctrine. They were big fans of Vatican II, the historic council on modernizing the Church that began in Rome in 1962 and ended in 1965—which dates also happened to bracket the onset of my puberty. When the nuns encouraged me to develop a personal, exclusive relationship with God, I took them seriously, framing my relationship in accordance with an instinct that the body is good, that it is connected profoundly to the spirit, and that the connection can illuminate a path toward the divine. If there is anything in my life that I would call a blessing from above, it is this instinct. My prayers questioning the virtue of my sexual feelings—most of which I'd had for as long as I could remember—were answered by a heavenly "Thumbs Up."

Soon after bolting from the confessional, I said goodbye to the plaster statues of St. Mary's and St. Andrew's and stopped attending mass regularly. I embarked on my own course of spiritual study and practice that flowered in college and continues to this day. I know there are many Catholics who, despite their objections and anger, continue to work inside the Church on issues relating to the body. But years after my breach, I am satisfied with my choice—even proud that it's in line with the kind of unmediated communion with the divine that early Church authorities attacked as heretical.

I had been as pious as any child could be in chrome-plated, split-level, postwar America. I learned my prayers, said them faithfully, and was always up for a mass or Novena. Like most boys with Italian immigrant grandparents, I had a crucifix on my bedroom wall, as well as a framed illustration entitled Christ Our Pilot, depicting Jesus standing behind an athletic, young sailor in a tight T-shirt at the wheel of a boat during a storm—Our Lord steadying the sailor's shoulder with one hand and pointing the way with the other. My room also featured an architectural niche that I made into a shrine, with cardboard-tube columns, a cigar box tabernacle, and two antique candlesticks I brought up from the dining room. I "said mass" there, complete with handmade wafers of pressed Wonder Bread, for a congregation consisting of my sister, my maiden Aunt Mary, and my grandmother, who sewed me up some vestments out of white dish towels. People said I might become a priest and this pleased me, since I liked the idea of doing good works and going around in a floor-length cassock.

My parents, though, weren't especially religious. During my childhood they'd made some effort to attend mass regularly with my sister and me, but by the mid-1960s, family-style Sunday mass was a memory. My father often attended mass in the prison where he worked as a guard, which was fine with me since he had a temper I didn't understand and often provoked, turning preparations for church excursions—or any excursions!—into horrible scenes. My mother, who read a lot and had her own questions about the earthly imperfections of the Church, grew into a classic, post-Catholic agnostic. She provided me with quite a beneficial example of thoughtful skepticism—she made sure, for example, that I knew what the discovery of the Dead Sea scrolls might mean for the future of Christian faith.

Nominally, it was the job of my Uncle John, as my godfather, to see to my spiritual development. Dear to all, overweight for most of his life, and devoted to collecting Waterford crystal, Uncle John was active in the parish. He counted the weekly collection, planned social events for the church hall, and organized trips for the parish priests. Unmarried, but with a lucrative position as a bookkeeper for a nearby resort hotel, he lived with my grandfather and my Aunt Mary—his and my father's sister—in my grandfather's house, which boasted a document of papal blessing on the dining room wall. In his bedroom Uncle John had his crucifix and his illustration of Christ, plus a framed, black-and-white photograph of a handsome priest named Father Flynn, who had been a friend of the family during the 1940s. Posed and lit as dramatically as a Hollywood star, Father Flynn always seemed quite glamorous to me—his having been "called to a parish in the city" sounded like some secret, papal mission. In addition to the gifts Uncle John regularly showered on both my sister and me, he brought back rosaries, prayer books, and other devotional items especially for me from New York, where he sometimes went for dinner and a show, with Father Gilbert, Father Fitzpatrick, or Father Healey, a mild, blond, young priest who arrived in our parish in the 1970s after I had moved away.

Uncle John seems to have had a special attraction to priests, though I can't imagine this ever included physical relations. I believe he was celibate all his life, and my family didn't talk about why he never married (even when, at his wake, in 1990, an adorable, young Puerto Rican employee of the hotel where he worked, showed up grieving). In the years before I stopped going to confession, Uncle John would let me come with him on occasional Saturday afternoon drives to nearby towns, where he would go to confession in other parishes. At the time, I assumed it had something to do with the modern architecture and pretty landscaping of these newer churches, and I was happy to ride along in his Buick convertible and have the opportunity to tell a strange priest about my heinous sins, which at the time included wishing my parents dead because they insisted I keep my hair shorter than my friends'; wishing my sister dead because she interrupted my friends and I when we were secretly masturbating; and, wishing certain of my schoolmates dead because they made fun of me on the playing field.

Between the ages of nine and twelve I was an altar boy. I was great at it and enjoyed it. I showed up for mass on time and knew my Latin perfectly. I outfitted myself sharply from the jumble of odd cassocks and surplices in the large closet where altar boy vestments were kept, and on the altar I was punctilious—hands crisply folded when not deftly lighting candles, pouring wine, or folding linens. I liked embodying the standard to which Father Fitzpatrick, who oversaw us, always said he wanted the other altar boys to aspire to.

There were fifteen or so of us. We all met on Saturdays in the sacristy, the room behind the altar, to practice Latin and receive our weekly assignments. I looked forward to being with this bunch of boys, because it was a more diverse group than the narrow stratum of classmates I normally hung around with. Composed of boys from different grades, even from different schools, our bunch was free of the habitual relationships that had gelled among my classmates, who had been together as an intact social entity more or less since the first grade, endlessly playing the same roles, choosing the same teams, courting the same girlfriends and boyfriends. I think this is why a certain preadolescent, homoerotic friskiness could bubble up so freely among us.

It bubbled up whenever Terry was around. Terry joined our group when I was eleven. Only eleven himself but as large as a teenager and almost as physically mature, Terry went to school in a neighboring district and was said to excel at all sports. This would have intimidated me except that Terry was friendly and outgoing, and treated me like an equal. I was not too young to have my first, deeply erotic thoughts about holding Terry's strong-looking body in my arms and spending the rest of my life with him. Terry's younger brother, Billy, was an altar boy too, and always followed his brother's lead—all the altar boys did ultimately—as when Terry introduced us to several crotch-grabbing games that were clearly favorites of the brothers in private. We all used to run around and play these games in the sacristy on Saturdays, while waiting for Father Fitzpatrick to arrive for our meeting. If Father was late, as he often was, he found the lot of us rolling around in a heap at the bottom of our vestment closet, squealing with laughter, our boners melting instantly at the sound of his stern but tolerant voice.

"Gentlemen, shall we begin?"

If the priest ever found anything wrong with our horseplay he never mentioned it.

One day, during a week when I was serving daily morning mass with Terry, I arrived early and found him already in the sacristy, standing with his back to the door, his hands in front of him, doing something I couldn't see.

"Greco!" he said, startled but apparently relieved it was me.

"Hey, you're early," I said. We were the only people in the building. The caretaker, who unlocked the doors, had come and gone. Not even the regulars had begun to appear out front in the pews. "What are you doing?"

"Fooling around," Terry said. He turned slightly so I could see that his hard cock was in his right hand. He was masturbating. His left hand held open the fly of his corduroy pants.

"Oh," I said.

"Had to," he said. "Ever wake up and just have to?"

"I guess," I said.

I had been masturbating for three years—either alone in my bedroom at night, or in secret places around the neighborhood with the kid next door, Bobby, who was younger than me and fairly immature. With Bobby, it was just play—as it was with my classmate Glenn, the first guy whose cock I ever touched, on a dare (in a school bathroom in the fourth grade—a moment that led to guilty tears that night after supper, and confession to my mother and forgiveness). I had not seen any other cocks except in locker rooms, where the presence of other guys prevented my acting on the curiosity that always struck me like a blow.

Glenn's, Bobby's, and those other cocks were like toys, though. Terry's was something else.

"Let's see it," Terry said, pointing with his chin. He knew I wanted to.

I took out my cock, and Terry and I stood facing each other. His stroke style was a little faster than mine, more mechanical. For a while I tried matching his pace but found it painful, so I went back to my own. We alternated between stroking and just holding our cocks, or letting them just stick out in the air hard, showing them to each other.

Terry's cock was larger than mine. It was also darker and curved to the right even when he wasn't touching it.

Is that what jerking off does to your cock? I thought.

Then Terry invited me to take hold of his, and as my palm wrapped around the shaft, it was as though a current much stronger than electricity began to flow into my body from that little appendage—a shock caused not simply by touching something normally hidden or forbidden, but by the unforeseen recognition that human flesh compounds power with inestimable preciousness.

I knew it wasn't Terry's soul I had touched, yet everything I had been taught about how the soul epitomizes a person's existence applied more to this human contact than any other I'd ever had. The moment was amplified, I admit, by the fact that Terry hadn't showered that day. Daily morning mass was at seven, and he had probably gotten up twenty minutes ago and biked furiously over to the church, as I had done. He was only eleven, but he smelled like a man. Smells like that would always guide me to sacred things.

"Now what?" I said.

"I know!" Terry walked over to the closet where the priests' vestments were kept and pulled open the double doors. There were mirrors on the inside of the doors and he positioned us so we could see both each other and our reflections.

"There," he said. "I figured this out in my mind during one of those boring meetings. Do you think Father Fitzpatrick does it like this?"

We knew we had only a few minutes to finish our business. We meant to shoot our loads into cupped hands, but Terry's positioning was off and half his load flew onto the lace sleeve of a priest's surplice. The milky glob hung there opaque and glistening like a moonstone. We laughed as we zipped up and used some paper towels to minimize the damage.

Father Fitzpatrick donned that very surplice ten minutes later. On the altar, Terry and I stifled giggles right through to the final benediction, when the sleeve waved as Father Fitzpatrick's hand made the sign of the cross.

I did wonder sometimes how Father Fitzpatrick "did it," or whether he did anything sexual at all. I had been taught that priests kept those feelings under the control of their vows, yet I had heard Father Fitzpatrick joke crudely about busty women and could easily imagine him, unlike the other priests I knew, married with kids and a real job, like selling cars. Years later my sister told me that Father Fitzpatrick once came into the restaurant where she was working as a waitress and, drunk, cornered her in a phone booth and started sputtering about what he would do if he weren't a priest. No priest ever came on to me—and I was never attracted to a priest that way until I met a sort of celebrity priest, another friend of the family.

A year after jerking off with Terry—who soon moved out-of-state—I was asked to accompany the choir on the organ at weekly services at St. Jude's "Within the Walls," which had just been built inside the prison where both my father and my Uncle Frank worked. I was one of my school's star music students and Father Madsen, the prison's Catholic chaplain, was a frequent dinner guest at my Uncle Frank and Aunt Fanny's house, just across the street from mine. Father Madsen—young, tall, and charismatically streetwise—had built St. Jude's by way of a well-publicized national campaign he created involving trading stamps. Ladies from all around the country, who would usually trade their supermarket stamps for gold-toned, starburst wall clocks and matching sconces, instead sent them to Father Madsen who, with the cooperation of the Trading Stamp Institute of America, turned them into cash and commissioned an in-the-round church of soaring, parabolic arches inside the prison. The priest and the arches appeared in lots of national magazines that year.

Father Madsen, or Mike, was always a hit at dinner. He showed up in polo shirts and sneakers, and joked around over beers with my aunt and uncle. I loved the effortless way he could swing from solemn: leading us in grace before dinner; to jolly: telling stories about dim prison guards versus wily inmates; to sentimental: describing repentant inmates who had built the benches and the baptismal font at St. Jude's with their own hands. I loved the way he made us see that condemned souls nonetheless deserved our love. Father Madsen's tales of growing up as a scrappy kid in the big city and playing basketball in public playgrounds made him a pretty regular guy and not likely to fall in love with me, but I liked being around him anyway.

The idea of my playing the organ at St. Jude's came up on a summer night when we were all sitting on my aunt and uncle's back porch after a barbecue.

"I can't pay you anything, Steve, but I'm sure this will accrue to your account," Father Madsen laughed, pointing heavenward.

"That's okay," I said.

"Is it safe?" Aunt Fanny asked.

"Sure," he said. "It's a great bunch of men. They'll love him."

Father Madsen winked at me.

"You'll love these guys—honestly."

"Alright," I said.

My father often came home with dreadful tales of violent men behind bars, so I was a little afraid of what Father Madsen's inmates might be like, but I didn't say anything because after years of hearing about these mythical men, I wanted to see for myself what they looked like. I had heard hushed references to "prison sex," and though I didn't know exactly what this entailed I knew it was between men and that excited me.

Father Madsen called my parents, and arrangements were made. It was a hot Saturday afternoon when my mother dropped me at the prison gate. I was in shorts and a T-shirt. A buddy of my father's showed me across the yard to the church. Inside, Father Madsen was conferring with the choral director, a music teacher from a nearby school. They greeted me and sat me down at the organ; then Father Madsen began the rehearsal by introducing me to the twelve men who were already sitting in the two pews on my left.

"This is Steve, guys. He's going to be playing the organ. Let's make him feel welcome."

The men responded warmly, with shouts of "hi," "hey," and "how ya doin'?" I saw that they were under the surveillance of two guards who stood nearby, chatting with each other.

So many of them are handsome, I thought. Such big, bright smiles. They seem nice enough.

They were all probably less than ten years older than me, wearing short-sleeved prison shirts that revealed veiny, muscular arms, some of which were tattooed. The population of that prison at the time consisted mostly of young black and Latino men from New York City. All had committed serious crimes, but any fears I might have had melted away instantly. Even at the age of twelve I found these men completely sexy in a way I couldn't define but knew was different from the attraction I felt for, say, certain members of my school's football team, who were mostly white and now seemed irremediably callow.

We rehearsed for an hour and a half. The church had no air conditioning. My pants were so short that I had to unstick the back of my legs periodically from the organ bench's plastic upholstery. I saw some of the men notice this; some kept trying to catch my eye. I could hardly stay focused on my musical scores because, well, I'd never seen so much brown muscle or felt so much masculine energy. A guy named Willie was the most appealing. An angelic-looking Puerto Rican just out of his teens, he had curly black hair, green eyes, chunky arms, and a terrific voice. There were several cues for a solo Willie sang that required special timing of my organ entrances. The choral director took us through them carefully, and after each one, Willie smiled boyishly, relieved.

After the rehearsal, as Father Madsen conferred with the choral director and the guards continued chatting together, the men stood up and started joking with each other as they waited for their instructions to move. Willie wandered away from the group and came over to say hello to me—probably a minor infraction.

"You play real good," he said. "You study music?" The liquid way he pronounced the 'pl' sound made me smile, as it sounded like music itself.

"Yes," I said, flushing. Talking this close gave me a chance to look at his hands, which were immense and square and tattooed with a cross between the thumb and forefinger. "Do you?"

"Am I studying music?" Willie asked.

Suddenly I understood what I was asking, given how different circumstances were for him and me. "I mean, do you get to study?" I said.

At that moment a guard came over for Willie.

"See you next week, Steve," Willie said with a click from the side of his mouth. I was surprised he remembered my name.

Father Madsen strode over and tousled my hair.

"Good work, buddy," he said, "Same time next Saturday?"

I nodded yes, eagerly. Then Father Madsen put his arm around my shoulder and lowered his voice.

"Only, no shorts next time, huh? It's the rules."

The priest winked. He didn't explain why I shouldn't wear shorts but at that moment I understood something—was blessed with something—that made everything in the seventh grade seem paltry. I got a huge erection which I then desperately tried to lose as I was escorted back to the gate where my mother waited in the car.

That night I masturbated thinking about wearing shorts with Willie, having boners with him, masturbating together. Somehow it didn't matter to me that, as Father Madsen had mentioned, Willie had killed his best friend and was in prison for life.

Willie wasn't in the choir when I went back to St. Jude's the following week, and I only played at the church for a few more weeks. By then, the Sunday mass was attracting so many guest dignitaries that a professional organist was deemed necessary.

I realize it's odd that I should credit the Church with helping nurture the happily sexual creature I have become—especially today, when so many stories of priestly pedophilia are coming to light. All I can say is that perhaps I fell through the cracks of coercion and repression—or perhaps a fuller exploration of sex and the Church would reveal as many good stories as bad ones. I take heart in the reports of good relationships between priests and other men (even boys!) that I read in Boyd McDonald's "Straight to Hell" anthologies and elsewhere. How far away my grandfather's funeral seems now. My aunts and uncles are all dead, as are Fathers Gilbert and Fitzpatrick, Sisters Dorothy and Mary Virginia. After visits to prehistoric caves in the Basque country and ancient ruins in the Bolivian altiplano, I feel more in sync, in my gut, with sun worship than with the Roman Catholic rites. Still, I attend mass every now and then, as an opportunity to meditate on my relationship with the Church, which I suppose will endure in some form until I die. For the last few years I have been making it a point to attend Easter morning mass at St. Francis Xavier, on West Sixteenth Street in New York—because Easter is my favorite Christian holiday and St. Francis draws a fairly liberal crowd, including a lot of openly gay people. I don't feel as much like an interloper at St. Francis as I do in other churches. Even though I don't assent to most of the tenets of Catholic doctrine or want to take part in the Eucharist, I feel as though I can sit there in good faith among people who have their own, individual formulas for assent while expressing the communal aspect of Christianity. Sometimes, however, in spite of my heresy, an episode of altar boy decorum will recur, as it did last Easter Sunday while I sat in a pew toward the back of St. Francis, waiting for mass to begin. I was obsessing over whether I smelled like sex.

It was a warm day and the church was packed. I was freshly showered and shaved, and had put on a blazer in an attempt to show respect for the occasion, which I had planned for weeks to attend. I was there by myself—my boyfriend was away for the weekend, with his family. The lady and gentleman seated to my left, at the end of the pew, were both dressed in suits and looked like the kind of people who might have attended a sedate dinner-dance at a country club the night before—or so I couldn't help thinking, as four hours earlier, at seven o'clock, I had been playing in a sweaty, all-night sex club.

The club had been filled with hot, horny men, and after two hours there my body had been anointed with several applications of piss, cum, beer, sweat, lube, saliva, and poppers, which produced a bouquet I found intoxicating but inappropriate for Easter morning in church. I had forced myself to go home, clean up, and nap for a few hours, particularly regretting that I hadn't gotten a second chance to play with the adorably punkish, pungent-smelling stranger in a tank top and Keds who arrived around six and, on his way inside, spent several minutes piggishly forcing his tongue down my throat.

It was heaven. The guy was short and compact, shaped like a gymnast, with smooth, untanned skin. He promised to come back after a look around, but we never found each other. I didn't get his name. I could swear the guy's saliva and sweat lingered in my nostrils.

Could that smell have survived a shower? I wondered as I sat watching final preparations on the altar, aware as well of the scent of my geranium soap, the herbal shampoo that the young woman with long, curly hair in front of me had used, and whatever makes well-worn wooden pews smell the same in every church in the world.

All seats were taken. The organ was playing Bach. The aisles near me had become choked with standees.

I'll bet that club stays open all day, I thought. Maybe that guy is still there.

But I didn't have to think long about going back after mass. I was craning to the left to see how many standees were jammed into the aisle at the end of my pew when I saw him—the guy from the club, standing not five feet away, dressed in the same tank top and a pair of jeans.

Jesus, he's come straight from the club, I thought. Good for him—I guess.

The guy looked out of it—propped against a stone pillar, eyes narrowed to slits, swaying occasionally. But there was something angelic about him, innocent—the light from a blue and red stained glass window fell onto his bare, white shoulders, bathing his body in a celestial radiance.

The smell was not lingering in my nostrils. It was coming from the man himself, and my pew-mates noticed it, too. The lady in the suit whispered something to the man. He looked over at my friend and smirked, then whispered something back. The two huddled a little closer together.

In that moment they became slightly less Christian in my eyes. I waved toward the pillar.

"Hey," I said in a whisper that I hoped would be loud enough to carry.

My friend looked like he was in some kind of trance, though it could have been prayer. He was having a hard time standing. I felt oddly self-conscious about relishing the contractions of his deltoids and lats as I watched him try to brace himself with one arm.

I caught the eye of someone next to him and indicated I was trying to get his attention.

When he looked over, I waved again.

"You made it! I'm so relieved," I said in a church-hush. "Come sit—I've done my best to save your seat."

At first he didn't recognize me. Then he understood.

I stood and asked the lady next to me to excuse our new arrival. There was really no room in the pew, but I was determined to squeeze my friend in close to me.

The lady and gentlemen both stood up as he shuffled past them in a parody of grace. The gentleman actually stepped out of the pew to admit my friend.

"Hey, funny meeting you here," the guy said as he slumped next to me. "What happened to you?"

He still seemed a bit unsteady, so I put my arm around his shoulders. His body was tighter and harder than I remembered. He didn't really smell that bad. It was just a very masculine funk.

"I left to take a shower," I whispered. "I had to come here. It's so great to see you here."

He grinned beatifically.

"I had to come, too. I always do," he said dreamily. "Good for the soul. I think about my soul even when I'm fucked up. Especially when I'm fucked up—right?"

The suits decided to leave the pew, which was tight. Another person took their place.

My friend looked upward and bumped his shoulder gently into my chest.

"Love the windows. By the way, what are you doing afterward?"

I wasn't doing anything.

"We can go to my place and get holy," I said.

My friend giggled.

The nuns taught us that any of us might be saints. My cock stiffened as the organ processional cranked up, horn and trumpet pipes blaring, and mass began.

A Cry for Vengeance

J.R.G. De Marco

I was about to betray every bit of Catholic doctrine I'd been taught which is why a horde of angry spirits hovered around me screaming with rage, their glowing, red eyes speaking of the vengeance they would call down on my head if I failed to resist temptation.

But how could I resist Kyle? Blond, green-eyed Kyle whose smile lit every dark corner of the church basement where he had led me and where we stood facing one another. Whatever I did would seal my fate for a long time to come. The choice was mine and I was scared. The ragged, spirits in their tattered white garments feared my choice and howled in painful anticipation.

It all happened years ago, but it might as well have been yesterday. It's still clear because the choice I made changed things forever. I knew I couldn't resist Kyle. I also knew that moment in the bowels of the church would come. It had to because I was different from other kids. I was like the people Sister Veronica had warned us about. She predicted this crossroads moment for all of us. For me, it had come early. It came down to me and Kyle alone in a dank space. And the fact of my difference engulfed that moment and promised to change my life. Of course, I feared that the nameless spirits would see to my punishment as the Catechism said they would.

Sister Veronica, five foot three with a face like a hatchet, had been teaching our sixth grade class about the intricacies of sin. I remember being amazed at how complicated it was. I'd always thought there was good and evil and that was it. You did bad things or good things and the bad things were sins. But it wasn't that simple. Sister Veronica made my head spin with all of the types, terms, and levels of sin. Actual sin and the near occasion of sin, mortal sins and venial sins, sins of omission and sins of commission. The Capital Sins were the source of all other sins and vices and I thought the logical consequence had to be capital punishment. But even these sins weren't the worst of the worst. No, she told us, there were certain sins which cried out to heaven for vengeance. Vengeance from the throne of God.

"There are four sins of this type," she hissed, "Murder is one. The taking of human life." She slapped her wooden pointer on her desk and I jumped.

Her burning stare made me feel as if I'd already planned at least one murder.

"Oppressing the poor is the second one," she intoned.

Even though I knew I hadn't done this one, I flinched when she smacked the desk again with her stick.

"Defrauding laborers of their just wages is another." Her eyes swept the room accusing us all as her stick slammed down on the desk again. I exhaled and realized I'd been frozen with attention.

"And the fourth," she paused and drew in a long shuddering breath. "The fourth I can hardly bring myself to mention. It is the most vile, the most horrid of them all, boys and girls." She surveyed the class and looked as if she would cry. "I can hardly say the word. But you need to know. The fourth is . . . the Sin of Sodom." Her voice was a whisper but her hands betrayed her disgust as they broke her pointer in two. One of the splinters landed on my desk and I nearly bolted from the room.

I had no idea what the Sin of Sodom was except that it had to be bad. Really bad.

We were instructed to memorize all the sins, especially those four, and to never, never commit them. I sat alone that night, Catechism in hand, trying to memorize every word, every comma, every little thing. When I came to the Sin of Sodom, I shuddered, imagining again what horrible things it could mean.

Sister Veronica must have realized that we'd all be wondering about this Sodom thing and so she brought in Father Di Orio to tell us about this most horrible sin. It being a priest's duty, she'd said.

He started in by reading us the Bible story of Sodom and Gomorrah in his gravelly voice. He put lots of emphasis in all sorts of places, raising his bushy eyebrows and snickering here and there. And when he told about the fiery end of the cities you could almost feel the burning buildings crashing down around you. However, by the time he was through we still had only a muddy picture of just what sodomy was. But we had a clear picture of the punishment for it—God had flattened Sodom and Gomorrah.

When some kid asked him for a better explanation of what exactly those guys in Sodom did, Di Orio squirmed, hemmed, and hawed. He said it was something sexual, something perverse which only the most horrible people did. It was a sin of perverted sex—not that regular sex couldn't be sinful, he noted, but this was especially bad because it was between two men or two women. It was so bad that it was an abomination. We were all stunned and no one thought to ask what exactly an abomination was. It sounded bad.

After Di Orio's visit, Sister Veronica reemphasized the "cry for vengeance" *coup de grâce.* I felt troubled because I realized that when I was a little kid I had flirted with the Sin of Sodom—at least as far as I could tell from Father Di Orio's description. I had sorta played with another boy's cock and he had touched mine. But all children do these things (so I overheard the family doctor tell my mother when she confessed her suspicions about me) and though I felt guilty, I never really felt that I had committed a sin or that I'd be condemned to Hell for all eternity.

What I learned when I was with that other kid was that it was *guys* I liked and *guys* I wanted. As I grew, that realization began to blossom, even as the sisters at school and the parish priests hammered away at us about the sinfulness of our lives and the utter blackness of a life lived outside God's grace. I began to feel the first twinges of guilt about what I had done and what I wanted to do even though I had no name for it at the time. And then came Sister Veronica and the Sin of Sodom and I knew that I craved a form of sex which was perverse, anathema, and an abomination.

After that lesson, I knew I was hurtling toward committing sins which, according to the Catechism, were "peculiarly wicked . . . and call down on those who commit them, the wrath and vengeance of God." And even though I hadn't really done anything, I knew I was doomed because I wanted to do these things and *that,* according to Sister and the Catechism, was just as bad as doing them.

Then it happened as it inevitably would. Kyle—a boy two years older than I—eventually made it clear that he wanted the same thing and he wanted it with me.

It started in the Boy Scouts. Kyle had shepherded me around when I joined. I'd liked the way he placed his arm around my shoulder. I enjoyed the closeness, which did not seem at all perverse to me. I suppose some might have thought Kyle was being a little too solicitous, a mite too helpful. I thought he was being just right, quite apart from the fact that he was a little older, a little taller, and had intense green eyes which made me feel funny inside. He had a rough and mischievous look, a sleek nose and a mouth which was lopsided when he smiled—and I liked it all. His manner was confident and at the same time sleazy in a boyish way. He was also a known quantity to everyone because his father was the sexton at the church where our troop held its meetings. Kyle himself knew every nook and cranny of the old building.

Kyle had made it clear that on our first overnight camping trip he would be sharing my tent in order to show me how to do things right. I couldn't wait. Apparently neither could Kyle.

One Saturday, after we had just served as altar boys at an early morning service, Kyle asked if I wanted to see the church basement and sub-basement. He promised lots of interesting things stored in the "catacombs" as he called them. He also said it might be kind of scary. I felt the hair rise at the back of my neck when I told him I wanted to see the catacombs.

We hung our cassocks in the vestry closet and he opened a large old wooden door which creaked on its hinges. A shiver passed through me and I felt a tingle in my crotch. Somehow I knew there was more to this basement visit than scary stories and interesting objects. I knew but didn't know and that was part of the thrill. Kyle, tough and cavalier, never let on that there was anything more to this than an adventure amid dank walls and plaster statues.

Damp air wafted up the stairs from the cool darkness below. He clopped down the wooden steps and pulled light chains, letting the bare bulbs swing and create monstrous shadows everywhere. I followed close behind, a little more afraid than I cared to admit. Old mahogany cabinets, with broken drawers, lined the walls. At one point around a darkened corner, before he could reach the next light switch, Kyle held out a hand for me. I gladly took it, shivering from fright. I could feel my teeth begin to chatter. Kyle, realizing I was frightened, squeezed my hand and said there would be some neat things to see up ahead. I couldn't answer and knew he didn't see me nod my head in the darkness.

He led me down another set of stairs, wooden and more rickety than the first. The dampness increased but the lights he turned on were softer and more gentle. When we reached the bottom of the steps he switched on yet another light and the room came alive. Tapestries with softly tinted Bible scenes, brightly colored procession banners—reds and greens, blues and golds, hung along the walls waiting to be used. A few tall statues, their mournful eyes peering into the distance, not noticing two small boys bubbling with anticipation. It was like a strange carnival where everything was silent and nothing moved. Though I knew that two levels up the church sat atop everything and that everyone up there, nuns, and priests, and parishioners were going about their business, I felt utterly alone with Kyle. It made me dizzy.

He must have felt the same way; he guided me around to a booth-like construction and stood before me smiling. I'm sure I seemed perplexed because he looked me up and down and then said, "You wanna?" I remember being unable to respond; deep down I knew what he wanted and that I wanted it, too, but I just looked at him.

He didn't miss a beat. "You ever jerk off with anybody?"

Finding my voice, I said, "No." Which was technically true.

"You wanna?" he asked again.

Kyle unzipped his pants and saw me watching. He was tempting me and, intent as I was on watching him zip down his fly, I began to hear the anguished cries coming from those spirits. Cries for vengeance were wailing their way to the Almighty because of what I hoped I was about to do.

I felt the familiar tingle in my groin, felt the pleasant sensation of desire mingled with the prospect of satisfaction. In a kind of dream state, I nodded my head and tentatively placed my hand on my own zipper.

Visions of Franny, a neighborhood "fag," sashaying down the street swished through my mind, accompanied by the sounds of angry spirits. Those raging spirits circled Franny, peering at him wide-eyed and shrieking their fearful condemnation. Would I end up an object of ridicule like Franny, who, every time he passed through the neighborhood was subjected to comments and catcalls and worse? Once someone hit him with a brick; it smashed into his head and sent him to the emergency ward. Would I become someone's target one day?

"C'mon," Kyle said, his voice husky, as he pulled out his cock. It was pink and hard and he gripped it in one hand. With the other he loosened his pants entirely and let them fall.

I felt light-headed. I wanted this to happen even though I knew I would burn in Hell. The cries and moans of the spirits assaulted me and I began to resent them. Who were they anyway to be crying for vengeance? Hadn't they ever been tempted beyond their means? Hadn't they ever sinned? Weren't they supposed to look at their own sins before they cast the first stone?

I wished them away but they wouldn't leave. They continued to shriek their cries for vengeance. Against me.

I was paralyzed with fear. Caught between the lure of Kyle's beauty and the possibility of painful, fiery, eternal vengeance. I felt like St. Theresa writhing in ecstasy when that roughly handsome angel appeared to her. She said she struggled until the angel pierced her with his flaming arrow. I always wondered about that.

"Wanna suck it?" Kyle's voice was raspy, tempting. He was a rough angel and he held a fiery, pink arrow. "Wanna?"

Was he crazy? Of course I did, but I had never done anything like that before. I wasn't even sure how to begin. He must have seen the uncertainty in my eyes because he knelt down and began to suck on me.

I wanted to faint with pleasure. The rush of spirit voices became a flood of tormented screams. The phantoms filled my head now, calling for Heavenly punishment. The Sin of Sodom was being here committed and I should be punished. Cast into the deepest, darkest, most filthy pit of Hell.

Kyle stood up, his cock still hard. "Wanna try it?"

Wobbly with pleasure, I nodded but felt the weight of the spirits pressing me back, trying to keep me from this temptation. But I didn't want to resist Kyle. I didn't want to hear the phantoms. So, I resisted *them* instead. They continued loudly trying to stop the inevitable. Even Franny swished across my mind. I could swear he looked at me and shook his head sadly. Or, did he smile?

I was about to compound the Sin of Sodom which Kyle had committed and about to make it my own. I'd also be making my bed in Hell.

As if watching from outside my own body, I saw myself getting down on my knees. Kneeling before Kyle, I peered at his cock, all pink and hard. I could smell the orange scented soap he'd used to shower that morning. All I had to do was open my mouth and move forward. I hesitated, filled with fear.

The rush of souls shouting for vengeance became deafening. I was about to commit a "peculiarly wicked" sin and thereby blacken my soul. Anything good I'd done would be wiped out by this sin which was worse than other sins. I reeled back on my knees, nearly ready to run.

But something unknown stopped me. I don't know what or who.

Kyle's cock stared at me and I saw its little eye glistening now. How could this be bad? I steadied myself and took a breath. The scented soap and the smell of his flesh filled my nostrils. The noise in my head and in my heart was louder than anything I'd ever heard as I bent toward Kyle. The din increased as I opened my mouth and took him in.

In an instant, the screaming stopped.

The silence was glorious. No one called for vengeance. It was just me and Kyle and we were locked together in a bond which I have come to think of as sacred. With one simple move, in the dim depths of the church basement, I stopped those ghoulish souls in their heavenward streak for divine retribution. I had stilled their cries for vengeance.

They return now and again, angry, vengeful, and wanting to hurl me into Hell. They shriek and scream but I know how to stop them now. Sister Veronica wouldn't be happy. But I am.

Excerpts from the Journal of a Canonical Bastard

Pansy Bradshaw

06. september 1954

today i am born. my earliest memory is of my mother screaming "somebody help me hes trying to stick rice up my ass" then she breaks water. i am born blue. because i am in "extremus" i am baptized by a roman catholic nurse in the delivery room. she names me john for my father. my mother screams "jesus christ."

october 1954 all saints church

because i have survived my family has decided to have a "real" baptism. family members zoom in for close ups. @the reception an elderly catholic aunt gushing with piety ejaculates to the priest "isnt it lovely father another little angel for heaven." my fathers mother exhales from her smoke & says "oh shit."

addenda

i come from a long line of mixed marriages. all the women in my family marry protestant men. all the men marry protestant women. they all have quiet nuptials in the sacristy hidden behind the high altar. the protestant spouses signing away their own convictions promising to rear their offspring in the one holy roman catholic & apostolic church.

my parents break with tradition opting not to marry in the church. my parents are married by a justice of the peace. i am a canonical bastard.

1960

my father is gone. he was a drunkard & a violent man. he had sex with men for money. i dont know this yet but i will learn about it later. when i do i wont be suprised.

my stepfather is a drunkard & a violent man. he too has sex with men for money. more news to learn later. he is also a lutheran. he makes my mother my brother & me attend mass in his "church." i believe we will be killed by god just for entering this place. the gates of hell will open & we will all be dragged into the pit of fire forever. the pastor is a nice man. satan disguised as an angel of light. he is married. he has children. he has sex with a woman. there is no end to their godlessness.

1961 all saints school

i sit next to the boy who lives next door. his name is james. he has brown hair & eyes. he has beautiful arms. freckles dot his nose & cheeks. we are constantly together. our physical contact isnt sexual but it is erotic. erotic is not a word i know yet. the sisters keep an eye on us. they separate us. this separation extends to our play outside school as well. i feel lost without james. i am seated at the front of the class. james at the back. our eyes forward on sister & the crucified image of christ.

1966 beloved disciple school

i sit next to rupert. he carries a pocket missal with him @all times. i do this too. you never know when you will have to baptize a pagan accident victim or an infant in extremus. its hard to gauge ritual preparedness. rupert keeps a pectoral crucifix in his desk which he kisses often. when he does this his face flushes red. i know the feeling.

rupert loves to talk about the saints. me too. when he speaks he touches his breast with the fingertips of one hand. to make a point he touches my breast with the fingertips of the other hand. the saints use this same form of touch. a posture of sanctity. it can be seen in holy images. when he touches me this way i feel as though a wound is being probed. tenderly.

sometimes when rupert is praying his head tilts slightly backward. his mouth is open but his lips do not move. he stretches his arms wide. cruciform. a saint in ecstasy . whenever i touch him i am touching jesus through rupert.

1967 public school

this is where "publics" get what they call an "education." this is the school of iniquity. it is the same school my stepfather attended. he says the sisters will make me a pussy. i hate him. i try to kill him with poison. i fail. he beats me with a 2x4. he rapes me. when i go to confession i am allowed only to mention my hatred. my attempt @patricide. the priest chides me in a good natured way to love my stepfather more. in my heart i can see that vatican II is leading us toward lutheranism. i bear my stigmata quietly @school. people pretend not to see.

interim

my stepfather is gone. for some reason i am clueless about his departure. more to learn later. there is already another man in my mothers life. he looks @me strangely. he wears a military uniform with a green beret. when i tell him it looks like a girls hat i am on the floor so fast i never see his fist coming. i thought i was giving him a compliment.

1968 beloved disciple school

together again rupert & i are inseparable. sunday after mass my mother lets me visit rupert. his parents have a proper catholic home. there is a holy water font next to the front door with an image of the infant of prague. the water is fresh. every room has a crucifix. every room has a statue of the bvm. a portrait of the holy father is in the living room. i am in heaven.

rupert invites me to his room. he shares this room with his older brother lawrence. lawrence is home on holiday. lawrence is a seminarian & a scoffer. a product of the spiritual unbalance of our times. he smirks as i enter. he gets up to leave. he calls us faggots as he exits. rupert retorts "if you dont like it stop fucking me." i almost gasp but do not. "fucker" rupert says with exasperation. he shows me all his cool stuff. a relic of saint rupert. a vial of water from lourdes. a crucifix with a fragment of white linen touched to a piece of wood from the true cross.

i want to marry rupert & say so. "dont be silly" he replies "boys dont marry boys." when i think about it i realize i have never noticed it @any catholic wedding. i tell him we will have to be missionaries together in india. "maybe" he says.

rupert sends me to his closet to find a box with more relics. while i am searching he says "look what i have." when i turn to see he is kneeling @my feet. he is naked. he has the body of an ascetic. with one hand he is touching his breast with his fingertips. the posture of sanctity. with his other he is holding his penis. the shaft is enormous. it is drooling spit. the scent of his body rises up to me. i feel as though i will faint. when i do my head slams into the door jam.

@school i bear my stigma quietly. rupert stays away. i try not to think about what happened. i do anyway. @recess rupert tries to talk with me. his words fail. i do not walk away. he gives me a small paper package. inside is a red scapular. i already wear the brown scapular & i tell him so. "the brown scapular is for pussies" he says "people who wear the brown scapular are afraid to really suffer the torments of christ."

the following saturday after confession the priest vests rupert & me in the red scapular of the passion. together rupert & i dedicate ourselves to christs suffering on the cross. we never speak of what happened.

interim

@home my new stepfather has his way with me often enough. he isnt really my father nor is he really married to my mother. while i am being dominated by this man i keep my eyes forward on christ. if jesus can endure the cross i can endure this. what he does to me can only bring me pleasure. for christs sake.

1973 outside the convent of our lady of mercy

rupert & i are sitting in his truck parked next to the convent wall. the streets are empty. we are seniors in high school. rupert is going to europe after graduation. i am entering a monastery in new york. we are smoking cigarettes. the windows are down. i am tense. i am trying not to be. rupert is leaving me to travel europe with a woman. i want to die. he puts his hand on my leg. he leans across the seat & gently kisses me. i do not resist. neither do i participate. before i know what is happening he has his mouth on me. i do not stop him. i do not want to. suddenly a sister is standing @my window "why are you here so late" she asks. my mouth opens wide as everything around me becomes bright white. i shout @the top of my lungs. my body is wracked with convulsions. sister backs away as rupert pulls back scrambling into a driving position. sister bolts like lightning for the convent gate. careening down the street rupert burns rubber. "jesus christ" he screams "what did you do that for."

interim

i have seen rupert only a handful of times in the decades since that night. our visits always strained & argumentative. once i went so far as to insult him via post card. a vengeful act i deeply regret. an abbot with whom rupert & i were close attempted a reconciliation. the evening @the monastery was amicable enough. we promised to keep in touch. i never saw him again.

shrove tuesday 2007 @my computer

i am trying to finish this piece. i am crying. the work of putting memory to paper has taken a lot out of me. this story has given birth to others. stories which had lain dormant. stories now rising up demanding a voice in print. to my left are my dictionaries. to my right bookshelves fill the wall. on the top shelves are a collection of scriptures with their commentaries. on top of those is another book. leather bound with colored ribbons marking its gilt edged pages of feasts & fasts. i stand & stretch. my whole body aches from sitting so long. i reach for it. the pages are all marked appropriately for the observance of the approaching deadline. i open to the section for evening prayer. there rests a holy card. a baroque image of the archbishop saint of salzburg. the banner beneath reads in austrian "der heilige rupertus." i found it once in a store that dealt in paper antiquities. when i asked the price to buy it the proprietor gave it to me saying "this one is not for sale. you may have it."

over the years i have been a monk. a whore. an artist. a writer. a political & religious radical. a teacher. a preacher. a dispenser of sacraments. i have rarely been a saint. not in the best sense of the word. i have had many lovers. through it all it is rupert i have carried with me. secretly. until now. bearing him in my heart.

ABOUT THE EDITORS

Amie M. Evans is a widely published, creative nonfiction and literary erotica writer, experienced workshop provider, and a retired burlesque and high-femme drag performer. Her short stories and essays have appeared most recently in *Entangled Lives: Erotic Memoirs; Ultimate Lesbian Erotica 2006; Show and Tell; Call of the Dark*; 2006 Lambda Literary Award nominated *Rode Hard and Put Away Wet; Best of the Best of Lesbian Erotica 2;* and *Ultimate Lesbian Erotica 2005*. She also writes gay male erotica under a pen name. Evans is on the board of directors for Saints and Sinners GLBTQ literary festival. She graduated Magna cum Laude from the University of Pittsburgh with a BA in literature and is currently working on her MLA at Harvard. She is the author of "Two Girls Kissing," a column on writing lesbian erotica, which can be found at www .erotic-readers.com and is co-author of a writing tips column, "Unsolicited Advice," with Toni Amato, which can be found at www.sasfest .org. She can be reached at pussywhippedproductions@hotmail.com.

Trebor Healey is the recipient of the 2004 Ferro-Grumley and Violet Quill awards for his first novel, *Through It Came Bright Colors* (The Haworth Press), and is also the author of five poetry chapbooks and a collection of poems, *Sweet Son of Pan*. His short fiction and poetry have appeared in numerous journals, 'zines, anthologies, and reviews, including *The Chiron Review; Long Shot; The James White Review; Van Gogh's Ear; Holy Titclamps; The Lodestar Quarterly; The Blithe House Quarterly; VelvetMafia.com; Ashe!; Queer Dharma; Signs of Life; When I Knew; Quickies 3; M2M; Wilma Loves Betty; Out of Control; Pills, Thrills, Chills and Heartache; Skin and Ink; Best Gay Erotica 2003, 2004, 2006; Best Gay Erotic 2;* and *Best American Erotica 2007*. Healey wrote a hit single for the Homocore punk band, Pansy Division, and was awarded a writing residency at the Morris Graves Foundation in 2004. He lives in Los Angeles. www.treborhealey.com.

Contributors

Austin J. Austin is like a virgin in the way that abstinence is like a circuit fisting party. Austin, a sick(ly) pervert, writes to examine intersections of illness, wellness, world, and body. A fat fuck and kinktastic queer, Austin's been an independent sex industrialist (focusing on phone and pro-Dommeing), and a recovering Catholic (complete with Jesus fetish and Holy Water collection) for over a decade. Austin and partner head Acsex (www.acsex.org), helping to make sex accessible for folks all along the disability spectrum. Visit Austin on the Web: www.beatgoddess.com.

A. Lizbeth Babcock lives in Toronto and has done extensive work in the queer community, including counseling students in Canada's only alternative school program for LGBTQ youth. She left the Catholic school system at age 16 to attend an alternative arts program where she met teachers who encouraged her creativity, fostered the development of her queer identity, and changed her life forever. Her work has also appeared in *Best Lesbian Erotica 2007*.

Helen Boyd is the author of *My Husband Betty* (Thunder's Mouth, 2004) and *She's Not the Man I Married* (Seal Press, 2007). She lives with her partner Betty in Brooklyn, and her blog (en)gender can be found at www.myhusbandbetty.com. She grew up in a parish run by Jesuits, which may account for her impertinence.

Pansy Bradshaw works full time as a nanny in Dillon, Montana. co-author of "Betty & Pansy's severe queer review of San Francisco" he is also the author of numerous poems, articles and short stories many of which are in the possession of the Kinsey Institute at Indiana University. He is a regular presenter for the religious studies seminar at the University of Montana western. He also serves as chaplain for home health & hospice at Barrett Hospital. He wears pearls with plaid.

Thomas Burke is the author of *Where Is Home* (Fithian Press, 2005). His work has been published in reviews including *The James White Review* and *Harrington Gay Men's Fiction Quarterly;* and in anthologies including *Bless Me Father* and *Stories of Catholic Childhood* (Plume/Penguin 1994). He is Assistant Professor of Humanities at Dominican University of California and lives with his partner in San Francisco.

Mary Beth Caschetta is a recipient of the Sherwood Anderson Foundation Fiction Award and the W.K. Rose Fellowship for Emerging Artists. Her award-winning stories have appeared in *Quick Fiction, Small Spiral Notebook, Mississippi Review, Seattle Review, Bloom, Blithe House Quarterly*, and *Red Rock Review*, among others. She is the author of a short story collection Lucy on the West Coast: And Other Lesbian Short Fiction (Alyson Books 1997). Caschetta lives in Massachusetts with her partner (and wife), the writer Meryl Cohn, and their standard poodle named after the lesbian writer Violette Leduc.

Louis Flint Ceci is a former high school teacher and college professor turned software engineer. He has had poems published in *Colorado North Review,* fiction and non-fiction in *Diseased Pariah News,* and scholarly essays in *College English.* He had brief careers as an actor and a freelance science journalist, and owns and operates Beautiful Dreamer Press. He won the Gold Medal in the Poetic Justice Poetry Slam at the 2002 Gay Games in Sydney, Australia.

Maria V. Ciletti's fiction credits include "Summer the First Time, 1985," (in *My Lover, My Friend,* Alyson, 2003); "Unexpected Pleasures" (in *Awakening the Virgin 2,* Alyson, 2003); "The Things You Do for Love" (*Skin Deep 2,* Alyson, 2004); and, "Jane Doe" (Bella Books, 2005). Her first novel, *The Choice* (Haworth Press) was released in May of 2007. Maria is a medical administrator and lives in Niles, Ohio, with her partner Rose.

Joseph R.G. De Marco lives in Philadelphia. His work has appeared in the *Advocate, In Touch, the New York Native,* and the *Philadelphia Gay News,* among others. His award winning article, "Gay Racism," has been anthologized in *Black Men, White Men* (1984) *Men's Lives* (1990) and *We Are Everywhere* (Routledge 1997). His stories and essays appear in the *Quickies* series (Arsenal Pulp 1998, 1999, 2001),

Men Seeking Men (Painted Leaf 1998), *Charmed Lives* (Lethe 2006), *Hey Paesan* (Guernica 1999), and *Paws and Reflect* (Alyson 2006). His e-mail address is joseph@josephdemarco.com.

Anthony Easton is a writer and artist whose work deals with issues of the body, sexuality, religion, gender, and language. His work has been published in several daily papers, *Geez* magazine, *Xtra, Xtra West,* and the *Red State Reader*. His artwork has been shown in New York, Chicago, and Toronto. He lives in Edmonton Alberta, a bleak Canadian "city" of mostly oil refineries and cowboys.

Ramón García's poetry has appeared in a variety of journals and anthologies. He has forthcoming work in *Eclipse: A Literary Journal, Mandorla: New Writing from the Americas* and the *Los Angeles Review*. His short fiction has appeared in *Story, Rosebud, Harrington Quarterly* and the anthology *Virgins, Guerrillas and Locas*. He has been a recipient of two National Endowment for the Arts fellowships at the MacDowell Colony, a research grant from the National Endowment for the Humanities, and a residency fellowship from the Virginia Center for the Creative Arts. He is Associate Professor in Chicano/Latino Studies at California State University, Northridge.

Stephen Greco's first book, a collection of erotic fiction and non-fiction entitled *The Sperm Engine* (Green Candy), was published in 2002 and nominated for a 2003 Lambda Literary Award. The book was praised by *Out* magazine for its "breathless bravura." Greco's first novel, *Dreadnought,* is a serialized best-seller on Amazon's direct-download program, *Amazon Shorts*. Greco is at work on a second novel.

Jane M. Grovijahn is an Associate Professor of Religious Studies and Women's Studies, who currently teaches at Our Lady of the Lake University in San Antonio, Texas. Catholic and queer to the core, her focus in life and work is directed by desire for God, absolute love of nature, good food, and justice in all things, especially for our bodies. She maintains a regular practice of watching cartoons on Saturday mornings.

Mallory Hanora is a young, radical, feminist queer currently living, working, studying, making art, and performing in Boston. She is part of the movement for Reproductive Justice and struggles for the human right to choose to not have a child, have a child, and raise a child in health, equity, and joy. Mallory is a member of Reflect and Strengthen, a collective committed to positive social change through creative expression and community building. Mallory loves dancing, hip hop, haircuts, hoop earrings, and making out.

Emma Day Jones resides in Northern California where she is attending college. She is currently working on the completion of a text that provides for the staging of the images presented in this essay.

Lisa M. Kelley lives, at this moment in time, in Northern New York State with her partner and their daughter. Her home is a place of love, laughter, and music, and her writing gives her spiritual quest various forms. She is a member of The Bay Area Poets Coalition and her written work appears in such publications as: *POETALK*, *Dyke Fan*, and, *Illuminations: Expressions of the Personal Spiritual Experience*.

Kevin Killian is a San Francisco novelist, poet, art writer, critic and playwright. His books include *Bedrooms Have Windows, Shy, Little Men, Arctic Summer, Argento Series,* and *I Cry Like a Baby*.

Beth Kiplinski has published two chapbooks of poetry: *There Are Others* (Slipjack Press, 2004) and *In Deed* (Forked Tongue, 2005). She lives with her partner, son, and three dogs near Seattle on an in island in Puget Sound.

Jim Leija is a performer, writer, and filmmaker living in Ann Arbor, Michigan. His performances have been seen at Dixon Place in New York City, the Ann Arbor Film Festival, the Performance Studies International Conference at Brown University, as well as venues in Toronto and Chicago. His recent video work will appear on the Michigan Public Media channel as part of a series showcasing local filmmakers. He received his MFA in Art and Design from the University of Michigan. For updates and information please visit www.jimleija.com.

Susan J. Leonardi is the author of *Dangerous By Degrees, The Diva's Mouth* (with her partner, Rebecca Pope), *And Then They Were Nuns*, and the forthcoming *Nun Country*. She writes and lives in Davis, California, and figures that whatever else you'd want to know about her (and maybe more), you can find in the essay.

Jeff Mann's works include two collections of poetry, *Bones Washed with Wine* and *On the Tongue*; a book of personal essays, *Edge,* a novella, *Devoured,* included in *Masters of Midnight,* a collection of poetry and memoir, *Loving Mountains, Loving Men,* and a volume of short fiction, *A History of Barbed Wire,* winner of a Lambda Literary Award. He is an Associate Professor of Creative Writing at Virginia Tech in Blacksburg, Virginia.

Alistair McCartney was born in Perth, Western Australia, in 1971. His work has appeared in numerous journals and anthologies, including *Fence, The James White Review, Wonderlands* (University of Wisconsin Press), *Between Men* (Carroll and Graff), *4th Street, Mirage#4 Periodical,* and *Aroused* (Ed. Karen Finley). The writing featured in this publication is from his first book, a cross genre novel titled *The End of the World Book,* forthcoming from The University of Wisconsin Press (Spring, 2008). He teaches Creative Writing and Literature in the BA Program at Antioch University, Los Angeles, where he lives with his partner Tim Miller.

Susan McDonough-Hintz is a freelance writer living in Massachusetts with her partner of thirty years. Her articles have appeared in *OutWeek* and *Next* magazines. This is her first published poetry since she received the Fountainspray literary award for poetry in college. She is currently working on a collection of autobiographical vignettes about growing up at the Jersey Shore.

Nora Nugent has not been mistaken for a good Catholic girl in a very long time. She lives in Southern California with her spouse of nineteen years. Her articles, poetry, essays, and short fiction have appeared in the alternative and LGBTQ press over several decades. "My Heart, Also Sacred" is excerpted from a nearly-complete novel about a smart and sensitive tomboy's determination to make sense of a bewildering world.

Doreen Perrine has been published in various anthologies and literary e-zines including the *Harrington Lesbian Literary Quarterly, The Queer Collection*, and *Raving Dove*. Her plays have been performed in such New York theatres as Here Arts and WOW Cafe. A member of the International Women Writer's Guild and the Golden Crown Literary Society, Perrine is also a mixed-media painter who coordinates a local writer's opportunity, "I Love You, Greene!" in

Greene County, New York where she resides with her beloved and three cats.

Artist and writer, **Ernest Posey,** a native of New Orleans, now lives and works in rural Mendocino County California. He has had over two dozen one-man shows of his paintings and mixed-media sculptures, and has been a TV director, graphic designer, gallery director, college art instructor, and mediator. His first novellas, *Hormone Pirates of Xenobia* and *Dream Studs of Kama Loka,* were well received by self-abusers everywhere.

Wesley A. Russell Jr. was born in Marin County, California in 1929 to an anticlerical French-in-name-only Catholic flapper, who wed a previously unbaptized convert for the sole purpose of being married inside Our Lady of Mount Carmel church in Mill Valley, California, to please her mother, making her husband promise no children for ten years. Within eight years, however, Wesley was born. He received the Sacraments and his education through the Sisters of the Holy Names, and his prom date ended up a nun. Wesley spent two years in Korea before pursuing a career in engineering-architecture and computers, eventually becoming a certified nurses assistant in AIDS hospices. He was in a forty-nine-year partnership until he was widowed and has been in his current partnership for the past five years. Always a queer, his last confession was in 1951, and he is now a born again atheist. Free at last.

Salvatore Sapienza's critically-acclaimed debut novel, *Seventy Times Seven* (Harrington Park Press), is loosely based on his experiences as a former religious brother in the Catholic Church, where he taught at an all-boys high school and ministered to people with AIDS, working alongside Father Mychal Judge, the New York City fire chaplain who died in the World Trade Center attacks. Sapienza has written several cover stories for *The Gay and Lesbian Times,* and his work has appeared in *Ashe Journal, Oasis Magazine,* and *Velvet Mafia.* Sapienza currently resides in the gay resort town of Saugatuck on Lake Michigan, where he owns a bed and breakfast and is currently working on his second novel. See www.70x7book.com.

Vince Sgambati is a longtime activist in social justice issues, including LGBT politics. He is a former teacher and staff developer in an urban public school district. He currently writes an online monthly column called "Vince's View" (prideandjoyfamilies.org). Several of his articles have also appeared in online and print magazines such as *Lavender, PrideSource* and *Out In The Mountains*. His writing will appear in an upcoming non-fiction collection of stories about gay men and fatherhood called *Donors & Dads* (Haworth Press). He lives with his partner of thirty years, their ten-year-old daughter, his ninety-five-year-old mother, and three furry friends.

Sr. Soami, formerly known as Sr. Missionary Position, was one of the four founding mothers of the Sisters of Perpetual Indulgence in San Francisco in 1979. On the occasion of the Order's tenth anniversary, he altered his name to Sr. Missionary P. DeLight, in honor of the first Sr. Missionary Delight, John Glorioso, who died of AIDS in 1989. In 2002, he honored another deceased brother and AIDS activist, David Baker, a.k.a. Beautiful Dove, with the adoption of his new name, Sr. Iamosama DeLite, the Sodomite of the Most Holy and Beautiful Dove, Rumi Sufi Heart Now—or for short, just Sr. Soami. www.thesisters.org

Tom Spanbauer was born and raised on a farm in Idaho and received his BA from Idaho State in 1969. He spent two years in the Peace Corps in Kenya, and one year as a high school English teacher before working odd jobs to support his writing habit. In 1986, he completed his MFA at Columbia. He is the author of four novels: *Faraway Places* (Putnam, 1986); the cult classic, *The Man Who Fell in Love with the Moon* (Grove, 1991), which received the Pacific Northwest Book Sellers Award; *In the City of Shy Hunters* (Grove, 2001); and, *Now Is the Hour* (Houghton-Mifflin, 2006). Tom is a survivor of AIDS and has been teaching a workshop in Portland for seventeen years called *Dangerous Writing*. http://www.tomspanbauer.com

Therese Szymanski has been short-listed for a Spectrum and a few Lammies and Goldies, and made the Publishing Triangle's list of notable lesbian books in 2004 with *Back to Basics: A Butch/Femme Anthology*. She's written seven Brett Higgins Motor City Thrillers; edited *Back to Basics, Call of the Dark, Wild Nights, Fantasy,* and *A Perfect Valentine;* has novellas in *Once Upon a Dyke, Stake Through the Heart* and *Bell, Book and Dyke,* among others, and will kill anyone outside of her blood relatives who attempts to call her "Terri."

Charlie Vazquez is a Puerto Rican-Cuban writer and artist raised and living in New York City. He is the author of the queer punk adventure novel *Buzz and Israel* (Fireking Press, 2005), two novellas (*Spittles the Punk Rock Clown* and *Corazón*), three original screenplays, multiple queer art essays, short comedic fictions (*Leslie of Los Angeles, Tanglefoot Magazine* Issue No. 1), and various published erotica, including contributions to Alyson's *Straight? 2* (2003), *Fast Balls (2008),* and *Best Gay Love Stories: NYC* (2006). He enjoys reading, Oregon, warm sand in Baja, and daydreaming, but his boyfriend might say otherwise. www.firekingpress.com

Ed Wolf's writing has appeared in numerous publications, including *Beyond Definition: New Writing from Gay and Lesbian San Francisco; Art and Understanding; Rebel Yell: Stories by Contemporary Southern Gay Authors; Coracle Poetry Magazine; Poetry Motel; Crack Magazine; Prentice Hall's Discovering Literature; Christopher Street;* and *The James White Review*. He has been nominated for the Pushcart Prize and was named Outstanding National HIV Prevention Educator of 2005 by www.thebody.com

Gregory Woods was educated at a Roman Catholic boarding school, the Oratory School, in Berkshire, England. He is now Professor of Gay & Lesbian Studies at Nottingham Trent University, England. His poetry collections are *We Have the Melon* (1992), *May I Say Nothing* (1998), *The District Commissioner's Dreams* (2002), and *Quidnunc* (2007), all from Carcanet Press. His critical books include *Articulate Flesh: Male Homo-eroticism and Modern Poetry* (1987) and *A History of Gay Literature: The Male Tradition* (1998), both from Yale University Press.

Raised Catholic, **Emanuel Xavier** never met his real father and was thrown out of his home at sixteen by his devoutly religious mother for being gay. He survived the brutal streets of New York as a hustler and drug dealer to become the celebrated author of the novel, *Christlike,* the poetry collection, *Americano,* and editor of *Bullets & Butterflies: queer spoken word poetry*. He has been featured on *Russell Simmons presents Def Poetry* and costarred in the feature film *The Ski Trip.* Emanuel is a recipient of the Marsha A. Gomez Cultural Heritage Award and a NYC Council Citation for his many contributions to gay and Latino culture including the House of Xavier and annual Glam Slam poetry competition.